BLACK
COUNTRY
MUSIC

BLACK
COUNTRY
MUSIC

LISTENING FOR REVOLUTIONS

Francesca T. Royster

UNIVERSITY OF TEXAS PRESS

AUSTIN

The poem on page vii is © 2016 by Vievee Francis. Published 2016 by TriQuarterly Books/Northwestern University Press. All rights reserved. Chapter 1 is a revision of the author's earlier essay "Black Edens, Country Eves: Listening, Performance, and Black Queer Longing in Country Music," *Journal of Lesbian Studies* 21, no. 3 (2017): 306–322. Chapter 3 is a revision and expansion of the author's earlier essay "Who's Your Daddy? Beyoncé, the Dixie Chicks, and the Art of Outlaw Protest," in *Popular Music and the Politics of Hope*, edited by Susan Fast and Craig Jennex (Routledge, 2019), 63–75. An earlier version of chapter 4 was published in the *Journal of Popular Music Studies* 32, no. 2 (2020): 18–27.

Requests for permission to reproduce material from this work should be sent to:
Permissions
University of Texas Press
P.O. Box 7819
Austin, TX 78713-7819
utpress.utexas.edu/rp-form

∞ The paper used in this book meets the minimum requirements of ANSI/
NISO Z39.48-1992 (R1997) (Permanence of Paper).

Library of Congress Cataloging-in-Publication Data
Names: Royster, Francesca T., author.
Title: Black country music : listening for revolutions / Francesca T. Royster.
Other titles: American music series (Austin, Tex.)
Description: First edition. | Austin : University of Texas Press, 2022. | Series:
   American music series | Includes bibliographical references and index.
Identifiers: LCCN 2022002698
ISBN 978-1-4773-2649-7 (cloth)
ISBN 978-1-4773-2650-3 (pdf)
ISBN 978-1-4773-2651-0 (epub)
Subjects: LCSH: Country music—History and criticism. | African
   Americans—Music—History and criticism. | African American country
   musicians. | Music and race—United States.
Classification: LCC ML3524 .R69 2022 | DDC 781.6420973—dc23
LC record available at https://lccn.loc.gov/2022002698

doi:10.7560/323526

To Annie and Cece, with love

I am becoming as roots reclaim
this soil, as what is felled takes on

a form it could not have imagined,
whose seeds had always rested below

like a sorrow of banjoes.

—Vievee Francis, "Happy?"

CONTENTS

WHERE MY PEOPLE AT?

"SORRY, I'M JUST HERE FOR THE BBQ." That's what Black person after Black person told me when I came up to ask them what it is like to be one of the few Black people at the Windy City Smokeout, a country music and barbecue fest in Chicago's West Loop, one Sunday afternoon in early July 2014. I located the Smokeout by the smells, of course—rich hickory and maple, crisping pork and chicken, charcoal and pepper and tomatoes—and by the sound of the bass thumping down through my chest, the sound that for me united the country rock pounding through the speakers with my own beloved genres of jazz and funk. Yet as I got closer and recognized the tune—Lynyrd Skynyrd's 1974 anthem "Sweet Home Alabama"—my heart gave a lurch. That song has been part of a contentious conversation about the South's legacy of racism and the role of music in perpetuating that racism, a defensive clapback to Neil Young's critique of southern slavery and its aftermath in his 1970 song "Southern Man." Hearing it here reminded me of all the reasons I felt wary as a Black woman entering this country music space.

To my ears, "Sweet Home Alabama" signifies the acceptance of white supremacist violence in the mainstream. The song shimmies up close to the minstrel tradition in its nostalgic evocation of "sweet songs about the Southland"; and that line "I miss Alabamy once again" gives me Al Jolson flashbacks. "Sweet Home" name-checks Birmingham's George "Segregation Now, Segregation Forever" Wallace.[1] And Lynyrd Skynyrd has performed the song on stage in front of a Confederate flag.[2] For the African American vocalist Merry Clayton, who recorded background vocals for the song, "Sweet Home Alabama" evoked painful memories of racist violence: of the 1963 Birmingham church bombings that killed four little Black girls,[3] and of Governor Wallace's segregation showdown at the University of Alabama, where he famously blocked the schoolhouse door to prohibit two Black students, Vivian J. Malone and James A. Hood, from entering. In a 2013 interview, Clayton says that she and her African American singing partner, Clydie King, first refused to sing on the recording. But they rethought their performance as a kind of a protest: "We couldn't stand on the frontlines, but we could certainly sing 'Sweet Home Alabama' with our heart and soul," she says.[4] And you can hear the protest in their vocals, the righteous passion of their full-throated gospel timbre, and the controlled fury in their vibrato.[5] In contrast with Ronnie Van Zant's laid-back, good-ole-boy delivery, Clayton's and King's cries provide a powerful counterpoint and create a sense of layers of Alabama experiences in the song.[6] As I scanned the Smokeout crowd for Black and Brown faces, Clayton and King's righteous "Alabama-ma-maaaaaaa!" in my ears, I thought both of the contentious history that surrounds country music and of the power to reclaim and transform it.

The questions that I wanted to ask the scattered Black people that I saw—"Why do you like country music? Why are you here?"—were ones that I was also reflecting on for myself. Since I'd decided to lean into country music and to write a book about it, I was growing to love Black and Brown country music's ability to capture difficult and complex stories in their lyrics and sounds, sometimes by hiding in plain sight. I found myself drawn to resourceful stories of making do and sometimes failing, like the Black and Brown sounds of country-soul crooner Freddy Fender's "Before the Next Teardrop Falls."[7] I found something familiar in the gritty texture of experience in the voices of my favorites, like Tina Turner's cover of "Help Me Make It Through the Night" and Linda Martell's hurts-so-good yodel on "Bad Case of the Blues." I loved the stories of family survival and loss that I hear in the Carolina Chocolate Drops' "Leaving Eden." And in Valerie June's crackle-voiced, contrary, slowed-down waltz in "Tennessee Time," I heard a reclamation of country speed and somatic experience in the face of northern migration. This was country music that you wouldn't necessarily hear on stage at the Grand Ole Opry or on Country Music Television, though lately it's been getting more attention from these venues. Some of these musicians wouldn't even call their music "country music," though they are in conversation with country as a genre. This music shares common aesthetics with country music, together with soul, gospel, blues, and rhythm and blues.

But when I first arrived at the Smokeout, I was so nervous that I sat in the car for several minutes before going in. It was my first country music fest, and I wasn't sure what or whom I'd encounter. The lineup was of all white musicians, with the exception of Chase Rice's multiracial backing band. Walking to the entrance, I hesitated as images of all-white crowds waving Confederate flags, hopped up on Coors and loose-meat sandwiches, two-stepped though my brain.

The Black security guard, a young man about the age of one of my college students, took my ticket and gave me a curious look, then averted his eyes, a smile playing on his lips. He and the other guard, also Black, snickered and shook their heads as I passed, and suddenly I was back in the seventh grade, awkwardly attempting the dance of the moment, "The Spank," at the end-of-year dance, the line of boys along the wall assessing my rhythm and not-quite-funky hips. Already, I felt that old shame of not being quite "Black"

enough, the old ear-burning feeling of being watched and mea-
sured by men, one of the first feelings that I had in my body that
told me that I was queer.

The crowd near the main stage was mostly white and mostly
young, in couples and in small groups. They wore a mixture of
styles, though cowboy boots were worn by many folks, in spite of
the heat. I saw a sprinkling of Black spectators and felt some relief.
But each person that I approached was polite, but firm. "Sorry, I
can't help you. I don't really like country music," the relaxed Black
woman sitting alone at a picnic bench told me, giving me a warm
smile. She was dressed in a white skirt and blouse and strappy sandals with medium heels. Perhaps she had come over from church.
She watched the crowd over her sunglasses and ate her chicken
wings. "Sorry, I don't know a thing about country music," said the
muscular Black man with a carefully shaved goatee. He was with
an older beefy white man in a golf shirt who glared at me as if I
were picking a fight.

Was it possible that everyone was just tolerating the music to
get at the food—a small, albeit tasty selection of BBQ vendors
from around the city? It's true that as I pulled up to the Fest, I
saw a group of three African American men leaving the site with
comically huge bags of barbeque, but they carried themselves with
the weary, satisfied air of folks just getting off work. Maybe they
were part of the preparation crew for the festival, getting things
ready for the crowd. They rolled down the windows of their gray,
beaten-up Honda, blasting hip-hop as they left.

Since Chicago is a place where you can easily find cheap, de-
licious barbeque in many neighborhoods in the city, and the admission to the festival was forty dollars a pop, I find it difficult to
believe that the people I talked to would only come for the food.
Maybe I was interrupting their groove, the chance to sit outside
on a hot, sunny day—one of the few in this unseasonably wet, gray
summer—and enjoy their "Q" without interruption.

Or maybe I was asking a fundamentally uncomfortable question, bringing to light an awkwardness that most of us, as we navigate white spaces, might try to ignore or suppress in order to enjoy ourselves.

COUNTRY'S QUEER PLEASURES

Why is it that listening to country music is so loaded for many Black listeners like me? Country music performance spaces, such as bars, concerts, festivals like this one, and even the internet, can be places of community and alliance across racial lines, but they can also evoke and memorialize visceral memories of racialized violence; lynchings; the indignities of Jim Crow; gender surveillance and disciplining; and the continued experience of racial segregation in urban, suburban, and rural spaces in the North and South. In these ways, loving country music is ambiguous, amorphous, risky, and sometimes lonely for many of its performers and listeners. For example, in a recent conversation, Holly G., the Virginia-based Black and queer creator of the blog *Black Opry*, a space for Black country performers and fans, shared this with me:

> Country music is the only genre of music where all the memories I have of it are alone. I hear a song and I can remember where I was and what I was doing but it was always by myself. Other songs you can remember, "Oh, I was in a club, or I was in someone's house and I remember hearing this. But all my memories of country music so far have been solitary. Because it's always had to be that way. That's why the work of creating a space for us [Black country performers and fans] is so important.[8]

Being a Black country music fan can feel lonely and sometimes dangerous. It sometimes feels unsafe to listen to such personal, vulnerable music in public spaces not of our own creation. This lack of safety is shaped by the ways country music has been weaponized to uphold whiteness and white culture. Black country music fans and performers must often tread lightly as they cross these racial boundaries. Perhaps this is why, until recently, the African American presence in country music has been more or less "hidden in the mix," as Diane Pecknold puts it,[9] with Black country fans always feeling as if they are the only ones in the crowd, and Black country performers being treated like the exception to the rule. This state of Black country is an extension of the larger dynamic of the ways that Black bodies are both hypervisible and invisible in US culture, as Claudia Rankine puts it so well in *Citizen*, where she describes the erasure of Black humanity as both systemic and ordinary: "The diminishment of self is a low flame, a slow drip."[10]

For some of us, loving country music—or even just having an intellectual curiosity about it—is the *other* "love that dares not speak its name," to evoke that old-fashioned description of queer, closeted life. Stephanie Shonekan, a Nigerian American professor of musicology and the author of the book *Soul, Country, and the USA: Race and Identity in American Music Culture*, describes the "raised eyebrows, the disbelieving half-smiles, the gasps of laughter" and "the incredulous bemusement" that she's received when she's talked to colleagues about her interest in bringing together soul and country music in her work.[11] The Black queer Southern Gothic performer Amythyst Kiah sings in her anthem "Black Myself," "I pick the banjo up and they stare at me, cause I'm Black myself." Yet country music and culture *is* also Black culture, whether it's the banjo itself, an African instrument and source of creative sustenance for Black people, enslaved and free; or the cut-loose vision of the Black country music pioneer Rissi Palmer in her video for her hit song "Country Girl," natural curls flying, singing with her grandma; or the soul and hip-hop artist Solange Knowles in her video for "Almeda," slyly twirling a Black cowgirl hat, and including cowboy culture as one of the "black-owned things" that "still can't be washed away." For many artists, Black and country go together naturally. This natural connection is reflected in the Black country music songwriter, novelist, and poet Alice Randall's comment that country

> relates as well to Alice Walker as it does to William Faulkner. . . . The people are rigorously honest about so much of the complexity and conflict of life, and through that, they create their own healing.[12]

What Randall suggests here, that the connection between country music and Black culture is both "natural" and "healing," is nothing less than revolutionary, challenging dominant thinking that country music is inherently a white cultural form that should be protected from the corrupting force of racial, cultural, and generic mixing.

To put Black artists and fans at the center of this inquiry is to irrevocably shift country music as a genre. It forces us to re-member, reengage, and hopefully transform country music's racial past. The music industry's segregation of old-time music into race records and hillbilly music in the early twentieth century still informs the ways the genre is policed. ("Hillbilly," with its own racially abject, if nostalgic associations to white rural poverty, was modified into country and western, and then just country in the 1950s.)[13] Centering Black people brings to the surface the genre's performative roots in blackface minstrelsy, and, digging below that traumatic layer, the sonic importance of the music of everyday Black folks, pre- and postemancipation, to its sound. Centering Black people and Black culture in country also forces us to engage the racial dynamics of its present, including the continued amnesia about country music's multiracial past and the narrow path allowed Black artists and other artists of color who seek recognition in the industry. You can hear that call for recognition in Lil Nas X's irresistible chorus to his 2018 song "Old Town Road": "Can't nobody tell me nothing"—a rebel yell of a different kind, of Black self-love and persistence; a claim to joy even when that joy is denied by the gatekeepers. Each of the artists explored here—Darius Rucker, Charley Pride, Tina Turner, Beyoncé, Valerie June, Our Native Daughters (Rhiannon Giddens, Amythyst Kiah, Leyla McCalla and Allison Russell), Lil Nas X, Mickey Guyton, Rissi Palmer, and DeLila Black, among others—tries multiple tactics to navigate this difficult and sometimes traumatic musical landscape, some by working insistently to find a home within the country music industry, some by pushing its edges, and others by creating spaces outside of it, in order to change the ways that Black country music and its history are seen, heard, and felt.

Part of my own journey toward understanding country music and my place in its history has been to learn the banjo. After a year of white teachers in all-white classes, I began weekly lessons on African Traditions in the Banjo, taught by Súle Greg Wilson, a Black banjoist, percussionist, dancer, and storyteller, and a founding member of the Carolina Chocolate Drops. It was in my lessons with Súle that I began to hear what I had always suspected: that this not only is our music to claim now but has always been our music, even when it goes by other names: country blues, blues, folk funk, string band, old-time. One week, Súle instructed me to put a small dangling metal earring on my banjo, just above the bridge, to create an African buzz and feeling when I played, and I felt like I was being initiated into a secret circle. Another day, we laughed, trading verses to our own "Got Two Weeks to Finish This Book" twelve-bar blues, then launched into the theme to *The Beverly Hillbillies*. One week, we worked our way through a syncopated version of "Shortnin' Bread" and "Lil' Liza Jane," songs I remember hearing on old racist *Looney Tunes* or *Tom and Jerry* episodes from the 1930s and '40s—when an exploding rifle turned backward would turn Elmer Fudd into a blackfaced pickaninny, or when, on *Tom and Jerry*, that faceless maid, only shown from the knees down, brown feet shoved into worn slippers, would scold "Massa Tom." But these were also the songs that my mother would sing lovingly to my sister and me before we fell asleep when we were little. Súle's flying fingers gave the songs style and bite, landing hard on the lower D string on the upbeat (what the Godfather of Funk James Brown calls "Keeping it on the One"[14]) to create a deep drone, and I felt like we were both exorcising something and reclaiming something. Afterward, Súle leaned toward the Zoom camera conspiratorially and whispered, hazel eyes twinkling: "After my concerts, always, people, Black people, would come up to me and say, 'You know, I actually love this music.' Or 'This was the music that I listened to at my grandmother's house.'" I laughed as Súle imitated these guilty Black audience members, voices lowered and eyes shifting like they'd committed a crime. Like me, they loved this music, and at the same time, they felt a little like they were doing something wrong.

In these ways, the pleasures that country music offers some Black listeners might be connected to Eve Kosofsky Sedgwick's still resonant and productive formulation of "queer" as "the open mesh of possibilities, gaps, overlaps, dissonances and resonances, lapses and excesses of meaning" when the constituent elements of identity—here race and class, as well as sex and gender—"don't signify monolithically."[15] This is one way that I want to use queer in this book—as a way of capturing the layered, sometimes conflictual experiences of pleasure that country music can bring to its Black performers and listeners. I am also deeply shaped by and indebted to José Esteban Muñoz's writing about queer utopia as the space of the "not yet," in his influential book *Cruising Utopia: The Then and There of Queer Futurity*. Muñoz emphasizes the ways that queer writers, artists, performers, and everyday people in their lives create a future in full recognition that we haven't yet made the world that we want.[16] This version of queer, as both grieving and joyful, seems very important to the history of Black country music, which artists continue to make despite the facts of invisibility, historical erasure, and lost contracts and gigs. It's this form of queerness that shapes the artists who continue to bring their best work and create spaces for listening and thinking and collaboration, despite an industry that often "does not love them back," as the queer performer and curator Karen Pittelman has put it.[17] And finally, I want to think of queer as the way that my own stance as a critic and storyteller is in conversation with other queer storytellers and critics, especially Black feminist storytellers—some of whom are musicians. And here, I'm thinking about Daphne A. Brooks's powerful book *Liner Notes for the Revolution* and especially her discussion of the Black feminist musicians who were also critics, writing, recording, and interpreting through their music stories of Black resistance and change, sometimes between the gaps of the white gaze.[18] While these critic-musicians are sometimes but not always queer in identity, they are queer in their inventive, insurgent methods, including collaboration.

NEW BLACK COUNTRY STUDIES

This book comes at a watershed moment when country music's relationship to Blackness seems to be at a point of transition and new awareness, giving rise to a careful movement of artists, scholars, journalists, and fans. One conversation changer has certainly been the country artist turned podcast host Rissi Palmer, who hosts a weekly Apple Radio podcast, *Color Me Country*, an impressively well-researched show exploring the history of Black, Brown, and Indigenous people in country music in the past and present; interviewing country performers, journalists, and others invested in this scene; and curating wonderful playlists of music. Forums like Kamara Thomas's Country Soul Songbook and Holly G.'s *Black Opry* blog are evidence of a new presence of younger queer BIPOC country music fans, artists, and content makers pushing conversations about country music, race, and queerness on social media and at in-person gatherings like Kamara's Country Soul Songbook Summit and Holly's Black Opry Fest. These online and in-person spaces create experiences of safety where in the past there's been precarity; connection where there's been isolation or ostracism; creativity where there has been containment. Holly G. tells *Country Queer*'s James Barker:

> I want Black artists to have a place where both their work and identities are celebrated. I want Black fans to have a place where they can show up and enjoy this beautiful artistry we're celebrating without wondering if the space is safe for them. I want Black people with the goal of working in the industry in any capacity to see that there is a path for them, even if we have to create the path ourselves.[19]

Scholars like Karl Hagstrom Miller, Diane Pecknold, Charles Hughes, Stephanie Shonekan, Erich Mann, Kim Mack, Michael Awkward, Nadine Hubbs, Geoff Mann, Adam Gussow, Dena Epstein, and others have challenged historic narratives that have erased Black artists from country music, bringing out the ways the country music industry has both reflected and contributed to the larger cultural logics of Jim Crow segregation, appropriation of Blackness, and erasure of Black history.

Moreover, the work of Black country artists themselves situates them deeply in this erased history in order to bring it to light. In the hands of Black artists, country music makes possible a way of indexing lost or purposefully erased experiences of place, history, and violence, whether it's from inside the country music industry, on the margins of it, or solidly on the outside of its gates. We hear this, for example, in the mournful, bluegrassy version of "Down in Mississippi," by the Independence, Missouri, mother and son duo Madisen Ward and the Mama Bear from their 2015 album *Skeleton Crew*. Madisen and Mama Bear trade lines over their two acoustic guitars, supported by a cello, the spare peal of a harmonica, and crickets:

> Way down where the leaves won't grow
> The blackbirds call themselves big crows
> All the laws made by Jim Crow
> Way down in Mississippi

Eschewing nostalgia, the song weaves a beautiful, if grief-filled, fever dream of bodies beaten down by sharecropping and what feels like an inescapable dread of looming violence. Country music scholars like Geoff Mann, Richard Peterson, and Nadine Hubbs have debated the role of nostalgia in country music and its role for white listeners in particular.[20] Black country music artists for the most part refuse such nostalgia. Instead, we hear the spirit and the sound of the fugitive, evoking slave escapes and rebellions and the Great Migration, as well as ongoing fights for freedom. So, too, in the Carolina Chocolate Drops' song "Leaving Eden," the narrator laments the joblessness and hard times that have beset Rockingham, in the Piedmont region of North Carolina (the birthplace of Rhiannon Giddens): "Our fathers' land of Eden is paradise no more"[21]—but perhaps, the song suggests, it has never been a paradise. In her song "Freeway Bound," the Oakland cowgirl Miko Marks turns to the promise of concrete highways after her dreams have been not just lost but "knocked down to the floor." In her ballad "My Kentucky," Kamara Thomas travels all over the United States, from the mountains of Kentucky to Chicago to the tip of Mexico, in a vain search for a home where she can live and freely love her "lily-white Olivia." As I discuss in chapter 6, Lil

Nas X says in an interview that his "Old Town Road" is a no-place, an imaginary space for dreaming and escape. If there is an Eden to be found in this music, it is one of one's own design.

Yet despite these shifts in critical and artistic conversations on country music and Blackness, there is still the "commonsense" idea operating that country music is consummately white in its consumption, production, and sound, and that's reflected in the programming of commercial country radio and the gatekeeping of recognition and labeling by organizations like the Country Music Association and the Grammys. As Geoff Mann suggests in his essay "Why Does Country Music Sound White: Race and the Voice of Nostalgia," creating and maintaining this commonsense and pervasive notion of country's white sound has required the erasure of African American, African, Mexican, and other histories, as they're entangled with this music.[22] These erasures are part of the history of producing whiteness while reducing Black musical agency.

This structural gatekeeping in turn shapes and limits fans' access to Black country history and awareness. Despite the fact that Black musical traditions and innovations are foundational to country music, many people, I suspect, would still be surprised to know that there is a considerable African American country music community. Many would be surprised to know the depth of this archive and history, and that throughout the twentieth and twenty-first centuries, there have been African American country performers. In addition to Charley Pride, perhaps the best-known Black country artist, a whole new, multifaceted generation of African Americans is performing country music, from Darius Rucker to Rissi Palmer to Rhiannon Giddens, Dom Flemons, and the Carolina Chocolate Drops to Cowboy Troy to Lil Nas X to Mickey Guyton to Queen Esther. In the UK, DeLila Black and Yola perform Americana and country, while Kaia Kater and Leyla McCalla bridge Afro-Caribbean folk and North American country music. The sounds of Black country are complex and often hybrid, including the country soul of Mavis Staples, Al Green, Millie Jackson, Bobby Womack, Ray Charles, and Swamp Dogg; the country trap of Breland, Lil Nas, and Chiyanti; the country folk of Laura Love, Kamara Thomas, and Lilli Lewis; the Black bluegrass of Jake Blount, Jett Holden, and Gangstagrass; and the country-punk interventions by DeLila Black and Brittany Howard. The early roots of country and blues are so intertwined that they are sometimes difficult to detangle. Rumor has it that the threat of country music's Black roots showing was enough for the Grand Ole Opry to prohibit drums in their performances for decades. The place of Black country music as both foundational and marginalized, I argue, has everything to do with the often-erased legacy of blackface minstrelsy—America's first commercially successful popular music.

GONE MISSING: BLACKFACE MINSTRELSY AND COUNTRY'S HAUNTED HISTORIES

Looking at minstrel traditions head-on is important for understanding the fraught racialized histories of country music and bluegrass. As the musician and cultural historian Rhiannon Giddens tells *Time* magazine:

> "It had such a gargantuan effect on American culture, world culture," Giddens says of the genre, which took root in the 1820s and '30s. "This was the first time that tunes were written down. So I've been going at it from a musicology point of view, rather than looking at it as blackface and running screaming from the room."[23]

It may well be that country music's early associations with "coon songs," blackface performance, and other aspects of minstrelsy are some of the reasons that Black listeners have "run screaming from the room" of country music—whether we know these facts consciously or just "feel" them. Or we may be uncomfortable because of the ongoing ways that country music has been used to shore up white supremacy, nationalism, and jingoism. White supremacy has been weaponized through country music performances like that of Fiddlin' John Carson, who performed at KKK rallies, and by George Wallace, Richard Nixon, George Bush, and Donald Trump.[24] But the line of descent to minstrelsy is even more direct: Emmett Miller, a blackface performer, recorded the first version of Hank Williams's "Lovesick Blues."[25] Live country music radio shows like the *National Barn Dance* and the *Grand Ole Opry* included blackface performances as a mainstay in their early years and through the late 1950s. As Louis Kyriakoudes notes,

> The role of blackface minstrelsy is usually mentioned and then quickly dismissed as peripheral to early country music and the Opry. In fact, "blacking up" was central to the creation and popular appeal of both the musical genre and the radio program. Pioneering country artists regularly included blackface singers, dancers, and comedians in their acts. Vernon Dalhart, the first country performer to sell a million records, toured regularly with blackface fiddling virtuoso Adelyne Hood. Hood's mammy persona eventually attracted the attention of the Quaker Oats company, who hired her to play "Aunt Jemimah" on the radio. Alton and Rabon Delmore, popular Opry stars of the early 1930s, also included a blackface duo in their tours.[26]

At the same time, Black musicians who were also performing in blackface in the nineteenth and twentieth centuries, like Master Juba, George Wallace, Bert Williams, and the banjo master Gus Cannon, often used the space and captive audience of minstrel shows for creative innovation, artistry, and sly critique under the

radar of white listeners (what Daphne Brooks calls "Afro-alienation acts."[27]) Indeed, the historian and Carolina Chocolate Drops
member Dom Flemons, in his essay "Can You Blame Gus Cannon?," writes about the complexity of fully hearing Gus Cannon's
performances, in Cannon's own time and now. As he first listened
to Gus Cannon's album *Walk Right In*, a 1963 recording of some of
his earlier minstrel tunes from Stax Records (that font of country
soul goodness), Flemons found himself sorting through layers of
meaning:

> In his music I heard minstrelsy, but I could also hear a novel, le-
> gitimate black art form developed from minstrel roots. And not
> only that. Cannon's music was linked to both popular music and
> traditional blues and folk—he played country songs, he played
> popular songs, and he incorporated traditional music into his
> repertoire before there were any copyright or industry stan-
> dards for codifying song ownership. He played what he liked,
> it seems, though that's not to suggest that he wasn't influenced
> by a popular demand for minstrelsy entertainment. He was a
> professional musician, after all.
>
> With these ideas floating in my head, further questions
> arose: Did Gus Cannon feel belittled by his profession? Did he
> feel he was doing a service? And who was his audience?[28]

I have a similarly layered response as I watch the Black country
sensation Blanco Brown, whose infectious 2019 song "The Git Up"
became a number-one hit on Billboard's country music charts right
around the time that Lil Nas X's "Old Town Road" was booted off
for not being country enough. In the official video, Brown gleefully
begins his day checking TikTok to see that his own dance has become viral. Strapping spurs on his sneakers, he travels through an
unnamed, mostly white small town, inviting various town members

to "git up" with him. I pause at that gesture of putting the spurs on the sneakers. It speaks to the agility that Brown himself must embody, skirting between segregated worlds, as an openly country-loving Black man. I confess I feel a melancholy haunting of country music's close connections to minstrelsy behind this video, especially in the way that Brown is inviting these white participants to learn his style, to imitate his own ease and joy and flow. As he instructs his listeners to "get real loose," and "lean back put your hips in it (it's simple, you can do it)," maybe he's not doing anything that other Black performers haven't done before (from "The Loco-Motion" to "Da Butt" to "Gettin' Jiggy wit It" to "Watch Me [Whip/Nae Nae]").[29] I think about the ways that minstrelsy also had its own dance crazes, most notoriously "Jump Jim Crow." American pop music's history is peopled by many Black artists initiating white consumers, as well as the rest of us, into Black movement, style, and attitude. But there's something about the video's setting in a mostly white, small-town space that makes me feel protective of Blanco Brown. Like Flemons listening to Gus Cannon, I wonder who else is watching Brown, and what they're thinking.

And yet, as I watch Brown as he dances from crowd to mostly white crowd, from a retirement home to a fire station to some gathering in a cornfield, open-faced and agile, my final impulse is to embrace him as an example of Black joy and resilience. In his dance moves—saucily rolling his neck, slipping and sliding and dropping it low, his jaunty two-step with a little voguing thrown in—we see a sampling of current Black dance moves set to a twang, a performance of creative freedom. When he gets to the lines

> This next part's my favorite part 'cause it's time to shine
> Gon' and do the 2 step then cowboy boogie
> Grab your sweetheart and spin out with 'em
> Do the hoedown and get into it (whoo, whoo, whoo),

he's so light on his feet that I believe him when he says this is his favorite part.

In 2020, during the same summer that George Floyd was killed, Blanco Brown had a near-fatal motorcycle accident, sustaining massive head injuries. In an interview one year later, as he struggled to get back on his feet and restart his career, he told the *Tennessean* that as he was waiting for help, "I smelled my own blood. That's when it all hit me. I got to stay strong through this one."[30] His words remind me of the vulnerability of the Black body and how important and hard-earned those expressions of Black joy in "The Git Up" can be. But I am also thinking of the words of the young Black New Orleans–based storyteller zandashé l'orelia brown:

> I'm exhausted by strength. I want
> support. I want softness. I want ease.
> I want to be amongst kin. Not patted
> on the back for how well I take a hit.[31]

I hold this complex legacy of minstrelsy, too, as I think about the musical career of one of the first Black country music stars, DeFord Bailey. In Bailey's story of mainstream success on the stages of the Grand Ole Opry in the 1920s and 1930s, we see a blueprint of Black country music experiences that will echo across time—a pattern of Black innovation, controlled visibility, and unceremonious removal. Bailey was a wildly inventive harmonica player, able to tease out sounds of humans, animals, and machines, to pick up tunes from all over—blues, old-time, show tunes, and spirituals—like a magnet, and to create a full spectrum of notes. From David C. Morton's biography of Bailey[32] we learn how he was able to use his music and his charisma to catapult himself out of the backbreaking jobs of domestic labor to play for others for a living, first by playing at one of his employer's tea parties, and, later, after being discovered by the wealthy insurance mogul George Hay, for the radio show that would become the *National Barn Dance* and then the *Grand Ole Opry*. But like many other Black performers during this period, Bailey tells a story about wild popularity and denigration: being cheated out of his fee; getting hard looks on the streets of Nashville from white children and adults alike; being encouraged to do schtick, despite his great talent—such as one routine inspired by his diminutive size, in which he was wheeled onstage in a baby carriage, then popped out to play his harmonica; going on tour and being made to sleep in a car or even rougher circumstances, separate from the white people he was touring with; and always being guided and controlled by the white benefactors who gave him airplay. Eventually, Bailey was unceremoniously dismissed from the show and went on to open his own shoeshine business in his home community in Nashville, playing occasionally for friends and at a few public events before his death in 1982.

It makes me wonder about that music, about what we could have heard if Bailey's talent hadn't been so contained. Compared to the multiple recordings of his white *Grand Ole Opry* contemporaries, Bailey only recorded thirteen songs, even though he knew hundreds, which his biographer Morton documents. What would we know that we don't know now if Bailey could tell us more, and if he had recorded more? How would country music sound and feel different?

In Bailey's signature song, the deeply country harmonica solo "Fox Chase," I hear sonic and lyrical connections to Black struggle and Black life, and a kind of political investment in music as a site of freedom that is both forward and backward looking. What if we had more of those? Bailey performed in the *Grand Ole Opry*'s earliest days, sometimes as the only Black performer, and most certainly as its first Black star. He opened each *Grand Ole Opry* radio performance with "Fox Chase." Is it just a coincidence that his best-known song is about being hunted? I hear in the rising rhythm footsteps, the whoop and barking of the hounds, the panting of the fox, and the echo of retreating space, and in the urgency of the song itself, which clocks in at only a few seconds over a minute, an echo of the slave chase. There is certainly the funk of Black living in Bailey's breath control, in his immediate translation of the drama of survival, in the bleak power relations of fox versus dogs and human hunters, and especially in the way he allows his instrument to become the animals. I hear it as a coded understanding of the constraints of his situation. Nothing is wasted in this performance. Nothing is to be thrown away, even as he slips under the radar, with the ducking and bobbing and the slipping of the yoke that we might see in the glide and beauty of Blanco Brown's dancing, too.

"IT'S MY COUNTRY, TOO!" WHO'S COUNTRY AND WHOSE COUNTRY?

Perhaps it was the deliberate efforts of the recording industry to follow the Jim Crow rules of the nation that made DeFord Bailey the exception rather than the rule in his time. Mainstream popular music wouldn't see another Black country star like Bailey until Charley Pride in 1967. But in 1962, the rhythm and blues star Ray Charles recorded *Modern Sounds in Country and Western Music*, an album that exposed the sonic and historic links between country music and rhythm and blues, covering iconic country songs like "You Are My Sunshine," "You Don't Know Me," and "Your Cheating Heart" and making them his own, changing forever the way they would be remembered and performed.[33] Charles was a vocal fan of country music, and made the album despite warnings from his label that it would flop. He writes in his autobiography, *Brother Ray*, "I just wanted to try my hand at hillbilly music. After all, the Grand Ole Opry had been performing inside my head since I was a boy in the country."[34] Charles's album initially did not get airplay on country radio stations,[35] but eventually his version of Don Gibson's "I Can't Stop Loving You" stayed at the number-one spot on Billboard's Hot 100 chart for five weeks. The result was an album that has itself become an icon. "He kicked country music forward 50 years," Willie Nelson told the *Tennessean* in 2006, by bringing together rhythm and blues and country music commercial classics in innovative ways.[36]

As I explore in chapter 2, Charley Pride signed his first contract with RCA in 1966 and went on his first major tour during the heat of civil rights strife. To forge a career in country music took incredible talent, perseverance, and savvy, supported by collaboration with white country artists like Willie Nelson and Mel Tillis. Pride was often praised by promotors and by other artists for sounding whiter than white country artists. Pride grew to become one of RCA's top-grossing artists, with twenty-nine number-one hits on Billboard's country music charts. He appeared on *Hee Haw*, multiple awards ceremonies, and other television appearances, yet he has also written in his biography of being hounded by racists, bomb threats, financial predators, and a deep personal depression.

During this same volatile period of social change that Charley Pride was navigating, the Black country artist and South Carolina native Linda Martell burst on the scene with a spirited earthy voice and a mean yodel. Martell was the first female solo Black country music artist to appear on the *Grand Ole Opry*, in 1969. Martell had hits with "Color Him Father" and "Bad Case of the Blues." Her first and only album, *Color Me Country*, appeared on Plantation (yes, "Plantation"!) Records, a label name that proved to be apt for her experience there. Though she publicly said that her career ended with that one album because she wanted to take time off to take care of her four children, Martell has since spoken out that her label disinvested in her, putting Martell's promotion budget into the career of the white female artist Jeannie C. Riley, who scored a big hit in 1968 with "Harper Valley P.T.A." Martell has also spoken out about repeated racist heckling from audiences and cancellations of concerts by bigoted promoters who feared that fans would rebel if they found out that she was Black, and about being counseled before her appearance on *Hee Haw* by a television executive on the pronunciation of her own song lyrics. After leaving country music, Martell eventually divorced and moved to the Bronx, bought a soul and disco record store, performed on cruise ships, moved home to South Carolina to drive a school bus, and performed in her band, Eazzy, on the weekends.[37] She has since become an influence on current country music artists, especially Rissi Palmer and Mickey Guyton.

The sound of country soul was one that was shaping the music industry in the 1960s and 1970s, but as Charles Hughes documents in his book *Country Soul*, racial crossing and borrowing both challenged and reconfirmed racial segregation, often benefiting white musicians more than Black ones. Hughes examines this history of racial crossing and borrowing in the country music and rhythm and blues industries, particularly looking at the shared studio musician work of what he calls the "country-soul triangle" of Memphis, Tennessee; Nashville, Tennessee; and Muscle Shoals, Alabama. One way those constraints are made visible is through Black artists within the country-soul triangle who attempted to cross over into country music but without the success of Charley Pride or Ray Charles, including Joe Simon, Millie Jackson, and Bobby Womack.[38]

According to Hughes, Womack once joked that the original title of his album was *Step Aside, Charley Pride, and Give Another Nigger a Try*.[39] The country music scholar Chelsea Burns writes that Bobby Womack was dropped from his label, United Artists, after recording *BW Goes C&W* in 1976, and was told by record executives quite straightforwardly, "You can't write that." The album sought to engage and build a Black country music listenership while also demonstrating a deep knowledge of the harmonic, melodic, and rhythmic conventions of previous country music recordings.[40]

Within contemporary country music in the past twenty years, we see artists who have focused on making their mark on the Nashville mainstream industry, like Darius Rucker, Rissi Palmer, Mickey Guyton, Yola, Priscilla Renea, Kane Brown, and Blanco Brown. As my discussion of Rucker in chapter 2 demonstrates, this work of staying visible in the mainstream requires great psychic work. Black country and string band revivalists and archivists like the Ebony Hillbillies, the Sankofa Strings, the Carolina Chocolate Drops, Our Native Daughters, and Rhiannon Giddens and Dom Flemons in their solo work have been deeply involved in exploring the roots of country music in their albums, public appearances, writings, and lectures. (Some of this work is explored in chapter 5.) At the same time, there's a set of country-adjacent artists who exercise a freedom in defining their own genres, like Valerie June: "organic moonshine roots music" (who will be discussed in chapter 4); Amythyst Kiah: "southern Gothic alt-country blues" (explored in chapter 5); Cowboy Troy: hick-hop; Lil Nas X: country trap (discussed in chapter 6); Gangstagrass: a super-catchy blend of bluegrass and hip-hop (best heard as the theme of the television show *Justified*); and Brittany Howard: what she calls "sad dance hall"[41] with her supergroup Bermuda Triangle.

Whether it's the creation of a bifurcated market of "hillbilly records" and "race records" in the 1920s by "talent scout"/record executives like Polk Brockman and Ralph Peer,[42] or the recent slapdown of Lil Nas X's "Old Town Road" from the country charts for not having enough "country music compositional elements" (to paraphrase *Billboard*'s rationale to *Rolling Stone*),[43] definitions of country music have depended on apartheid logics of racial separation, appropriation, and erasure. But when you center the experiences of Black musicians and listeners, the very definitions of country music must change.

With this history in mind, for many artists, being recognized as "country" by gatekeepers of the industry is important, not least because there are financial repercussions. The costs of not being "country enough" have meant being kicked off the country charts (like Lil Nas X), not being nominated for major awards in country categories like the Grammys (as happened with Beyoncé's "Daddy Lessons"), not receiving country music radio play (as has happened for both Darius Rucker and Ray Charles when they first "crossed over" into country music), not being promoted by one's label, or even losing control of decisions to shape one's career (as happened in the careers of Linda Martell and Rissi Palmer). These are all dimensions of undercutting Black creative agency. The response of current Black artists has been strategic and often multipronged. Some artists have been less interested in Nashville and the commercial industry and have eschewed the category of country altogether, negotiating the genre at a slant through Americana, roots, and folk. Some, like Priscilla Renae, sought a career in mainstream country music and pop, as she did after first establishing herself as a go-to songwriter for a range of powerful popular artists such as Rihanna, Mariah Carey, and Madonna. Some artists, like Rissi Palmer, have chosen to record on independent labels. Some use social media like Instagram and TikTok to share their music, as has Mickey Guyton, who has used her own efforts to supplement those of her label, Capitol Records, to get her songs released and heard.

Perhaps because of the challenge of country visibility for Black artists, country songs about being country have become a staple for Black musicians. I think this is more than a defense of their country legitimacy. I think it's an attempt to wrest these definitions out of the hands of those in power and to create and expand country music identity, sound, and style. So in Rissi Palmer's song "Country Girl," she challenges the idea that you can't make and love country music if you're not rural, don't speak in a drawl, can't claim "kin" from the US South, or, as Rissi's own dancing body reminds us, are not white. And as Kimberly Mack discusses in her essay "She's a Country Girl All Right," Rhiannon Giddens uses autobiographical storytelling to talk about her own particular country experience in the Piedmont region of South Carolina, in her own "Country Girl" song. And she does so less as a way of essentializing what "country" means than as a way of reminding us that country culture and country music can be Black, "subverting historically inaccurate racialized notions of country music authenticity."[44] Kamara Thomas, in her 2020 Country Soul Songbook Summit, a community for country artists, journalists, and conversation makers, uses in its posters, bumper stickers, and social media sites the slogan "This *is* your mama's country music," a claim to Black country community and roots that is historic, intersectional, and queer-centered.[45]

The goal of this book is to capture all these impulses: the shame, pride, and dogged work; the sly satire and the bold boasts; the contrary rhythms and powerful reclaimings; and always, the desire to create something that moves us. Bobbing like a forgotten bottle in the waters is this question, "But is it country?" Sometimes, as I hope to prove in this book, that question is only the beginning of the story.

CHAPTER ONE

UNEASY LISTENING

Tina Turner's Queer Frequencies

[handwritten:] Tina turned goes country to escape an abusive relationship

WHEN I WAS A TODDLER, my Chicago-born parents packed up the family and moved south to Nashville, reversing the migration that their parents had made decades before. My father, the first in his family to go to college, had a new job teaching English at Fisk University. My mother was reluctant to leave Chicago and her family and friends, but she agreed to make Nashville our home for a while. When my parents divorced ten years later, my mother decided to return to Chicago, bringing my sister and me with her. My mother was ecstatic, having missed her family and her home, and was ready to begin her own independent life. But I wasn't so sure. I was twelve then, and Nashville was the place where I had spent most of my childhood.

In Chicago, after our return, I remember frequently cutting through the vacant lot across the street from our apartment building on my way home from school and pretending I was in a Mountain Dew commercial. I'd look up at the leaves of the Chicago cottonwoods, watching the sun streaming through, blocking out the buildings and the glints of broken glass on the periphery, and I'd imagine I heard a harmonica and the slide of a steel guitar. I'd picture myself on a rope swing, my strong arms suspending my body over a creek, toes dangling, and my friends would be laughing with me as they played in the water, and there might be the sound of banjos. We'd be a mixed crowd, boy and girl and Black and Brown and white, and there would be no tension (unlike in my still-segregated elementary school and neighborhood). I'd be wearing cutoffs, and they'd hang down smooth below my knees, no chub rub in this fantasy, and maybe I'd be wearing a bikini or maybe I'd be wearing nothing at all on the top, my body muscular and hard and soft and voluptuous all at the same time. Somehow the body that I was in fit in with the music, laid-back and sun-kissed, dangling over that water with all the time in the world: "Give me a mountain and nothing to do, / Give me the sunshine, give me a Dew," the mellow voice on the Mountain Dew commercial sang.

In my real life, my body was changing in ways that I wasn't quite ready for, everything widening and softening. I was a tomboy of sorts, not really good at sports but loving the gruff companionship of boys as well as the more lively sociability of girls. But that year the boys that I loved for their friendship were growing uncomfortable with me, eyes drawn to the breasts that I wasn't sure I wanted. What I knew I wanted was for time to slow down, time for play, for the lazy, hickory-smoked days of summer barbecues to stay with me. I was also learning how to make my body small that year, how to block out the sound of catcalls from passing cars as I walked, how to make myself ignorable.

I usually listened to the pop station on my clock radio, but when I'd hear a countrified moment of a song—the mandolin solo in Rod Stewart's "Maggie May," say, or the Eagles' "Desperado," or the Rolling Stones' cowbell opening to "Honky Tonk Women"—I would catch a moment of time slowing down again, and I would feel a sweet longing for a time and place where my body felt my own again, right in its skin. I hadn't found that freedom in Nashville or Chicago, but I heard it sometimes between the frequencies of the music.

BLACK WOMEN HAVE almost always had a complex relationship to countryness and, with that, country music, whether they are from the North; the third-generation product of the Great Migration, as I am; or still living in the South. As the National Book Award for Poetry winner and self-described Affrilachian poet Nikky Finney writes in her poem "Brown Country":

> I love country
> For the tender story
> For the blazing heart
> For the ache and sorrow sweetness

But this pleasure in the music is always in tension with the lived experience of racial and gendered violence. In the poem, Finney describes the feeling of "dozens of crawling all over me eyes" that she still feels when stopping at an all-white country rest stop, getting gas for her car as a Black woman alone. She imagines (or maybe actually sees) a man in a cowboy hat bringing his buddies to the window to look at her, and the music she loves is transposed into an assault: "they zip their pants / up and down like a fiddle." Scanning the green landscape, she has a vision of her grandfather, "untying himself from all the trees / He pops and stretches his many necks back into place." Despite her love of and craving for country music, she acknowledges, "This is the music we were lynched by / These are the hangman's songs."[1]

In "Nutbush City Limits" (1973), the first song that Tina Turner penned herself and recorded at Bolic Sound Studio, the Inglewood, California, recording studio complex built by her husband, Ike, and written in the depths of the worst days of her infamously violent first marriage, she reaches back to her own country Tennessee childhood. In her memoirs *I, Tina* and *My Love Story*, Turner says that as a child she turned to the backwoods and fields of Nutbush as a place of escape from her parents' often-violent

[handwritten note:] who is making country music racial is important
— if white, exclusionary
— if black, rememberiring

arguments. But in the song "Nutbush City Limits," rather than giving us nostalgia for a place simpler and greener than Inglewood, a country escape, Tina's very first lines describe small-town life as a series of oppositions, with a palpable tension lurking just beneath the surface—just like her present one:

> A church house, gin house
> A school house, outhouse
> On Highway Number Nineteen
> The people keep the city clean

She describes Nutbush, Tennessee, daily life as having a tightly choreographed rhythm: church on Sunday, picnic on Labor Day, work the fields during the week, a careful schedule allowing little room to get out of line. Turner is matter-of-fact: get caught drinking in this dry town and you get a stint in jail without bail, and "salt pork and molasses is all you get in jail." Specific details help us imagine this as a hard-won lesson for her. It also makes me wonder if there were more lessons that we're not hearing about. In *I, Tina*, her first memoir, written with Kurt Loder, Turner details that feeling of surveillance in Nutbush, making it explicitly racial. For Black people in Nutbush in the 1940s and 1950s, everyday relationships with white people were polite but undergirded by fear:

> There was segregation of course. I don't know how it was for others, but for me, I remember the white people as being friendly then. Now, a lot of that was because the blacks "knew their place," right? As a child, you were brought up to respect white people. It was always, "Yes, ma'am" and "No, ma'am" to them. "Yes, sir" and "no, sir." And you always went to the back. That was the way it was. And yes, always a tinge of fear; it was almost by intuition that you knew the nice white people from the bad ones, and when to really stay clear. . . . The whites had a

fear instilled in the blacks so they could control them and keep them respectful.[2]

While the presence of white supremacy goes unnamed in "Nutbush City Limits," the song dramatizes how it feels to live under the conditions of control and fear: "You have to watch what you're puttin' down," the song tells us. If there is affection for the town to be found in "Nutbush City Limits," it is affection told from the point of view of a survivor.[3]

Musically, "Nutbush City Limits" is a perfect marriage of rural and urban, country girl and city slicker, Tina and Ike. With Tina Turner's blues shout wedded to a whomping 4/4 country beat, perfect for line dancing, and Ike Turner's citified, sly, fuzzy cat-scratch rhythm guitar, a bold horn section, and a funkily psyche-delic Moog synthesizer solo that evokes the tasty Moog lick that the Ohio Players came up with the year before in "Funky Worm" (1972), "Nutbush City Limits" brings together many genres that influenced them: country, rock, rhythm and blues, and funk.

When Tina and Ike Turner bring their musicianship together in live performances of this song, the result is wildly infectious, even if sometimes strained. A 1973 performance of "Nutbush City Limits" on the German music show *MuzikLaden* dramatizes that strain. They lip-sync, the rest of the revue stripped away. It's just Ike and Tina on stage, and we realize how important the rest of the band is for keeping spirits high. Ike incongruously plays an acoustic guitar, unlike the electric guitar that we hear on the recording with the rest of the band. Ike seems sullen behind his dark-tinted glasses, looking up only occasionally to scowl. There's a nervous energy to Tina Turner's performance; she's dancing quickly and a little frantically, perhaps missing the backup support of the Ikettes. She is skinnier than I've ever seen her, in a stylish skin-tight red jumpsuit. Because the performance makes use of the recorded version of the song, we can't tell what her voice sounded like at that moment, but her face looks tense and weary.[4]

When Tina Turner sings "Nutbush City Limits," "Honky Tonk Women," "Help Me Make It Through the Night," or other songs that are part of her country music repertoire, her relationship to "country" as both an idea and a sound is complex. These songs might be heard as declarations of independence, distinguished from the rock and soul that she usually recorded with Ike. The fact that her little-known first solo album, *Tina Turns the Country On!*, is made up of country music cover songs at a time when there were very few successful Black country music performers is itself a powerful statement of artistic daring. At the same time, we hear her reworking stories and reworking history through these country songs—a chance to use country music to express her difficult, sometimes traumatic experience of home. Each of these songs returns to a troubled time and place that still might threaten to mire her, like Finney, in the swamp of history. These songs voice a desire for mobility in the face of constraints of genre, race, and violence. This desire to breach barriers creates a tension that energizes some of the most poignant and powerful aspects of Tina Turner's performance style: her bluesy shouts and cries; her strong jaw and neck, arm muscles, and legs; her leonine strut; her constant high-energy dancing, in formation with her wonderful backup singers or in impromptu solo jigs; her effective use of hair to accent her swooping, extending the line of her body or punctuating with a shake; her pouts and satisfied grins; her expressive face streaming with sweat—all declarations of independence. They give the impression of a spontaneous outburst of feeling, and at the same time we see someone working very hard—the realities of constraint.

Turner's move to St. Louis, and eventually to California with Ike, from Nutbush is part of the larger exodus of African Americans from the South known as the Great Migration, which spanned from the early twentieth century through the 1970s. The African American historian Darlene Clark Hine describes a hidden history of the Great Migration: Black women fleeing violence from white employers and neighbors, as well as violence in their own families and homes. Faced with cultures and laws that devalued or simply didn't believe Black women's pain or even that they could be raped (due to stereotypes of Black women's sexual excesses), Black women created a "culture of dissemblance," a mask of openness and availability that hid these stories and their lingering trauma, shielding the women's inner lives from their oppressors.[5] In addition to the racial tension that Turner describes in Nutbush, her home life with her parents was a physically and sometimes emotionally violent one. And Tina's experience of domestic violence continued even after she moved from the South to the North with Ike.

I am using Hine's concept of a culture of dissemblance as a lens to look beyond the mask of sexual openness in Turner's performances, particularly in her country songs. Perhaps by returning to the "home" of country, as both a sound and a place, she asks us to see it as an imperfect home, troubled by white surveillance and the threat and reality of violence. We might also think about country's wedding with the urban in these songs as a kind of incomplete transcendence of these tensions—after all, northern cities were also the site of white surveillance, poverty, and violence for those who left the South, including for Turner herself. Perhaps in "Nutbush City Limits" and in other country songs, Turner is asking us to think about the birthplace of this culture of dissemblance in order to exorcise it. Turner's fans, especially her Black female fans, might recognize these complex feelings, some that might be less accessible to women whose families left southern country life in earlier generations but who might still recognize the aftermath in stories about back home that are interrupted with the shaking of a head or a vow to never go back.

THE NASHVILLE THAT I grew up in, in the mid-1970s, was in a strange place that seemed to want to be both old and new. The official parts of the city—downtown and on the rows of streets where the recording studios were—embraced the image of itself as cosmopolitan and young and cutting edge, with fern bars and jazz and alternative rock and country clubs. The university neighborhoods of Vanderbilt and Fisk brought multiracial streams, joining and mixing with each other: grocery stores and cafés, and white kids and Black and Brown and Asian kids riding to the 1000 Oaks Shopping Mall together on banana-seat Schwinns. Newscasters and folks from the Chamber of Commerce emphasized that Nashville was not yet the Deep South but part of the Middle South, kissing cousin to the Midwest and Mid-Atlantic states. Part of this newer view of the city was the kitsch image of "country": Minnie Pearl on *Hee Haw* with her wide-brimmed hat with flowers and price tag, pig-in-overalls salt and pepper shakers, jokes about buxom young women in haylofts. This pop version of old Nashville declared its ironic hipness, its newness, while at the same time evoking and distancing itself from the rural towns immediately around it.

But there was also a grander image of Nashville linked to an older, more refined, and definitely more plantation-flavored past, encouraged by the city's proximity to the Hermitage, Andrew Jackson's stately home. You could feel it in the richer neighborhoods, vine-covered colonial mansions with lawn jockeys now (mostly) repainted white. A not-too-distant Jim Crow past remained like molding water stains underneath the wallpaper, its tense, ancient fumes bubbling and buckling the smooth surface.

I was aware, even at a young age, of the tensions between Black and white. Our next-door neighbor sometimes flew the Confederate flag on special occasions, and even though I had a huge crush on his daughter Leslie, who was my age and who also liked me and who wore her dresses way too short, I understood that I shouldn't ask to sleep over at her house and that it was important to ignore her when she asked me to show her my underwear. I knew that I needed to be at the top of my mostly white class at school, and even though I was encouraged to think of myself as just as smart as any of them, I put painful hours into perfecting my letters until my fingers ached after getting a C in handwriting. Expectations ran high.

For my sister and me, as Black girls growing up in Nashville then, country music was part of the grammar of living. You couldn't escape it no matter your race or class or the kind of music you listened to. The local commercials featured it: ads for car dealerships, flour, amusement parks. Sausages made just outside of the city featured a little freckled, red-headed white boy in a straw hat chasing a hog across the side of the package to the tune of a banjo: "Take home a package of Tennessee Pride!" The locally made public service announcement warning people not to litter created a persona called "Tennessee Trash," a white man with squinty eyes, tattoos, and curly dark brown, Brylcreemed hair, throwing cups and cigarette butts out of his Pontiac as it roars down the highway. The music was a pretty good imitation of Johnny Cash. The local television station's morning show had a house band that featured a wicked slide guitarist with long muttonchops. My elementary school class field trips included the Grand Ole Opry, Music Row, and the set of *Hee Haw*. My gaps in knowledge of old and new country favorites were filled in by the commercials from K-Tel records that ran during *Looney Tunes*: Marty Robbins and Tom T. Hall, Porter Wagoner and the Carter Family, Crystal Gayle and Mac Davis, Merle and Willie and Waylon and Dolly and Tammy. We were on a first-name basis.

I was on a first-name basis with Tina, too. But she was glamorous to me, and that didn't mean "country" in my mind. My sister and I would stuff socks into our shirts to give ourselves busts, and we'd put on the strawberry-blond wig that one of our babysitters

left at our house, and we'd shimmy and pretend that we were surrounded by equally glamorous backup singers and lots of dry ice.
We'd fight over which one of us got to be Tina, and who had to be
the quiet Ike in the background. We'd hike up our jeans to show
our legs and tie our shirts up to show our belly buttons, and my
mother would laugh at our performances and then quickly go back
to the book she was reading. I would always sense in my mother's
laughter that there was something about Tina's performance of
glamour that made my mother nervous. Or maybe it was okay to
play at being Tina, but not to *be* her. Not to become someone else's
victim, I grew to understand.

WHEN TURNER TAKES ON the voice of the "Honky Tonk Women"
in her 1970 cover of the song, I hear a critique and revision of
the myth of Black women's sexual availability. In her version, the
Tennessee honky-tonk is a space where sexual violence must be
escaped, or at least bested.

"Honky Tonk Women" when sung by Mick Jagger and Keith
Richards is about white men's sexual adventures. It is a sonic
pledge of allegiance to country and to blues, and to an imagined
rural, raucous life of excesses of alcohol, sex, and the company of
trickster women. It was first recorded by the Rolling Stones in
1969 on the 4th of July, as a single, and then together with "Country Honk" on *Let It Bleed* later that year. Wikipedia tells me it
was written while Mick and Keith were vacationing in São Paulo
and were influenced by the rural bars, country people, and music
of that region. We might hear that in the beat of the opening
cowbell, but it is Tennessee that they reference in the song's lyrics—Memphis and Jackson specifically—and it is American blues
and country that we hear in the song's beat, guitar, and chorus, the
influence of the blues kings (and Stones idols) Muddy Waters,
Howlin' Wolf, and Robert Johnson, as well as the country laments

of Hank Williams and Jimmie Rodgers. While the song didn't name Black women as the subjects of this trickster sexuality (as did "Brown Sugar," recorded a few years later), it fits into a history of sexual conquest and dissipation linked with rural poor and often Black spaces like honky-tonks, juke joints, and bars.

But when Ike and Tina rerecorded "Honky Tonk Women" just a year after the Stones, they made it their own, reclaiming the spirit of blues and country from the British rockers. The song became a permanent part of Tina Turner's repertoire, too, and she changed the lyrics, telling this story from the point of view of a honky-tonk woman instead—someone, like Turner in "Nutbush," making the most of constraining circumstances. She described a "gin-soaked man" who "tried to fool me upstairs for a ride." This speaker may or may not be a sex worker, but when she tells us from her point of view that he carried her upstairs as she "leaned right across his shoulders," we get the sense that that trip upstairs might not have been fully voluntary. This implication of rape changes our understanding of the line "And I just can't seem to drink the man off my mind." When Turner performed the song live in 1982 at the Apollo Theater in New York City with the Ikettes and the rest of the band, she loaned the song a spirit of world-weariness beneath the high energy. She tells us about the gin-soaked man in Memphis and a VIP in New York City, but in this performance, the song feels less about her exploits with these honky-tonk men and more about her camaraderie with her dancers and musicians. Tina trades some lines with her longtime pianist Kenny L. Moore, who adds his own commentary—like "It was bad, huh?" and just "Yee haw!"—together with some ragtime-style piano licks, and I am reminded of Fats Waller (who began his career playing piano in a New Orleans brothel). Turner and her backup singer-dancer Ann Behringer and longtime Ikette LeJeune Richardson perform some shimmies and urban cowgirl two-stepping and form a chorus line with high-leg can-can kicks, leaning on one another for support.

On this evening, Tina owns this song together with her band, even though she does not erase its history.[6]

WHEN I ENCOUNTERED "country" Black people for the first time, we were visiting the home of the family of one of my mother's co-workers, folks who lived outside the city in a small, dim house surrounded by acres and acres of land. It was so alien to me, as if my own grandparents' migrations from South to North had occurred centuries, rather than decades, before. Their home was cool and dark, lit by electricity, of course, but with a kind of dampness that seemed to swell the grain of the kitchen table and that I associated with poverty, and in my memory I still mix up the smell of decaying wood with the smell of the hickory smoke that sank deep into my hair and skin for days afterward. I remember drinking water from a sulphury well, offered in a Dixie cup, and running among the just-bursting corn that framed the house instead of a lawn.

But most of the Black people who were in my life as I grew up were cosmopolitan, a mixture of academic and global and bougie: my parents' Black activist friends associated with Fisk University, where my father taught, or the public library, where my mother worked, and my very proper third-grade teacher, Miss Cooley, whose carefully coiffed hair, stately bearing, and smart wash-and-wear polyester pantsuits recalled those of Miss Diahann Carroll.

When we moved back to Chicago after my parents' divorce, country music receded into the background. If someone called you "country" in Chicago when I was a teenager in the 1980s, it was an insult; it could mean not combing or pressing your hair, or wearing curlers or slippers in public. It might mean eating food that announced itself too loudly: pickles or potato chips drenched in hot sauce, or hard-boiled eggs, watermelon, or even the watermelon Now and Laters—penny candy that clung to your teeth and threatened to take out your braces, if you had them. Bringing what you enjoyed and relished in private into the public space of the school yard, the sidewalk, or in front of the corner store seemed to be the violation. Because who didn't enjoy these things in the privacy of their own home? That we all indulged in some of these practices at least some of the time was irrelevant to the insult. Indeed, it added to the specific flavor of the name-calling.

It's my hunch that many northern Black people's discomfort with and rejection of country identity and country music have to do with a distancing from rural life and the South associated with a painful past: sharecropping, slavery, land loved and won and stolen, often violently; from rural community ways; and rural-identified ways of hearing the body, sutured over in the experience of migration to the North, successful or not. As the performer Valerie June put it in an interview with *Austin City Limits*, "A lot of the music that makes us who we are today—we had to leave that because of different memories that we didn't want to have anymore."[7] It's that negotiation with past trauma and violence that colors Turner's country songs as well.

My father told me that his mother loved country music and would listen to Chicago's live broadcasts of the *National Barn Dance*, which was recorded right here in the 1940s and 1950s. But she would never have admitted to her neighbors that she listened to this music, which was considered—maybe especially—by recent southern immigrants to be even less sophisticated than jazz and R&B, and, moreover, "white people's music." A generation later, my own mother liked Glen Campbell—and she had several of his albums, though she rarely played them for us. Later, when she got older, and we left for college, she openly listened to everything. But I still don't remember poor Glen being pulled from the stack. Maybe that voice reminded her of her past marriage and the emotional pull of that time in Nashville. I do know, though, that there is something in her favorite Aaron Neville soulful croon that reminds me of Glen. (Or is it that Glen reminds me of him?)

I HEAR TINA Turner's first solo album, *Tina Turns the Country On!*, as a Black feminist reclaiming of country music and her own country self—in ways that reject nostalgia in favor of the naming and healing of loss. She recorded the album in 1974, a year before her final break and divorce from Ike Turner and at the beginning of the renaissance of her career. It's also a moment of growth in the Black feminist movement. *Sula*, Toni Morrison's novel of a Black woman in search of her own psychic and sexual freedom, was published just the year before, in 1973, to hungry readers. In 1974, Labelle was taking over and funking up the white boy rock scene with her album *Nightbirds*, bringing together rock and glam and funk, as well as a distinct commitment to exploring Black women's sexual subjectivity in "Lady Marmalade" and other songs. Nina Simone, in exile to avoid arrest for unpaid taxes in protest of the Vietnam War, recorded her last album for RCA that year, her good-bye to the racism of the United States, fittingly titled *It Is Finished*. The Combahee River Collective was founded in 1974, as was the National Black Feminist Organization, with Michele Wallace as a founding member. (She had not yet written *Black Macho and the Myth of the Superwoman*, which wasn't published until 1978, but she might well have been living it.) This moment was ripe for Tina Turner's own ambitions for a solo career that would reflect boundless sound and genre possibilities: rock, R&B, funk, as well as a return to the country music that she herself had lived—a country girl, also referenced directly in "Nutbush City Limits." And though *Tina Turns the Country On!* didn't chart very high, its emotional punch and innovation earned it a nomination for a Grammy for Best Female R&B Vocal Performance (but she was beaten by the unbeatable Aretha Franklin).

When I think about Tina Turner's decision to make this first solo album a country one, I wonder about the ways that her own "countryness" might have been disciplined out of her at earlier points of her career. This was dramatized in the 1993 film about her life, *What's Love Got to Do with It*. We watch as Turner (played by Angela Bassett) is shamed by her church members for singing loud and raw in the choir as a child; as she's mocked by her city relatives for being too "country"; as she migrates north as a teenager. In one scene, Ike (played by Laurence Fishburne) molds Tina's mouth to create the "proper" sounds for a burgeoning singer, to be more stylized as "nice and rough." Ike also tells her that her voice is mannish, and these disciplinings of her voice and body to be both more citified and more feminine seem connected to me, conveyed by the sophisticated urban dance moves that she's taught, and by the high heels that she must learn to move in, and which become her trademark.

In *Tina Turns the Country On!*, Tina has the chance to meditate on and occupy and signify those past pressures, and to reengage traditional country modes of lyricism and nostalgia and the yearning for freedom in an extended and public way, something that has been difficult for other Black women to accomplish as either fans or performers. A cover album, including songs by Hank Snow, Dolly Parton, Bob Dylan, James Taylor, and Kris Kristofferson, it is Turner's attempt to uncover, to create and shape a career of songs that she really liked and that she says represented her own tastes.[8] The album was recorded at Ike Turner's Bolic Sound Studios, but with an outside producer and outside musicians, including artists who performed with Elvis Presley, like James Burton on guitar and Glen D. Hardin on piano. On the album, she finds ways to meditate on yearning, desire, and complex, even inhospitable, visions of home.

At barely thirty-six minutes, this is a short album, and on the surface these covers are love songs. (On the back of the album, Tina is naked but for a flowered bed spread. Might that bedspread be seen as the mantle of country music? As a symbol of the songs themselves, which both conceal and reveal her own vulnerable, raw feelings?) Given the song choices and the barely controlled anguish in her voice, I also hear this album as a story cycle of suffering and liberation.

We see this theme of suffering and liberation explored in the album's very first track, P. J. Morse's "Bayou Song"—a song that vividly captures the feeling of being pulled under by a tide of poverty and violence. In its portrait of the everyday experience of domestic despair, it welcomes a connection to Tina's now notorious relationship with Ike. Unlike the everyday life of this financially successful couple, the song depicts the Bayou as the setting for material poverty, with dirty windows and hungry babies. But we might also think about how the song's description of the weary muscles of someone who works with her hands and back ("too tired to eat, too hungry to fight") might also capture the experience of someone who sings and dances strenuously for a living. The song also expresses the soul poverty of being in a physically and emotionally abusive relationship that Turner describes in her memoir *I, Tina.* Turner reflects on her life in 1973, around the time that *Tina Turns the Country On!* began its production:

> I remembered what marriage had meant to me when I was a girl—the loving husband and wife, the happy children. My God, I thought, how had things gone so wrong? The kids would all run and hide when Ike came home, the man was so mean. He had his problems, too, of course: he was getting older, and thick in the waist; and I know he was worried about his nose—the cocaine was starting to eat through the tissue between his nostrils. But he wouldn't stop taking the stuff. He got so crazy with that scene in the studio that me and the kids couldn't even celebrate the holidays anymore. At Christmas, it was like, "Don't buy me any motherfuckin' presents." You'd be wrapping gifts in the bedroom and he'd come in and kick them all over the floor—"Get this shit offa this bed! All these fuckin' holidays . . ." Ike never had a way with words, as you can tell.

So this was my life, and I was starting to see it real clearly now.[9]

In "Bayou Song," I am especially moved by the repeated image of the speaker's similar feeling of hopelessness:

Windows dirty
I can't see out them
Sitting and smoking and thinking about it
Lord I'm so tired.

The lyrics, along with Tina's mournful, sometimes angry voice and the supportive chorus of female background singers, also encourage a reading of the song as a yearning to escape. The song paints a portrait of the weary, cyclical labor it takes to make a marriage work. But the song ends on a resistant note, with a series of curses, in a call and response with the backup singers: "Let the bayou bog starve by itself," and "Let the bayou bog drink itself to hell."

Turner powerfully works the angle of commiseration with her African American female background vocalists: Jessie Smith, Pat Hodges, Clydie King, and Merry Clayton (the latter pair whose vocals provide the powerful countervalence to "Sweet Home Alabama") here and elsewhere. In country music, as well as in rock, background singing has been one of the few places where Black women have been visible. Background has often been the place for Black women's voices to interject shape and add soulfulness and grit to male-dominated musical genres like country and rock. I'm intrigued by Tina's play with the shifting status of these voices in her performances by centering their call and response, so that their voices are always in conversation, repeating, supporting, confirming, maybe also bringing out a new nuance in a harmony, each song never quite a solo. The background vocalist call and response embodies an ethics of care that also has an erotic charge. More than backup, the voices of Smith, Hodges, King, and Clayton amplify and confirm Tina Turner's country intervention. They form sonic solidarity to counteract the violence that she sings about in "Bayou Song."

In addition to exploring violence and solidarity in her country storytelling, Turner explores Black women's eroticism, taking on roles that are typically masculine. When I listen to Tina Turner's cover of Kris Kristofferson's "Help Me Make It Through the Night," the next song on *Tina Turns the Country On!*, I am immediately drawn into her low, controlled register, the way her voice's vibrato shows its muscularity. She takes me through the seduction, guiding me to take the ribbon from her hair, to loosen it, and for me, the listener, to lie right down beside her. Her voice is husky, whispered, as if there might actually be someone listening in the next room this early-morning hour—a husband, or her children. I am drawn into the song directly, and the song's suggestion that we might be doing something that we know we will regret later is pushed aside for the moment, as I let Turner's voice work on me. Sure, as the song builds, she says most clearly, "I need a man." But by then, my own gender seems irrelevant. There is even the possibility that I can be that man, at least in this shadowy light, this moment of emotional desperation. I am nearly convinced that this could work, or even that I could be her lover beyond that night. This is not a clean seduction, a romance freed from guilt or the twists of desire. (And in that way, it is much like some of my own early relationships.) Indeed, even as the song presents our time together as a problem, one that promises to hurt one of us, my role in it is necessary. I'm going to help her "make it."

The song fits into the ways that I've been moved by Turner before, by her voice, by her very direct address, by her combination of muscularity and vulnerability, the sheer exhaustion suggested by the labor she gives to every line of a song, the journey to what is nice and rough. I have been taken through scenarios of love and romance with Tina, positioned as a protector (in "What's Love Got to Do with It," the film and the song itself), as co-conspirator, as empathetic listener, but usually not as the lover. But this is the first song that soundly places me in the space of lover so effectively. Even given the traditionally heterosexual constraints of country music as a genre, Turner's delivery lets me in. And some of that has to do with how I recognize the need expressed in the song as, in part, my own. The need for a reprieve, to feel comfortable in one's own skin and body.

Kris Kristofferson's "Help Me Make It Through the Night" has been covered by women before: by Tammy Wynette and Rita Coolidge, among others—but this rendition so interestingly ingests and transmogrifies Kristopher's own stylings: his growls, his own cries, his craggy performance of the chinks in the armor of white masculinity, equal parts vulnerability and masculine gruff, this time translated as Tina's blues shout, forced to a whisper. The song's performed breakdown of long-built-up strength has its own resonance when sung by a Black woman—tapping the history of violence and assumed obliviousness to pain—the strong Black woman and the unrapeable Jezebel both. This makes the invitation, and the entry, emotionally fraught and powerful for me as another Black female listener.

Turner creates a space to be a fan of country music that may have felt barred to me before. And perhaps this is possible in part because I am entering into the moment of Tina's solo debut, her first, her own moment of risk and new definition.

In the film *What's Love Got to Do with It*, we watch Turner learn choreographed steps, fit her feet into impossible shoes, but we also watch her shine, sparkle, and especially shake. We hear her control in the performance of losing control as she gives her trademark wail in "A Fool in Love": "Whoa, there's something on my mind. Won't somebody please, please, tell me what's wrong?" In "Proud Mary," we hear her tell us about working for The Man "every night

and day," but we also watch her dance the sorrow out of that statement, roll out the pain. But it's still there, the pain behind that
story of "Proud Mary," and it comes out instead in "Bayou Song,"
and in the whispered desperation of "Help Me Make It Through
the Night." In the tradition of the blues, shouters are able to sing
without amplification, and I am reminded of the force behind that
power, the skill as well as the force of a history of pain deferred,
reassembled, undammed, and then let go.

In *Tina Turns the Country On!*, Turner is a kind of root worker,
able to dig deep to access emotion and muscle and spirit. Through
country, as well as R&B and rock, she exorcises rage and pain with
her outsized sound on this album. Turner takes a country music
repertoire, already seemingly worked to its limit by talented others,
and defies those limits. She creates new meanings and speaks specifically to her own and other Black women's experiences, spoken
and unspoken.

Turner included "Nutbush City Limits" in her live repertoire for
almost three decades. It was one of the encores chosen for her
2008 Fiftieth Anniversary Tour, her last before her retirement
from touring. These performances, which spanned her years with
the Ike and Tina Turner Revue and her solo career, were testimony
to her resilience and to the variety of her musical influences, from
the Beatles' "Get Back" to Phil Spector's "River Deep—Mountain
High" to her own "Private Dancer" and ending with "Proud Mary"
and "Nutbush." At the Chicago performance, one of the last shows
of the tour, Turner closed with a lively rendition of "Nutbush City
Limits." Running up an elevated catwalk that extended over her
fans, she didn't seem ready to quit—she seemed poised to crowd-
surf, this sixty-nine-year-old, bending to touch some of the audience's eager hands and then, repeating those lines, "Nutbush
City, Nutbush City Limits," arms raised in triumph, until she is
drowned out by applause.[10]

CHAPTER TWO

LOVE YOU, MY BROTHER

Darius Rucker's Bro-Intimacy

IN 2005, THREE YEARS BEFORE he would launch his wildly successful country music career, the Hootie and the Blowfish front man, Darius Rucker, appeared in a Burger King commercial for the Tender Crisp Chicken Bacon Cheddar Ranch Sandwich.[1] Nattily dressed as a Black cowboy, Tex Ritter style, complete with acoustic guitar, purple rhinestone shirt, white hat, and white cravat, Rucker performs in earnest and a little goofily, head bobbing to a tune reminiscent of "Big Rock Candy Mountain," seemingly unaffected by the bevy of mostly white women cavorting around him, jumping through hoops of red onions, bending over showily to pick burgers from trees in vinyl short-shorts, fondling bricks of cheddar, buckets of white ranch dressing sloshing between their two-stepping legs. In this pubescent (or maybe prepubescent) "have it your way" fantasy of free-flowing women, food, and color, Rucker plays the "straight man," of sorts, while perhaps serving as an object of desire himself, the promise of his own compact, muscular body still contained by the taboo role of Black and country, but waiting to be discovered, unwrapped, and undone, at least in the world of fantasy. In the fantastical world of the "Tender Crisp Chicken Bacon Cheddar Ranch" commercial, Rucker promises the guilt-free pleasures of numerous sensual freedoms. Rucker yodels: "I love the Tender Crisp Bacon Chicken Cheddar Ranch, no one tells you to behave. / Your wildest fantasies come true. Dallas Cheerleaders give you shaves." Never breaking his earnestness, Rucker performs a contained but still visually available talisman of desirable Black masculinity (both tender and crisp), one that promises to enjoy these transgressive pleasures and emotional releases with you. If Wendy's once asked, "Where's the beef?," in this commercial, Rucker is definitely *it*.

Might Rucker, in his very performance of "straight man" in the face of excess—an imaginary wingman to audience enjoyment, seemingly unaffected himself—be offering up his own "Afro-alienation act"? This is a term coined by the performance studies scholar Daphne Brooks to describe the ways that Black artists have used the space of performance, including music, to enact freedom under constraint. In her book *Bodies in Dissent: Spectacular Performances of Race and Freedom*, Brooks looks at nineteenth- and early twentieth-century African American performers who, through their gestures, voices, and other aspects of "rehearsed methods," are "registering the disorienting condition of social marginalization"—sometimes under the radar of their white audiences.[2] From the minstrel performer Bert Williams to the escaped slave/abolitionist/magician Henry "Box" Brown, who escaped from slavery by shipping himself in a box across the Mason-Dixon Line, these Afro-alienation acts are part of a history of using performed roles of Blackness "to transform the notion of ontological dislocation into resistant performance so as to become the agents of their own liberation."[3] With this lens, what seems like Rucker's complicity might actually be fierce focus; what seems like laid-back ease might actually take great labor; and what feels like a disposable joke, perhaps at the expense of its star, might instead be a blueprint for navigating the minefields of race, gender, and sexuality, particularly in predominantly white, patriarchal, and capitalist spaces such as country music.

Since the Burger King appearance in 2005, Rucker has become one of country music's most popular and lucrative stars, with several songs that have reached number one on the country charts, sold-out stadium appearances, a Country Music Association Award, and a Grammy for best country solo performance in "Wagon Wheel," in 2014. That same year, he was inducted into the Grand Ole Opry Country Music Hall of Fame (one of only three African Americans—along with DeFord Bailey and Charley Pride). Rucker's career reflects a savvy negotiation of the still very tightly patrolled world of mainstream country music, where racial mixing and sexual and gender nonnormativity are still taboo. And indeed, in his transition to country music, Rucker has worked hard to craft an authentic country image that links him to the South, including his album *Southern Style* (2015), and to country musical traditions, especially connections to the white country artist Radney Foster and the duo Foster and Lloyd,[4] to Black country classics by Al Green ("For the Good Times"), and to Charley Pride. Rucker has entered the country world, I'd argue, through a combined strategy of likability (as Joe Posnanski once wrote in an NBC Sportsworld profile of him, "Rucker understands there's power in niceness"[5]) and a focused, sometimes steely professionalism. In particular, the critic Will Hermes describes Rucker in *Rolling Stone*: "Rucker's clean-cut, matter-of-fact amiability was a key to Hootie's triumph—and it certainly helped him connect with a mainstream country audience, too. But in addition to being a nice guy, he's a stone-fierce competitor—just like his buddy Tiger Woods, whose wedding he played."[6]

DARIUS RUCKER AS BRO

I see in Rucker's friendly amiability the consummate "bro." As a bro, Rucker has found a register through which he can safely navigate these sometimes treacherous waters of racial mixing, as both a buddy and a conduit to censored feelings and emotions. One male interviewer admitted to listening to Rucker's music after a romantic breakup, while eating a carton of ice cream. Rucker has performed for Barack Obama, hangs out with the football player Dan Marino and the NBA star Dirk Nowitzki, and is a close buddy to Tiger Woods. (In addition to performing at Woods's wedding, he performed at Woods's father's funeral.) Rucker is an ardent and emotional sports fan and famously confessed that when he used his teary voice in "I Only Wanna Be with You," he was crying for one of his favorite teams, the Miami Dolphins, which had recently lost a game.

Broness, I'd argue, is itself a transmogrification of Black cool and the projection of Black bodies as spaces of feeling, playfulness, manliness, and even unity. While the prototypical bro that we see in popular culture might be the white Wall Street stockbroker or white fraternity brother, I'd argue that it is a culture of manly intimacy that builds itself on white constructions of Black intimacy and soulfulness, ease, confidence with the body (negotiated through hugs and high fives), and hipness. It is, of course, an appropriation and a shortening of earlier Black slang use of "Brother" as a term of endearment and Black racial unity with roots in the Black Power movement (as in "Give me five, my Brother!"). "Bro"'s whitening process might even include an ironic layer, some self-consciousness of the "love and theft" of Blackness[7] to construct these often exclusively white spaces of male social privilege. And yet, it is also a form of masculinity that solidifies patriarchy, and that depends on the protection of all-male spaces to create a kind of heteronormative intimacy.[8] As a Black "brother" who is also a bro, Rucker—and his music—is able to circulate in these privileged spaces as both guest and projected source of power.

We see the power of Black brohood to earn its place within contested spaces on the cover of Rucker's 2015 album, *Southern*

Style. Rucker leans on an iconic white picket fence, cross and wedding ring his only bling, relaxed and easygoing (and easy on the eyes). Or we see it as we watch Rucker on stage at the Grand Ole Opry, with faded baseball cap and tight NASCAR T-shirt, hugging his friend Brad Paisley, wiping away the tears of happiness because Brad's just stunned him with a surprise invitation to become the newest Grand Ole Opry member.[9] Or on a 2012 appearance on the *Today Show*, where, after a performance of "Wagon Wheel," Rucker gives away a paid mortgage to a wounded war vet. There he is "Lifting Lives" on a celebrity golf tournament. Observe Rucker lending country "cred" to Lionel Richie's own 2012 country crossover album, *Tuskegee*.[10] As the two sing a duet on a live countrified version of the R&B tune "Stuck on You," with added flourishes like fiddles and slide guitar, the two men—the only Black ones on the American Country Music Awards stage—share a brohug. In the duet, Rucker's sound is fuller, more rounded, even more emotionally accessible than Richie's more sharply stylized, more nasal falsetto. The performance frames Rucker and Richie as two men who are intimately connected, a performance of musical friendship and emotional bonding. At the end of the song, Richie improvises, "Mighty glad you stayed around, Darius, I love you to death, my brother," a testament to their connection and a comment on Rucker's staying power in country music, perhaps.

If brohood performs a kind of intimacy and ease of body that white culture has always admired and appropriated from Black male culture, Rucker's Black brohood savvily makes powerful use of these codes to travel through the white spaces of country music. His performance of Black brohood reveals the performative nature of Blackness and shows that as E. Patrick Johnson points out, "the concept of blackness has no essence"[11]—it is itself a performance, and the measure of its authenticity reflects the values and codes of power of the groups who recognize it. The success of Rucker's

Black bro forces us to face the ways that performances of Blackness and Black masculinity can be loved and admired by white audiences who might have a lesser commitment to the lives of Black people themselves. But intimacy can operate in unexpected ways. Might the highly performative nature of Rucker's Black brohood also leave open the possibility of shared intimacy with those of us who also occupy Blackness in ways that feel inauthentic to others' eyes, including Black queer women like me?

FOR A YEAR when I was in college in Kansas, I was friends with a frat house full of boys, mostly white boys. I think I'm going to be an anthropologist, I told myself, soaking in their chatter and heartache. I think I might be queer, I told myself, sitting on a lap because it felt easy and good.

One autumn morning that year I woke up in an armchair in a room with five sleeping boys. They were piled in a bunk bed a few feet away from me, the air thick with boy sweat and snoring. The TV was still on from a night of watching WWF professional wrestling and *Saturday Night Live*. My father, a professor at my university and the person I lived with, came to find me, and he stood in the bedroom waiting until I got up, hands on his hips, cold autumn light streaming from the window behind him so I couldn't see his face.

Once we got outside, my father told me I was too old for such play. Boys were men, and outside of this room were more men. Outside of this room was work and the right kind of love. I already knew outside, knew how to keep my hands in my pockets, head down from the wind. I knew about bus stops and cars slowing down and how to look into the middle distance. I understood the importance of being invisible on the street. But I wanted this room, these five boys. I chose to be there. Not lured. Wanted morning quiet with boy smells and me in this tattered easy chair covered

with someone else's dirty jeans, awake with my eyes closed, waiting for them to wake up.

Across from the park where I would sometimes go running was
Fraternity Row. You could tell which frats were tonier: the wood
siding of the Tudor-style house for one of the top-dog frats was
recently weatherized, and it had new, tinted windows. The other
frat houses, colonials mostly, were also recently painted, and bor-
ders of flowers appeared during parents' weekend. The boys who
lived in these frats would play touch football outside with their
shirts off, and they were tanned and muscled from the Nautilus
machines they must have kept in their basements. Sometimes girls
dressed in matching sweatshirts would come to visit them, bringing freshly baked cookies. But the frat house where my friends
were, what I called in my head the Fraternity of In-Between, had a
kind of permanent dustiness about it. It was painted an unflatter-
ing brown, and the hedges had been removed at the rotting root.
If you ran by, you might see a boy's legs dangling out of an open
window, while he was smoking and reading. You might see a shirt-
less boy with a farmer's tan, reddened arms, pale chest, pushing a
mower over the yellowing grass. The boys did their own gardening
and repairs, and so planks of unstained wood patched the worn
places on the house's frame and porch.

The Fraternity of In-Between was run-down, but not like the
Animal House in the movie, the clichéd party house worn into the
ground through rowdy behavior, all beer-canned front yards and
naked blow-up dolls thrown through broken windows. No, this
house was of another, more modest ilk. It was as though the house
had no idea that it could be seen by others, as if everything worth
noting about it happened inside rather than out.

Which goes against everything I had ever thought about frater-
nities. Wasn't the whole reason you joined a fraternity or sorority
to be seen, so that others could read the letters on your T-shirt,
recognize you, know where you stood in the order of things? That

was the feeling I got when I had tried pledging my sister's sorority soon after coming to college. She told me that a Black sorority would help me feel grounded in this mostly white college town, and I believed her at first. We were instructed to wear the same pink dress every day, and to carry an ivy plant wherever we went, and to recite the Greek alphabet while holding a burning match fast enough so that it wouldn't burn our fingers. I hated being told what to do, but even more, I hated my need to belong paraded so obviously in front of everyone. I dropped out as a pledge only a few weeks in, and when I saw my once–pledge sisters on campus, they would greet me with a masked smile.

The frat felt like much less pressure. The frat did do its frat things: Rush Week, pledging, theme parties: Hawaiian Luau Party, Twin Party, Desert Island Party, Room to Room Party, Homecoming. A professional photographer came and documented each one, and the themes and date were printed at the bottom of the photos, along with the Greek letters. There was a sister sorority that played practical jokes on them, and its members served as their dates for dances. I went to these dances, too, sometimes as a friend-date, or with the group of girls who called themselves the "Little Sisters" to the frat brothers.

The music that I heard around the frat was dominated by mid-1980s pop-country and prog rock: the Charlie Daniels Band, Kenny Rogers, Kansas (of course), and a whole lot of Styx. The DJ who played the big parties always included the Isley Brothers' "Shout!" to get people on the dance floor (an obligatory frat party staple, culled from the *Animal House* soundtrack), and there might be some Whitney Houston ("You Give Good Love") or Billy Ocean ("Suddenly") when the lights turned down low and it was time to slow dance. At the same time that I was exploring frat life, Darius Rucker, a year older than me, was playing frat parties at the University of South Carolina with his band, the newly formed Hootie and the Blowfish. I imagine that we might have been listening to some of the same music. Maybe both of us, as we worked those frat house dance floors, were conjuring up our own Afro-alienation acts.

My friends in my other life thought I was crazy. Todd, who was queer and came out after college, as I did, was at the time a solid misanthropist, and would say, "I don't know why you bother with those nitwits." He grew up with a few of the frat brothers in a small town in western Kansas, knew their parents, was picked or not picked for the same teams, belonged or didn't belong to the same high school cliques. They were part of the life that Todd wanted to leave behind. My friend Robin asked me point-blank over coffee, "Why would you want to be a part of a group that won't have you as an official member? Why settle for that kind of inequality?" We were sitting together at one of the student group tables, pamphleting in support of the people of El Salvador and waiting for Cyd, our mutual crush, to get off work at the student union to join us. I knew that even our most high-minded activism shared some of the same sexism, bromance, and sexual intrigue that I found in frat life. I shrugged. "I just like them," I said.

At the Fraternity of In-Between, I often felt like I was the audience to their romance with one another, watching, soaking it all in. In their water balloon fights, slaps, pinches, noogies, brohugs, backrubs, they were always touching one another, fighting off touching one another, or trying to touch one another. They slept, ate, dated, and studied with one another, sat next to one another in class. They were never far away from another brother, and would use that word, "Brother," often, and as if they meant it. As if they shared common flesh.

Maybe I craved being one of them. Oddly, many of the boys seemed not to have hit their final growth spurt yet. They were short and cherubic, or tall and scrawny, many of their voices still breaking. Sometimes, when one of them walked in from the cold, I was struck by the girlishness to be found in their soft, reddened cheeks.

There was no housemother, no figure of authority, and yet it was not a place that felt dangerous to me. When I look back now at my own ease there, I understand how unlikely this is. When I show my partner, Annie, the photos of me and the boys and the other odd girls who also hung out there, drinking directly from the spout of a keg or dancing in a sweaty throng to "Rock Lobster," she sees danger. I'd see danger, too, if I had been my own big sister or girlfriend. I would have been afraid for me, surrounded by all that competition and booze and concentrated male energy that the photographs seem to capture.

But what I sought there was the hidden quiet. After a party, we'd sit on the second-floor landing and talk about our parents, about where we came from. I'd insert myself into debates about the second inauguration of Ronald Reagan, bringing in my critiques gleaned from my Amnesty International meetings. We talked about love. I confessed to having a crush on the woman who brought the antipornography slide show to campus. She was older, maybe even thirty, and had a British accent, and she wore tight designer jeans tucked into tall yellow rubber Paddington boots. It was the first time I remember saying that I had a crush on a woman out loud to anyone, and I wondered, after I did it, if they had really heard me. After all, they mercilessly teased one of the brothers who got clothes catalogues from the store American Male, calling them his "porn," and I'd heard the word "faggot" lobbed around more than once. But when I said, "I love women," one of the boys simply nodded and said, "Yeah, I can understand that," like it was just another strange fact of my life that I was sharing, like living in a condo. Or maybe it was just familiar to them.

MAYBE DARIUS RUCKER has a bit of the "in-between," too. Through his performance of "bro" intimacy, Rucker disrupts gendered categories of masculine country performance that Richard

Peterson describes in his book *Creating Country Music*. Peterson discusses the two dueling codes of "hard core" and "soft shell" country music authenticity, in which "hard core," such as the rough-and-tumble but emotionally poignant sounds of Johnny Cash and Hank Williams Jr., is at a premium.[12] Hard-core country performances might include southernisms in speech; self-deprecation; untrained voice and personal involvement in the song, raw emotion, expressing personally felt experiences; and lyrics that depict humble beginnings. These performances also put a premium on the storytelling aspect of country music and the power of direct address to the audience.[13] Rucker manages to tap into some of the emotionality of "hard core" country performances with his facial expressions; his folksy, occasionally growly baritone; and his sometimes personal lyrics about love, God, and fatherhood—also a means of opening up static images of Black manhood that still dominate the media. Yet, like successful "soft shell" country performers (more often associated with "countrypolitan" or pop-country crossovers like Charley Pride, Kenny Rogers, and the Oakridge Boys), Rucker sings in a melodious regional accent only vaguely reminiscent of his South Carolina roots; his stage image feels crafted in its informality, a little distanced from the audience, an entertainer at heart. And characteristic of soft-shell performers, any entrée into his personal life—including his interracial marriage to Beth Leonard and their recent divorce—is controlled and decidedly sunny.[14]

As a storyteller, Rucker imbues his lyrics with the feeling of a good-humored Everyman who is still capable of being surprised by love. Loss is also occasionally part of his journey, but it is not at the center. His is not the voice of Johnny Cash, shaken and devastated by loss—the survivor. He lacks the loneliness of George Jones or Clint Black or Roy Orbison. His storytelling is conversational, accessible, and the voice he uses to tell his stories is earthy, warm, melodic, and moving, a voice that you might overhear singing in the shower. His most iconic gesture when singing is his pounding of his hand on his heart, a gesture of sincerity—from his heart to ours. This performance of earnestness might be its own Afro-alienation act, since claiming and protecting one's capacity for joy (as well as rage) continues to be difficult in these violent and still racist times. At the same time, this gesture of heart pounding captures the double message of the bro: masculine tenderness and bravado both.

Rucker writes or cowrites most of his songs, and his lyrics capture homey everyday details of domestic life—modern with a hint of the traditional. For example, in "It Won't Be Like This for Long," he shares the caregiving of his child with his wife; but the lyrics also include listening to his child saying his prayers before going to bed. This combination of modern and traditional is also featured in "Homegrown Honey," which at the beginning is about boredom while bar hopping in New York City, but quickly turns into a paean of the grooves and sexual energy of southern women:

> You shake it down to your roots
> Did your momma teach you how to do that thing you do

Similarly, the lover described in "Southern Style" (cowritten by Rucker) is a mixture of old-fashioned and contemporary, an outspoken fan of both Lil Wayne and Lynyrd Skynyrd, he says, able to move between these characteristically outspoken Black and white performers, but also traditionally religious, "a Billy Graham fan like her mother."

In many ways, Rucker's performance of Black masculinity evokes earlier notions of racial uplift, centering family, heterosexuality, and traditional Christian values, but there are glimmers of images of female agency, together with male vulnerability, to complicate and update the message (for example, in "It Won't Be Like This for Long," "If I Told You," and the Hootie and the Blowfish hit "Let Her Cry"). Rucker tries on images of dissolution in a few party songs, like "Going to Hell" or "Drinkin' and Dialin'," but just enough to allow him his "boys will be boys" bro-ness.

DARIUS AND CHARLEY

Perhaps Darius Rucker's greatest role model for success has been Charley Pride, whose warmth and performance of comfort in white and potentially difficult spaces a generation earlier was more than impressive: dueling banjos with Roy Clark, or cracking jokes on the set of *Hee Haw*. Rucker's successful early twenty-first-century crossing into country music has been made possible by Charley Pride's late twentieth-century career. It's a connection that Rucker himself makes repeatedly in his interviews. But as we see, Pride's negotiations require labor. The laughter, ease, and never-yielding professionalism of both performers are shadowed by the ever-present possibility of racial violence against them, threatened or real. Their double-conscious performance of likeability in anticipation of racial violence is a version of the "salvic wish" at the heart of Black respectability politics—that the internalization of "proper" behavior and white approval will save one's life and the life of one's family.[15] Rather than merely "calling out" the politics of Black respectability in Rucker's or Pride's approaches to success, I think it's more powerful to explore them, to see ourselves at the heart of them, and to admire them as sources of creativity. Their careers give us the chance to witness and hear the code-switching, masking, and humor that cut several ways, aspects of Afro-alienation performance, and to think about these performances as ones that we still might find in our own toolboxes of survival.

Charley Pride was the first African American country artist tied to a major label, signing with RCA in 1965. From the 1960s through the 1970s, Pride scored fifty hits on Billboard's country charts, and thirty of those reached number one. In the mid-1970s, he became

RCA's best-selling artist since Elvis Presley. In his 1994 autobiography, *Pride: The Charley Pride Story*, he talks about experiences of the violence that was often in the background of these successes, framing them in a genial, sometimes indirect storytelling voice, which favors understatement and humor. While he acknowledges the difficulty of getting concerts and engagements as a Black country music singer, especially early in his career at the height of the civil rights movement, he describes it in his gentle, self-deprecating way. For example, in response to concert organizers' fears of boycotts and racial violence, Pride says that he would open his first shows with this joking disclaimer: "Ladies and gentlemen. I realize this is a little unique . . . me coming out here on a country music show wearing this permanent tan."[16] In this we see an example of Pride's layered strategy: his seeming internalization of a white-centered view of race (where whiteness is the norm, tanned or otherwise) while making light of audience fears, and perhaps pointing to the ironic love of Blackness inherent in white idealization of tanned skin.

On his album covers, Pride serves up a visual image that is hopeful and earnest, though by no means apologetic. Album titles that pun on his name, like *Pride of Country Music* (1967) and *Pride of America* (1974), reinforce the image of his patriotism and his belonging. The cover of *Pride of Country Music*, his second album, features a color photo of him, hands relaxed on top of his guitar, wearing a charcoal suit and immaculate pressed white shirt, clean shaven and brown skin gleaming, a face hopeful and undeniably handsome with its deep cheekbones. His eyes look up and a little away from the camera, as if to ignore any haters in order to follow a shooting star on the horizon, which he himself certainly was by then. Pride's style echoes that of other well-respected Black male performers of the same period, including Harry Belafonte and Sidney Poitier, as well as the relaxed poise of Darius Rucker.

In their important study *Country Music U.S.A.*, Bill Malone and Jocelyn Neal suggest that Pride's success might be attributed to his timing, "the right singer at the right time in history."[17] But Pride's autobiography complicates this notion of a smooth and seamless entry into country music success. In *Pride*, he describes being heckled by Black soldiers on a USO tour in Germany for singing country music. He describes death threats, racist pranks by his white country costars, encounters with stalker fans, including one who claimed that he had the power to put her in a trance, and another who insisted that she was his missing white mother.[18] He writes with characteristic wry humor of moving a self-described Grand Wizard of the KKK to tears: "'Charley,' the guy said in a pronounced southern accent, 'That was a good show. I'm from way down in Georgia and I'll be darned, I ain't never heard a nigger sound like you in all my life. You put on a hell of a show.'"[19] Poignantly, he describes his struggles with a dark and sometimes immobilizing depression that "was as though a veil of dark gauze was drawn around me, wrapping me in paranoia, insomnia, confusion and dread. I believed someone was putting things in my drinks and trying to harm me."[20] Given the many micro and macro aggressions that Pride describes in his autobiography, such paranoia might have been justified. These moments speak to the ways Pride had to navigate not only the sonic but also the visual power of his celebrity—how his raced body, sometimes seen in incongruity with his voice, was read by others as meaningful, upsetting, and otherwise powerful.

In a memorable example of Pride's navigation of racial tensions, in the summer of 1967, Pride went on a concert tour with Willie Nelson through Texas and Louisiana, with his manager Jack explaining the logic that teaming up would help open doors for him in the South and help mitigate racial tension. Pride describes an incident at the beginning of the tour that has since become legend:

> We had a stop in San Antonio and we were all staying at the Roadway Inn. Jack and I drove up and there were a lot of people

standing in front of the motel. Willie was there, along with some of the band members and a group of fans.

As I got out of the car I heard Willie yell, "Hey, Supernigger, come over here."

As I walked toward him, everyone looked around nervously, maybe thinking there was going to be trouble. When I got to where Willie was standing, he grabbed me and kissed me with the whole crowd looking on. That broke everybody up.

Willie called me "Supernigger" for a long time after that. I think it was his way of disarming any racists who might be around, a way of taking the language of rancor and throwing it back at them as humor, the way Redd Foxx often did. In the same way that profanity is enfeebled by overuse, the buzzwords of hate can be neutralized by mocking them.[21]

There's so much that Pride doesn't say about this moment. Like that kiss—was it a winsome peck on the cheek? A full-on soulful smooch? An "offer-you-can't-refuse-you-broke-my-heart,-Fredo" power kiss? At any rate, I think it is worth noting that while Pride sees Nelson appropriating racial slurs to take away their power, he himself uses a markedly different tactic of dealing with racism through indirect response in his writing. For Pride, the psychic work of mediating others' intentions, good and bad, is often a more subtle labor.[22]

JASON WAS THE ONLY Black brother at the frat. A former football player, he carried his large frame with a delicacy and consciousness of space that I found moving. At group dinners, he'd often scrunch his body to make it smaller, hovering over his plate, careful to keep his elbows pressed tightly to his sides. While the other brothers were usually grubby, except when preparing for a date, Jason always smelled like cologne (Polo by Ralph Lauren, I learned later), and when it was hot outside, he showered twice a day. At first, I teased him for his fastidiousness, his arrangement of his ties in rainbow order in his closet, and the boar-bristle brush that he kept in his back pocket, to whip out at a moment's notice to maintain his shapely short Afro with its shag in the back. But it was clear from his awkward laughter that I had touched a nerve. Jason wanted to become a dentist, and he had a beautiful, wide smile that usually had the power to charm just about anyone, including those who underestimated him: his professors and classmates, store owners, his housemates. He'd flash it whenever he walked past me in the narrow halls, muttering, "Pardon me. Sorry," laying his hand lightly on my back as he passed.

One Sunday morning, Jason and I went with a group of the brothers to grab some breakfast at Country Kitchen, a towny chain diner a few miles from campus famous for their biscuits and gravy. We were the only Black people in the restaurant, and we sat next to each other, in silent support. The whole group of us were laughing and excitedly debating soap operas. (Everyone in the house was hooked on *Days of Our Lives*, but I was a diehard *All My Children* fan.) As Jason jumped up to summon our busy waitress, a pair of older white women sitting at a table near us looked over, alarmed. One crumpled up her napkin, wiping her orange-lipsticked mouth as if she had been poisoned. The two women quickly left the diner and hurried to their car, leaving behind their unfinished crullers and coffee. When we got back to the van, I asked the group, "Did you see that? Those ladies looked like we were getting ready to kidnap them!" The group made comforting noises, and patted Jason and me on the shoulders. Jason's roommate Chris said, "Who cares about a couple of little old ladies?," putting an arm around Jason and roughly knuckling his head, then put the keys in the ignition to drive us home. Jason chuckled softly. The ride back was quiet, and I switched my thoughts to schoolwork and home. As we pulled back into the driveway of the frat house, one brother piped up, "Actually, I forgot you all were Black!"

HISTORY IN THE MAKING?

Like Pride, in Rucker's visual images as well as his interviews, we see him navigate and often mediate racism in ways that are striking. For example, in several of Rucker's music videos, Rucker is cast in white worlds in ways where he is physically separated from the white people in them. The songs provide an emotional soundtrack, but the scenarios of romance and prosperity exclude him. For example, in "History in the Making," from Rucker's first country album, *Learn to Live* (2009), two white couples are the center of the action, one in the 1950s, one in the present. We watch them fall in love and make a home in a beautiful old white house. "History in the Making" has a promising title, offering a chance, perhaps, for commentary, direct or indirect, of Rucker's history-making presence as a country star. Instead, Rucker remains on the margins. As the song lyrics tumble from image to increasingly erotic image ("I just want to take this in/The moonlight dancin' off your skin"), Rucker's voice grows more passionate. Maybe Rucker is a ghost, haunting the couples' dreams. Maybe Rucker is meant to be the voice of the old house itself, the beautiful old wood paneling glowing like his skin. What is clear is that this narrative in the video isn't about Black domesticity, Black romance, Black family making, or Black history, at least not explicitly. But maybe it *is* an acknowledgment that the specter of Blackness is deeply tied to white history, to white (manifest) destinies, if the vision is one of symbolic and literal racial segregation.

This symbolic segregation of Rucker from the white people around him is a pattern that happens in many of his videos.

In the video for "Alright" (2009), set in Rucker's hometown of Charleston, South Carolina, Rucker is green-screened into scenes of white contentment: white people sitting on homey porches, white children playing on the beach, white tourists enjoying picturesque shopping areas. The only Black person you see in the town is Darius himself, and he's been spliced in. And the video for "Don't Think I Don't Think about It" (2010) features a break-up-to-make-up love story featuring a white couple. Throughout the drama, Rucker is stuck singing in a barn for most of the action.[23]

But in the video for "Wagon Wheel," his 2012 hit, we can see Rucker enacting a different, more critical relationship to whiteness. Like the others I've mentioned, in this video everyone except Rucker is white, but it takes that narrative of Rucker as an outsider to whiteness and explores it, dramatizing the process of isolation, risk, and persuasion. Rucker plays an itinerant musician who is traveling alone through a white rural town, attempting to make it to a concert, and to the white-appearing girl in the photo that he carries with him. The sepia tones and nostalgic sound of the video might remind us of the vulnerability of a Black male body alone in rural spaces, memories of lynchings and being run off land not too far below the surface.

Over the course of the video, Rucker hitchhikes his way through this rural space, marked by railroad tracks, quiet roads, and antique stores, sometimes meeting resistance from the whites who stop to give him a ride, but each time winning them over with his singing. As it happens, the stars of the reality show *Duck Dynasty* are cast as the townspeople (and I have to admit their long beards, hunters' gear, and gruff demeanors trigger my own anxious memories of traveling as a Black person through rural white-only spaces). In one scene, Rucker looks into an abandoned antique store and sees himself—a kind of curio. He watches himself singing and dancing

in the antique store, among the canned goods and farm imple-
ments. Then he sees others watching him: a white man wearing
an American Flag bandanna and two white women. Their expressions are ambiguous, ranging from curiosity to desire to envy.[24]

Rucker finally makes it to the bar, where ostensibly he's supposed to perform. We see his name on the marquee, but he's
barred by the white bouncer at the door. The white patrons of
the bar watch unmoved as Rucker tries to explain that he's the
headliner, but then the bartender—the white woman in the photo
that Rucker's been carrying all along—beckons to the bouncer to
let him in. When Rucker starts to perform, the crowd looks uncomfortable at first but then warms up. Rucker's expression as he
performs on stage is like that of a professor teaching his students
a hard-to-swallow lesson. He nods and encourages until, by the
time we get to the chorus, "Rock me Mama like a wagon wheel.
Rock me mama any way you feel. Hey, Mama rock me!" the audience is singing along. The song ends triumphantly.

And then, like Dorothy waking in her Kansas bedroom, it turns
out that it was all a dream! We see the "real" Rucker, waking up,
getting out of the bed on his tour bus. Ironically, the white skeptics
that he encounters throughout the dream are members of his own
band and entourage. With the cover of a dream, the video invites
us to peek into Rucker's psyche and acknowledges the riskiness
and labor of performing country music as a Black man. Rucker
shows us the continued existence of racial tension with his white
audiences, while he also offers his view of musical performance as
the path to shared joy and reconciliation.

FOR A SEMESTER, I abandoned my anthropologist's project of
just "studying" boys, and Jason and I tried dating. There was
something about those fish-out-of-water experiences that we

both shared that made me think we might have more in common. And he was very persistent. He gave me his class photograph and had written on the back in his best Spanish, "Te amo
por siempre" in romantic, loopy handwriting. That was followed
by tiny diamond earrings for my birthday with the note, "More
diamonds coming soon!" One morning near Valentine's Day, he
and his frat brothers came to my apartment to serenade me, Jason
on one knee, holding out a rose. No one had ever serenaded me
before, and I was flattered. But I also felt the wild urge to run
in the opposite direction as fast as I could. While it sometimes
felt powerful, in this new role as prize girlfriend I found myself
performing someone I didn't recognize. For Spring Break, Jason
took me home to meet his family. That first night, over an episode
of *The Cosby Show*, I heard his brother whisper to Jason, "You got
one of those yellow gals." They gave each other high fives. Once
his parents fell asleep and I crept from the guest room to his
childhood bed, Jason whispered to me that he had never touched
himself before, because God was watching, and I laughed in disbelief. The frost of shame, if there was any for me, was very thin
and easily melted, and besides, if there is a god, wouldn't she want
me to enjoy myself? When it was time to return to campus, his
parents prayed over our car to drive the devils out and called me
their daughter. I knew our days as a couple were numbered. But I
did find home for a while one gray Saturday afternoon later that
spring, just after the last, unexpected snowfall. I cornrowed Jason's
hair while I sat on his unmade bed, drawing a tic-tac-toe of a part
in his hair with my wide-toothed comb. This was a self, iconic in
its Blackness, that I recognized and courted, and maybe Jason
did, too. The warm smell of Ultra Sheen rose up from the bright,
vulnerable brown of his scalp, and holding him steady with my
knees like a drum, I was unsure if he was brother or lover or son,
and for that moment, it didn't matter.

THE ONLY BLACK GUY

Sometimes, I wonder if, despite his success crossing over to country music, Darius Rucker feels trapped by his image as "the only Black guy." I know I'm not alone in wondering that. Key and Peele, a comedy duo that has explored Rucker's image repeatedly, offers a poignant parody of Rucker's attempts to negotiate his white audiences. In episode eight of their 2012 season on their Comedy Central show, Rucker (played by Jordan Peele) appears onstage in Rucker's trademark laid-back T-shirt and bald pate, strumming his acoustic guitar to a mostly white crowd. While the skit doesn't mention Rucker's switch to country music, Peele's Darius sings a parody version of the Hootie and the Blowfish classic "I Just Want to Be with You" that clearly signals a departure from the group and his past music: "Don't want to go out with my friends no more / Don't want to hold your hands no more. / I don't want to be with you." But Darius is interrupted by an enthusiastic fan (a goateed and dreadlocked Keegan-Michael Key), who insists that Darius *is* Hootie. When Darius tries to correct him, like a patient teacher (again)—that there is no such person as Hootie, it's just a nonsense name for the band, "like Toad the Wet Sprocket," the fan doesn't quite get it. Maybe he's stuck in his own essentialized logic of "Hootie" (which might mean Black Darius) and the Blowfish (the white remainder of the band). Rather than accept change, Key and the rest of the audience come up with their own interpretation. Key announces to the rest of the audience, "We gotta pick, y'all! We gotta choose between Hootie *or* the Blowfish!" The audience then begins chanting, "Blowfish! Blowfish!" Darius is growing increasingly agitated:

"That hurts my feelings, y'all," he tells them.

"You said you're not Hootie," Key counters.

"I'm not, *sir*. But in the question you just asked, I was clearly Hootie."

"So you *are* Hootie."

"I'm not, though."

"He *is* Hootie!"

The crowd explodes in another round of absurd chanting of "Hootie!" Darius is crying now, and raises his arms in Christ-like supplication, offering his body to surf the crowd. "I *am* Hootie. I *am* Hootie," he sobs.[25] In this skit, not only does *Key & Peele* caricature the racially bifurcated logic of some Hootie fans, but it also speaks to the pressure on Rucker to keep his composure in public. Like Luther in *Key & Peele*'s "Obama Anger Translator—Victory" from the same season,[26] *Key & Peele*'s parody of Darius Rucker is a study of the pressure on public figures to keep composure while Black, but it also gives Rucker room to finally lose control. Rucker has expressed his appreciation for the skit and commented on Twitter and in other interviews that he finds this and other *Key & Peele* send-ups of his image "frickin' hilarious."[27]

Might Key's dreadlocked Hootie fan who feels the need to "choose" also speak to some Black music listeners' complex relationship to Rucker? Or perhaps even articulate an internal voice that Rucker himself might have to negotiate: whether to remain the safe and known Hootie, the beloved Black front man for an otherwise white band, or to venture out into a musical world that has expressed its preference for whiteness (i.e., country music)? Key's role as mediator of the crowd's opinion in the sketch is doubly interesting to me given Key's fluid racial performances. (Key and Peele are both multiracial and both play Black and non-Black characters on the show.) Key's dreadlocks, Rasta cap, and cowry shell jewelry could be sartorial signs of white hippy style *or* of African American Afrocentric hipness. Maybe Key's fan is a clueless white fan, or maybe he's a fellow fish out of water, navigating white spaces, too.

While a casual scan of Darius Rucker's YouTube video comments reveals a presence of Black fans—and I have grown to be one myself—Rucker has occasionally expressed frustration at not being seen or recognized by the Black community. In a 2014 interview with *Wall Street Journal Live*, Rucker laments that despite his success, he has never been invited to be on the cover of Black magazines like *Ebony* and *Jet*, and that his 2002 R&B album, *Back to Then*, failed to chart significantly (the album topped out at 43 on Billboard's R&B charts, and 127 on Billboard's Pop charts).[28] More recently, he's described his own family's initial bewilderment and even shaming of his love of country music, as well as shaming comments by Black journalists sent to interview him.[29]

Perhaps, as Rucker struggles to be fully seen and heard by both his white and Black audiences, transmogrifying any frustration or anger into something cuddly or at least palatable, something of himself threatens to get lost in translation. Is there room for Rucker to express the anger he's allowed in the *Key & Peele* sketch? In the Hootie and the Blowfish song "Hold My Hand," which Rucker says he sees as a protest song,[30] there's a smile in his voice as he reassures us that he has a hand for us:

> With a little peace, and some harmony
> We'll take the world together
> We'll take 'em by the hand.

But there is little room for rage or to point out injustice in this conciliatory song. In his pandemic-era hit, "Beer and Sunshine," even in the face of the "BS" on television, in the face of death and social unrest, the song has an upbeat beer buzz and casts an image of quarantine as flowing sunshine, hanging out in flip-flops, and putting golf balls off a dock. I am reminded of the African American writer Hanif Abdurraqib's essay "On Kindness," where he explores the ways that he's often described as kind, especially by white people, and especially by those that don't know him well:

I know, particularly when it is by people who aren't familiar with me, that what they are actually complimenting is the absence of that which they perceived, perhaps expected.

What I am saying is that I have been thinking a lot about Black anger lately, and what we do, and don't do with it. . . . I am interested in what we afford each other, in terms of emotions that can sit on our skin, depending on what that skin might look like.[31]

Is there room for Rucker's country music audiences to see rage sitting on his skin? This question gets raised in his video performance of his 2017 song "If I Told You."[32] The lyrics as well as the visuals of this video for the song hint at a moodier self. Filmed in black and white, the video shows Rucker always alone, recording in an empty studio, swilling back a glass of something on the rocks, or standing on a rooftop. Classically dressed in a crisp white shirt and black blazer, belting into a big retro-style microphone that suggests torch singing (or a nostalgic Gap ad), it would seem that Rucker is baring his soul. His eyes flash and burn as he sings to his lover,

What if I told you there is no fixing me
'Cause everybody's already tried.

Rucker's lover in the video, a white-appearing woman, is shown pensively haunting the same city, the same rooftop. But the two never occupy the same space, though sometimes the image of the lover is projected as a kind of thought bubble in Rucker's mind, a fantasy of past sunny beaches and blue skies. (In this way, the song continues the tradition of a kind of symbolic racial segregation in Rucker's videos that I discussed earlier.) As he asks her, "Could you love me anyway?," she doesn't seem to hear or respond to Rucker's sung questions. Whether he might be loved despite his anger or his moral struggles is left unclear by video's end. The song to me suggests the risks of Black men expressing anger—the risk of being misunderstood or abandoned.

BEFORE, AT THE Fraternity of In-Between, I could belong, but I could also be stealthy. Unincorporated, watching, I could be a part of the masculine energy of the house. Maybe I could be a bro, too. Or so I thought. But once I began dating Jason and then broke up with him, I lost my status as an honorary brother. It was impossible to regain my post as observer, outside of the dramas of frat life. Instead, I was the girl who had dumped their friend ("Bros before hos"), or else a potential conquest. There was no room anymore for friendship. Eventually, I distanced myself from the house and the friends I had there, immersing myself in schoolwork and politics and in other aspects of campus life. But sometimes, when I hear a certain kind of manly tenderness, a crack in a smooth croon, I still feel the loss of it.

RACIAL RECKONINGS

In the past, Rucker's public approach to his experiences of racism has been guarded acknowledgment, eschewing any show of outrage: "If someone doesn't want to listen to my music because of the color of my skin, I don't want them there," he said back in 2011.[33] More recently, though, he seems to be in a public process of racial reckoning. In the wake of the mass murders by the white supremacist Dylann Roof in his hometown of Charleston, South Carolina, in 2015, and then the murder of George Floyd in 2020, Rucker has begun to discuss racism in his interviews and in multiple venues.

In June 2020 on Facebook, he posted a statement to fans decrying the police brutality in the murder of George Floyd. "This whole thing just breaks me down to my core," he writes. A month later, in July, Rucker was interviewed by *The Today Show*'s Harry Smith, discussing the recent racist violence and its effect on his family.

In some ways, in the interview, he's the same Darius Rucker. The conversation takes place over a game of golf, that most genial of sports, and we watch as Darius gives Harry the gentlest of trash-talk with a chuckle, hitting the ball precisely over the resplendent green of the Troubadour Golf and Field Club, just outside of Nashville. In the interview, Rucker is reflective. He shares with Smith, who is white, that it was watching his children struggling with the death of Floyd that inspired him to alter his tactics of restraint. He fears for his young son and his daughters, who might also someday be stopped by the police, or shot by them: "I don't want that for my boy. I don't want that for my daughters. I don't want that for anybody." He shares that he's worried about losing fans in a sensitive profession of making country music, where "one sentence can end your career," citing the Chicks as an example. And he admits that his own success has not shielded him from police surveillance: "You become a rich Black man and you think that racism goes away. It doesn't. I mean, there's people who hate you more because you're rich."

That summer, Rucker made a series of public appearances that registered his dis-ease with the state of the nation, particularly the COVID-19 pandemic and the numerous spectacular acts of racial violence across the country. In addition to "Beer and Sunshine," a mostly lighthearted acknowledgment of the need for escape and comfort in "a world gone crazy," Rucker recorded "Why Things Happen," a collaborative song with two other Black male country music performers, veteran country star Charley Pride and the relative newcomer Jimmie Allen. Without explicitly naming racism, the three grapple with grief and the world's injustices. Rucker and Pride sing the first verse together:

> You'll never know when your last breath's
> Gonna fade like a July sunset
> Or how a tragedy like gravity holds you still
> While the world keeps spinnin'.
>   —"Why Things Happen"

While the song was recorded a month before the Floyd murder, the verse acknowledges a precarity relevant to the experience of living as a Black man in the United States. In this coming together of these three Black male country stars from three different generations, I hear an acknowledgment of a shared loss and an act of brotherly community-making.

In his November 6, 2020, conversation with Rissi Palmer on her podcast *Color Me Country*, Rucker takes on these struggles even more frankly. Perhaps this is possible for him because of the atmosphere of burgeoning race consciousness in country music, including public support of Black Lives Matter by Mickey Guyton, Dolly Parton, Chris Stapleton, and Palmer herself, and because of the extraordinary opportunity of being interviewed by another successful Black country music singer, a woman who has faced similar struggles in the industry (Palmer tells him at one point in the interview, "I really feel like you're telling my story"). In this interview, anticipating Rucker's historic cohosting of the CMA Awards and the election in progress between Donald Trump and Joe Biden, Rucker discusses the initial difficulty of getting airplay for his country music, the continued challenges of racism as a Black country music star, and his admiration of the growing body of successful Black country music artists. I am struck by Rucker's expansiveness in the interview, and his willingness to return to the difficult themes of racism that he downplayed in the past.

He tells Palmer, "I remember growing up in Charleston, South Carolina, in the early 1970s and being told that's just the way it is. And getting older and the things that I was doing, trying to do it, just saying to myself, that's just the way it is. And getting to Nashville, where they have their preconceived notions, and hearing that's just the way it is. I remember saying to myself you can put up with whatever happens to you here because what happens here wouldn't be one-tenth, one one-hundredth of what Charley Pride went through, so you put up with all the crap. Just—go get this."[34] But Rucker tells Palmer that he's decided to abandon this past, teeth-clenching self. "I'm not going to compromise my life and my career for someone's hate," he tells her.

BACK AT THE Troubadour Golf and Field Club, Rucker sits on a barstool, smile-frowning, a trick, perhaps of the sun in his eyes. His knees jut outward, opening his body to us, and his hands are folded at his lap into almost a fist. As Harry Smith presses him for more details, Rucker rubs his hands together—the only visible sign of nervousness, as he offers even more about his fears for his own family at the hands of the police. As the interview wraps up, he offers a smile, but his shoulders are just a little slumped, his back showing signs of a weight that's been carried, suggesting a core that has been broken, and that seeks a balm. "It's important to say that everything is not okay," he tells us.

CHAPTER THREE

HOW TO BE AN OUTLAW

Beyoncé's "Daddy Lessons"

ON NOVEMBER 2, 2016, a few days before the fateful presidential face-off in the United States between Hillary Clinton and Donald Trump, the fiftieth-anniversary presentation of the Country Music Association Awards (CMAs) featured an unlikely, if now notorious, collaborative performance: the R&B icon Beyoncé and her band joined the Chicks (known at that time as the Dixie Chicks: Natalie Maines and sisters Emily Burns Strayer and Martie Maguire) to sing Beyoncé's country music–inflected "Daddy Lessons," from her wildly successful 2016 album, *Lemonade*. This joining of a country and R&B performance was especially timely, given that the past year had seen an intensified and often volatile bifurcation of racialized public discourse. It was a moment that asked us to believe the lie that these performers are from completely different worlds. But as I watch Beyoncé performing this undeniably country song together with the Chicks, I am further reminded of the lesson explored throughout this book—that African American music can be and has always been a part of country music's sound and history. At the same time, Beyoncé's Black female country outlaw performance brings to the fore Black women's anger, freedom, and resistance through this song—beyond the worlds that their daddies may have dreamed up for them.

"Give it up for the Dixie Chicks," Beyoncé demands of the slightly stunned CMA audience, using her dazzling presence and authority to get the song going. She's rocking a sequined dress that screams "Sexy Ma Ingalls," hair worn Crystal Gayle straight. Maines, Strayer, Maguire, and Beyoncé trade a series of calls and responses of "Texas!"—the location of their shared roots, however distinct their individual experiences of that Texas might be. "Daddy Lessons" is a song about a rough-around-the-edges daddy, from a daughter's loving, if critical, perspective. Throughout the performance, Beyoncé and the Chicks convey mutual support and admiration, clapping and whooping it up in encouragement, harmonizing with one another, completing one another's' sentences, leaning into one another, even briefly sharing a mic (though it is rare for any diva to give up a mic). About four minutes and forty seconds in, the song segues into the Chicks' "Long Time Gone," their Grammy- and CMA-winning hit from 2002, their own song about daddys and old lessons that we might have outgrown. "Keep those hands clapping," Beyoncé instructs.

I WANT TO be an outlaw like Beyoncé. I want to show up where I'm not expected and rock the house, bring the people to their feet. Sing with my friends, lead a horn section, whoop and yeehaw, shake our bodies without shame. I want to swagger and twerk and ride a horse down my city street, like Beyoncé does on the videos for "Sorry" or "Hold Up." Stop traffic and borrow a bat to swing into a window or two, open up a fire hydrant so that the small children can dance with glee. Drive a monster tractor, crushing muscle car rooftops, all while balancing on glorious high-heeled sandals. Tired of being invisible, of being polite, of swallowing my words and pain.

Maybe by being born a Black woman, and a queer one at that, I am already an outlaw, whether or not I choose to be. There is a difference, of course, between the outlaw that others dream up for me and my own resistance. That difference means everything. "So it is better to speak, remembering/ We were never meant to survive," Audre Lorde wrote in her poem, "A Litany for Survival."[1]

THE CMA PERFORMANCE was noteworthy on many levels. This was Beyoncé's first appearance on the awards show, and she and her band were some of the very few Black people present at a ceremony that has always been predominantly white. (Also included on stage that year were the three-time CMA Award winner Charley Pride and the Olympic gymnasts Simone Biles and Gabby Douglas, who were presenters.) This was the Chicks' first appearance on the CMAs since being blackballed by many mainstream country music institutions and fans angered by their leftist politics.

Many country music fans and commentators took issue with Beyoncé's and the Chicks' performance at the CMAs, some alluding to Beyoncé's vocal support of Black Lives Matter[2] and the Chicks' criticism of George W. Bush during his 2003 invasion of Iraq.[3] Brad Paisley, country music nice guy, host of the 2016 CMAs and a controversial crossover artist himself,[4] tweeted his support the evening after the show: "Frequently country crosses over. But every now and then a major pop superstar wants to be a part of this, too. Welcome, Beyoncé." But the very first reply on Twitter to Paisley's message was that of an angry anonymous country fan: "Fuck Beyoncé she supports thugs plus her music is garbage."[5] Another angry fan tweeted, "Figures they would pair up. One who has no respect for the American military and another who has no respect for the American law enforcement. Ashamed they would be allowed to perform at the CMAs at all."[6] These angry tweets reflect an identification of Beyoncé and the Chicks with a progressive politics that some would claim to be counter to country music values.[7] After the CMAs, Natalie Maines reportedly said that she would never return to the Awards show, disgusted by the chilly treatment that Beyoncé received backstage and by the critiques of the performance by conservative country fans.[8]

Country music has made room for its white male country outlaws, even if it doesn't always make room for outspoken Black women. The outlaws movement of the 1970s—which included Waylon Jennings, Merle Haggard, Willie Nelson, and Johnny Cash—while not necessarily always progressive, did provide a space for a performance of anti-authoritarianism that was often allied sonically, and sometimes visually, with Blackness. Jason Mellard points out that outlaw country's turn to American roots music to demonstrate its authenticity includes Black traditions of old-time and blues.[9] Thus, the outlaws enjoyed an association with Black culture, though usually implicitly. As the Man in Black, Johnny Cash could stand up for injustices against incarcerated folks and other outsiders, his Black shirt, hat, and jeans trademarks for his heroically critical stance. Blackness's association in mainstream white culture with danger, illegality, and outsiderhood was put to use in Cash's career to lend an element of authenticity. These moments reveal how, for these white male outlaws, proximity to Blackness—particularly metaphorical Blackness—is the ultimate expression of outsiderhood. Perhaps in these examples we see a continuation of the ways that white artists have trafficked in Blackness by embracing "everything but the burden."[10]

"Daddy Lessons" thus became a lightning rod for public arguments about the politics of race, genre crossover, gender,[11] and country music, soon to be joined by Lil Nas X's "Old Town Road" in 2019.[12] But these debates weren't new; there was the country outlaw backlash against countrypolitan pop country crossovers in the 1970s and fan pushback against the "shotgun marriage of hip-hop and country music" in the form of hick-hop artists like Cowboy Troy, Kid Rock, Nelly, and others.[13] Despite the CMA protests and the rejection of "Daddy Lessons" for consideration for an award in the country music category by the Grammys,[14] "Daddy Lessons" features many country elements, including a harmonica solo, banjo, twangy guitar, a stomping 2/4 beat, plenty of yips and yeehaws, and a central country music storytelling trope: the outlaw, gun-brandishing daddy.[15] At the same time, the song includes sonic elements drawing from R&B traditions, including a brass section evocative of New Orleans second lines,[16] the instrumental and vocal structures of call and response, and, maybe most of all, an African American tradition of "diva" performance of spectacle: the audience command and sonic power that we see at play in performances by Nina Simone, Grace Jones, Diana Ross, and Beyoncé herself.[17]

WHEN I THINK of being an outlaw as a Black queer woman, I think of Lorde's book *Sister Outsider*, looking from the outside in, with bell hooks's oppositional gaze. I think about giving folks a piece of my mind, like Eula at the end of Julie Dash's film *Daughters of the Dust*; or roaring with rage on the back of a motorcycle like the righteous women of Lizzie Borden's cult dyke film *Born in Flames*. I think of the joy that can come from being an outlaw, what the Black feminist scholar Brittney Cooper calls "eloquent rage," the rage of an anger passionate, precise, and owned.

Despite these inspirations, I've struggled all my life with seeing and hearing my anger, and then with what to do with it. How to create thoughtful change with anger's pointed and strategic expression? And as the parent of a Black girl child, I struggle to find models for her to express her anger, especially as she grows older.

What does my anger look like right now, as I write this? It is not here on the surface but resides in my body, doing its violence quietly, churning acid in my stomach. Waking up after a night's rest, I am reminded by my aching jaw, teeth smarting from the grinding. When I stand, big and small arrows of pain dart down my back to remind me that I sat hunched over my computer all afternoon yesterday, trying to find the right words. How to write it, how to tell you so you can hear it?

BY THE TIME Beyoncé and the Dixie Chicks performed "Daddy Lessons" at the CMAs, *Lemonade* had already become a cultural phenomenon, embraced passionately by the Black women that I knew: my students, my colleagues, my friends. I came across passionate social media posts, blogs, and articles about the album. Candice Benbow, together with activists, professors, and pastors, created *A Lemonade Syllabus*, which began as a Twitter hashtag, #Lemonadesyllabus, and which has been used by many to teach lessons in Black feminism, reproductive justice, prison abolition, Black women's history, music, and culture.[18] I taught *Lemonade* in my own Introduction to African American Literature class that fall of 2016, and my students were excited for the chance to talk about *Lemonade* alongside Toni Morrison's *Sula* and Ralph Ellison's *Invisible Man*. The visual album first premiered on April 23, 2016, on HBO, then on Tidal (the streaming company owned by Jay-Z and Beyoncé), until it eventually made its way to iTunes and other sources on the internet, as well as being sold as a DVD together with the CD. Fans of modest means scrambled to view the visual album for themselves, so among my student and friend circles, we would share our passwords to Tidal or pass around the DVD so that we could all see the visual album in its entirety. The visual album carried us through the experience of suspicion, betrayal, anger, reflection, and healing that signified beyond Beyonce's individual and isolated expression of jealousy and vengeance, to something deeper that we were all feeling in this time of racial unrest. Many of us were enraged by the recent violent loss of Black lives to police violence: Trayvon Martin, Eric Garner, Sandra Bland, Philando Castile, and many others. Many of us were still smarting from Satoshi Kanasawa's infamous *Psychology Today* blogpost that suggested that men's rating of Black women as least beautiful was "human nature" and the social media firestorm that followed.[19] Perhaps beyond mere gossip, this was why so many Black women became obsessed with speculating about the real "Becky with the good hair"—the tantalizing "other woman" that Beyoncé throws under the bus in the song "Sorry."

A few months after the CMAs, I stepped up to serve as chair of my English department, a job that I was good at but also found stressful in its invisible labor of diplomacy: counseling a Black male graduate student who felt afraid on campus, ducking security guards' suspicious looks to find a safe place to read before his night class; and that same afternoon, listening while a white faculty member confessed that he was afraid of this same student's anger; writing in support of an indispensable administrative assistant whose hours were being chipped away, until she was forced into early retirement. On the drive home, I'd blast *Lemonade* from my aging Honda Fit's speakers, Beyoncé trading lines with the rapper Kendrick Lamar, their fury matching mine with a beat strong enough to march a protest to:

Freedom
Freedom
I can't move
Freedom, cut me loose!

Lemonade evoked a strong collective response among Black women like me who were stunned and heartened to see and hear its powerfully intimate expressions of pain, anger, and resilience enacted by this worshiped, seemingly invulnerable, diva. I heard it in that line from "Freedom": "I need freedom, too"—Beyoncé's insistence that she was not an exception because of her celebrity. As Melissa Harris-Perry writes, "*Lemonade* disrupted our inner ear, throwing us off balance as we confronted the breadth of all we have missed, ignored, and submerged by pushing Black womanhood, even our own, to the margins."[20] The album's imagery, sometimes jarring, sometimes intimate, moves from home movies of weddings and living rooms to surreal plantation landscapes to starkly lit spaces where entertainment and sex work seem to meld, speaking to the past and present violence that haunts Black women. The marriage of song and image is reinforced and amplified by pieces of poetry by the Somali British poet Warsan Shire. Shire's poetry reinforces and sometimes complicates the song's lyrics, read dramatically by Beyoncé herself in a voice hushed and immediate, as if she were curled up next to me, whispering in my ear.

WHEN I WAS in my thirties, a friend told me that she had been lured into a van and sexually assaulted. It happened in broad daylight, on a busy Saturday right downtown in the college town where we both lived, and by a man she knew only a little. I had seen him before, too, hanging out at my favorite café. Her assailant hung around the edges of our queer community and presented himself as a shaman, and that was how he convinced my friend to enter the van alone, where he also lived. My therapist suggested coming up with an "action," a protest to get my anger out—something creative. Together we imagined my going to the café where I had seen the man before. Maybe if I ran into him, I could have an accident. Something could spill. Hot coffee felt like it was going too far and might land me in jail, but I told her I could live with a very tall glass of ice water. I did go to that café a few days later, so sunny and bright, with plants and old couches where patrons put their feet up while they read, a place where I often did my grading, and I waited, teeth chattering with anticipation. I imagined the water, the floating ice cubes, landing on his lap with a splash and creating a dark map on his jeans. "There he is, folks," I'd say, laughing and pointing. I imagined the man starting up with surprise and outrage, and then, hopefully, with shame, branded with sopping wet pants. Maybe the water would ruin his books or his computer, I speculated. I thought of my friend, how she couldn't stop crying and shaking after it happened, and how I couldn't convince her to go to the police. She blamed herself because she went into the van willingly. After an hour, the man eventually showed up. He was a small man, dressed in an incongruous assortment of accessories, a cliché of lefty cool: a Black and white Palestinian scarf worn bandit style over a T-shirt celebrating some local jam band; greasy graying hair caught up in a scrunchied ponytail; at his wrists and on his chest were a tangle of woven bracelets, crystals, and amulets, announcing his shaman status to those of us who cared. As he scanned the café looking for a seat, I caught his eye and held it. He started toward me, as if I were inviting him to sit with me, and then stopped. "He knows I know," my heart whispered with glee. I may have lost my resolve to go through with my ice water protest, but at least I got him to look down first.

THE DADDY IN "Daddy Lessons" teaches his daughter to fight. In encouraging her to "be tough," learning how to shoot his rifle, riding motorcycles duded up in classic vinyl and leather, the father encourages his daughter to both defend herself and to take care of her mother and sister—that is, to take the place as the head of the family, a place usually reserved for sons.

When Beyoncé's and the Chicks' voices meld in harmony with those lines about the father, gun and head held high, there is glory and dignity in this image, and I picture someone who might be immortalized on a statue in a small-town square or, well, in a country music song. Except, of course, this is a Black daddy. And armed Black men are not usually the subjects of patriotic statues or most country songs. We are reminded of this daddy's Blackness both sonically and visually in the *Lemonade* visual album. At the opening of the visual, as the rhythms bring us into the song, we hear a chorus of male hoots and snaps and yeahs and gruff "go go gos!"—sort of a downhome version of the Black male voices on Marvin Gaye's "What's Going On." (In the version of "Daddy Lessons" performed with the Dixie Chicks, the background "yee-haws" have a different resonance, with a heightened female vocal presence.) As the trumpet solo begins, we watch a circle of young Black men, hanging out together, dancing, joking, and laughing in front of a corner store. We see a closeup shot of a young Black girl on a stoop, watching, thinking, and listening. The video then cuts to Beyoncé in a puffy-sleeved country-style dress cut in West African fabric. She sings and dances next to a seated Black man in a cowboy hat, a snappily dressed elder playing a red electric guitar. This sonic and visual fabric of male support bolsters Beyoncé's storytelling and figures Black men as collaborators as well as listeners.

Beyoncé's song recollects "Daddy" with affectionate nostalgia but also a questioning eye, one that acknowledges his human failings, his whiskey in his tea. When she sings

> Daddy made me fight
> It wasn't always right
> But he said, "Girl, it's your Second Amendment,"

in that "but" is the sense of struggle, of weighing two different versions of morality, one supported by Daddy and the Constitution, the other, her own.

As the song heats up, it shifts from a memory to a warning, this time to a man who is doing her wrong. As the song's attention shifts to this other man, the man who is hurting her, the song gets more ambiguous. Is Daddy one of the men who protects her from trouble, or is Daddy also one of the troubled men, like "you"?

The visual imagery of "Daddy Lessons" in *Lemonade* presents its own angle on the outlaw, archetypal but with a different framework shaped by Black experiences of freedom, as well as gendered violence and experiences of surveillance. Built in is a sense of contradictions between this white outlaw ideal, her father's sense of justice, and her own. A Black father and daughter ride together on a horse through a lush field. Later we see that man riding his horse down the street of a cramped, but orderly, Black neighborhood—denoting a quest for freedom within urban confines. Another Black man nestles his infant daughter against his chest in one shot and then, seconds later, takes a swing toward the camera. We see two young men stalking a residential street, checking for unlocked car doors, presumably to rob them. The cinematography is a little blurry, but the colors are Kodachrome bright, producing a nostalgia that is both sweet and bitter. We see the sweetness when the song cuts to a home movie, a small conversation between a young Bey and her father, Mathew Knowles. "What would you do if Granddaddy and Grandma were here?" her father asks her. "Have fun!" young Beyoncé replies. "Tell them!" the father demands. And at once, this earlier generation is summoned, whether living or dead, now also a part of the song. The video then makes a quick cut to an older Mathew Knowles playing with Beyoncé's daughter, Blue Ivy, creating a chain of memories of fathers and daughters. Although Beyoncé's actual father is not dead, the song enacts the desire to speak across time to the dead, to both love and grapple with daddys across the generations.

But those generational legacies are not always so sweet. In the interstitial section leading up to the song, we watch a little Black girl watching her mother and father fight. The scene has the blurs and emotionally imbued franticness of a barely suppressed memory.

As the argument escalates, the girl holds her head and ears, crying. Beyoncé's hushed voiceover asks, "Mother Dearest, did he bend your reflection? Did he make you forget your own name? Did he convince you he was a god? Did he make you sit on your knees daily? Do his eyes close like doors? Are you a slave to the back of his head? Are we talking about your husband, or your father?" In this sequence, men, specifically fathers, are both loving and unpredictable, and potentially violent. Beyoncé whispers, "I don't know when love became elusive. What I know is, no one I know has it. My father's arms around my mother's neck, fruit too ripe to eat." The image of her father's arms around her mother's neck is ambiguous, and could be one of affection, possession, violence, or maybe all three. Against the grain of nostalgia, "Daddy Lessons," as framed by the album's visuals and Shire's poetry, forces us to think about the perpetuation of patterns of violence across generations, even as the song also evokes tender memories of fatherhood.

A FEW YEARS after my friend was assaulted, I found James Baldwin's 1955 essay "Notes of a Native Son," in which Baldwin describes a similar desire for revenge. The essay begins with Baldwin's reflection on his father and on the rage that isolates him and ultimately kills him. In the wake of his father's death, Baldwin reflects on his own experience of rage and his description of a crossroads of racism and survival.

After being refused service by a waitress in a New Jersey café, Baldwin finds himself in a rage—not just at the waitress but at all the struggles of racism and poverty that hound him and his family. He writes,

> "We don't serve Negroes here."
> Somehow, with the repetition of that phrase, which was already ringing in my head like a thousand bells of a nightmare, I

realized that she would never come any closer and that I would have to strike from a distance. There was nothing on the table but an ordinary watermug half full of water, and I picked this up and hurled it with all my strength at her. She ducked and it missed her and shattered against the mirror behind the bar. And, with that sound, my frozen blood abruptly thawed, I returned from where I had been, I *saw*, for the first time, the restaurant, the people with their mouths open, already, as it seemed to me, rising as one man, and I realized what I had done, and where I was, and I was frightened.[21]

A chase ensues, one white man joining another and then another, and it looks like Baldwin won't escape the fury of the crowd, until his friend, also white, comes to his rescue, and holds that man and others off, and Baldwin is able to flee the scene. Even in that moment of breakneck struggle to survive, Baldwin has a moment of self-realization:

> I saw nothing very clearly but I did see this: that my life, my real life, was in danger, and not from anything other people might do but from the hatred I carried in my own heart.[22]

Baldwin both echoed the urge to strike out that I felt in that café that Saturday morning and confirmed my greatest fear, the fear of the scope of my anger let loose. When I sat poised with my own water glass, I wasn't sure where my anger began and ended. I knew it had been fed by many acts of violence before this one. Was I feeling rage at the assaults and indignities that I had also experienced by men? The racism of the town and my own invisibility in it? At that moment, what I yearned for was the calmness of putting pen to paper. I yearned to do what Baldwin does so well: to look shrewdly at violence, experienced individually and collectively, with my vision sharpened but not obscured by anger.

IN "DADDY LESSONS," Beyoncé invites us to tap into rage, without falling into the traps of patriarchy. She does so with a Black feminist eye aware of the complex ways that Black men and women are stereotyped as angry in excess. For example, Beyoncé's line "My daddy said shoot" is complicated by the vexed relationship between Black people, self-defense, and the right to bear arms. For Black people at most points in American history, the decision to retaliate against injustice with gunfire has been censored and controlled as an arm of white supremacy, from the moment Black bodies were brought to US shores as enslaved labor. In the 1960s and 1970s, the Black Panthers' embrace of the right to bear arms promised by the Second Amendment was a central aspect of their criminalization in the eyes of those who feared them, particularly the government of the United States. This deadly surveillance carries on into the contemporary moment, as we see vividly illustrated in the life and death of Philando Castile shortly after the release of "Daddy Lessons." On July 6, 2016, Castile was pulled over by police officer Jeronimo Yanez on the streets of a Saint Paul, Minnesota, suburb. During a search of his car, Castile was found to be in possession of a firearm that was legally registered in his own name. He was not brandishing the weapon. He didn't shoot his gun. Castile was fatally shot—seven shots at close range—by Officer Yanez in front of Castile's girlfriend, Diamond Reynolds, and her four-year-old daughter.

I want to pause for a moment on that daughter, who at four has learned a lesson about this daddy figure that she'll never forget.

And I want to pause on my own daughter, who is watching my face as I read about the alarming escalation of a protest by a group of armed, white pro-Trump protesters the week before the 2021 presidential inauguration. I try to hide my own anger and panic as I see images of the protesters storming the Capitol building, scaling structures in protest of the electoral college's vote for Biden. As a Black woman, I find it hard to ignore that these protesters, who successfully entered the Capitol's chambers of deliberation, took multiple selfies of themselves in various poses—including sitting at House Speaker Nancy Pelosi's desk, where they stole her computer—and were able to do so in a way very different from the system of surveillance and control of unarmed Black Lives Matter protesters in the past. The next day, my daughter's classmates are agitated as they discuss the protesters during their remote classroom's morning news hour. Cece and her classmates voice their fears that the election will be turned over. I measure my words to her carefully. I find myself echoing something my own father texted to me the night before: "Our system has seen worse and can take the pressure. Lawlessness won't win." I say "our system" in ways that sound confident in our own roles as African American citizens. (And I hear again that daddy in Beyoncé's song, "Girl, it's your Second Amendment.") But I'm not sure if I believe it.

Black folks' right to bear arms is complex, even more so when the Black person who defends themself is a Black woman or a Black trans person. It brings to my mind the cases of Marissa Alexander, Bresha Meadows, Ky Peterson, Tewkunzi Green, and other girls, women, and gender nonbinary African Americans who were imprisoned for shooting their attackers in cases of domestic violence. For example, Bresha Meadows, growing up in rural Ohio, had witnessed her father's beating of her mother all her life. She had been raped by her father when she was twelve. In an eerie mirror image of "Daddy Lessons," at age fourteen, she decided she couldn't take it anymore and took her father's gun and shot and killed him. Meadows was imprisoned, but with the support of activists in the Chicago-based prison abolition organization Love and Protect and the #FreeBresha campaign on social media, she was eventually granted clemency.[23] Meadows has gone on to college and has become an activist in support of other survivors of domestic violence.

Even as *Lemonade* alludes to domestic violence, particularly in the sections before, during, and after "Daddy Lessons," the approach is significantly different from the tactic the Chicks took in their 2000 hit "Goodbye Earl." This song is a darkly comic revenge tale about an abusive husband who puts his wife in intensive care and continues to do so despite a restraining order. With the failure of legal means, two high school girlfriends take matters into their own hands by murdering Earl—and not losing any sleep over it: "Earl had to die," they sing. The song gives a very specific description of feeding him poisoned black-eyed peas, wrapping him in a tarp, and tossing him into the lake, punctuated by jeers, "Nah, Nah, Nah!" (And on the video, the Chicks and their cast do a little do-si-do to celebrate.) "Goodbye Earl" gleefully encourages taking justice into one's own hands. But in "Goodbye Earl," female outlawhood has a very different charge, a "Thelma and Louise"–style fantasy of justice shaped by the presumed innocence of white womanhood.

As engaging and satisfying as "Goodbye Earl" can be,[24] Black women have a different fight. "Daddy Lessons" might be more clearly identified with a transformative justice approach that seeks to both critique and reengage with men. Drawing from a Black feminist consciousness, "Daddy Lessons" wrestles with both revenge and loyalty. The song's loving and critical depiction of Black men reflects the language of the Black feminist authors of the 1977 Combahee River Collective Statement—a text that is still key in Black and queer feminist movements such as the Movement for Black Lives: "Our situation as Black people necessitates that we have solidarity around the fact of race, which white women of course do not need to have with white men, unless it is their negative solidarity as racial oppressors. We struggle together with Black men against racism, while we also struggle with Black men about sexism."[25] The presence of white supremacist violence from the outside makes the experience of physical and psychic violence from Black men on the inside all the more poignant.[26] Ultimately, with "Daddy Lessons" as a turning point, Beyoncé's

Lemonade seeks a vision of full humanity for both Black women and Black men.

WHEN BEYONCÉ SINGS of daddies, of course I think about my own. How far he seems from the gunslinger in "Daddy Lessons": the first man I ever saw cry, this lover of Jesus and J. Krishnamurti, Langston Hughes and the *MacNeil-Lehrer Report*. My father's gentle hands can pound human voice and heartbeat out of a drum, but he never hit me or my sisters or my mother, and he convinced my mother to abandon her occasional spankings, too. I've never seen him lose his temper. Sure, I've seen him get stressed out at our Christmas parties when small children play with the ceramic nativity scene or teenagers put their pop cans on his pool table. I've heard him get terse with uncooperative customer service representatives, lowering his voice to a quiet, well-enunciated tone.

My father's gentleness is all the more noteworthy because of the physical violence that was a part of his everyday world, growing up Black, poor, and struggling on the South and West Side of Chicago in the 1940s and 1950s. His own household had been violent: his father sometimes beating his mother, his mother sometimes beating him. My father told me how, as a teenager, it was common to be confronted on the street by other men for money, so he developed the habit of carrying himself hunched and protected, and he never walked alone if he could help it. When he was in college, my father found out that he was good at boxing. Despite his light frame, he knew from his life as a drummer how to get inside a rhythm, the one-two of shuffling feet, when to hit and when to duck. He thought that maybe this would be a way to pay for school. He kept winning his fights until one day he was matched with a fighter much heavier than he was and with fewer scruples. A few minutes into the fight, his opponent reached behind his neck and gave him a rabbit punch, knocking him out cold. He realized that boxing could kill him. Instead, he put his energy into school, and then more school, and with the help of scholarships and a night job at the post office and a day job driving a bus, stealing naps between work and school, he finished college, and then graduate school, eventually earning a PhD. He told me that it took years of living in green, surrounded by the open space and green lawns of campus quads, to unfurl his insides. Sometimes, when he's debating a point at the dinner table, in his passionate precision I can see the ghost of that mean right hook. But whenever he wins an argument, he keeps coming back, gently turning the point over and over again to fully see the other side. From my daddy, I learned the lesson that to be gentle when life is otherwise is definitely a kind of a fight.

FATHERHOOD HAS LONG been a sore point in the Black community, where the history of rape and the breeding and selling of slaves made family structures difficult to sustain. And as bell hooks points out, for some Black thinkers during and immediately after slavery, successfully shepherding family and the larger community through a kind of "benevolent patriarchy" modeled on white heteronormative standards of US culture was the mark of freedom.[27] On the other hand, in governmental studies like "The Moynihan Report," in the 1960s, the "failure" of the Black community to thrive was blamed not on joblessness or other aspects of structural racism, but on a Black family structure caricatured as perverse and criminal, led by deadbeat fathers and matriarchal Black superwomen—and those stereotypes of the broken Black family remain with us. But we have also always had other versions of family in the Black community, models that have been devalued and criminalized by white culture, or that just go under the radar: daddys who don't live with their "baby mamas" but who are deeply involved in their children's lives; daddys and mamas who live together but aren't married; women-led households, multigenerational households, queer families. Maybe all of these could be considered queer, especially in the eyes of the law.[28]

Daddy lessons, as they've been defined traditionally in our white supremacist, heteronormative, and patriarchal culture, may not serve us. We might need to push beyond them. Within "Daddy Lessons," Beyoncé calls up family memory and names how those histories shape her current views of love as well as her fears for its loss. But maybe "Daddy Lessons" might also be a jumping-off point for reinventing what daddying can mean, for ourselves and for those we love. What might it mean to daddy ourselves? Perhaps this version of daddying can have a sharpened eye for justice. It can be gentle but also persistent, like my own daddy. We might be daddy for our daughters and sons, our partners, ourselves, and those outside our immediate family, claiming a more expansive vision of home.

Beyoncé rides on her horse, sky blue and crisp behind her, the afternoon sun almost blinding. At first, our view of her is framed by a car window, a car driven by an older Black man who smiles at her kindly as he watches, the gold from his sunglasses glinting in the light. Other shots from the song show a little girl riding with her daddy right behind her, holding her in the saddle, but as "Daddy Lessons" progresses, Beyoncé rides alone. The sun dapples her box braids and jeans and her simple white T-shirt, and she looks neither right nor left, but moves with the horse's steps, upright and with grace, ducking an overhanging branch.

In the end, I see Beyoncé offering a revised model of rage that can be generative, and also inclusive and justice seeking, one that parallels the Black feminist view of "mothering." Can we hold the lessons of daddys without being bound by them? What other frames can we see? As a queer Black feminist, I have gained strength by recent formulations of the revolutionary power of mothering ourselves. In her anthology *Revolutionary Mothering*, Alexis Pauline

Gumbs is inspired by the Black feminist mothers before her, like Audre Lorde and June Jordan and Toni Cade Bambara, writer-activists whose vision extends beyond blood bonds, even beyond their deaths. These authors teach us that to mother is to bring care regardless of blood, reaching always outward, loving always with an eye to new possibilities—the transformation of our own hearts and of the world. Gumbs writes, "The radical potential of the word 'mother' comes after the 'm.' It is the space that 'other' takes in our mouths when we say it."[29] If mothering ourselves necessarily means transforming past ways of being a family, of partnering and loving, maybe we can transform our daddy lessons, too. This is the direction that I see over the course of Beyoncé's *Lemonade* as she moves from narratives of intimate hurt, betrayal, and grief focused on the nuclear family to collective grief, healing, and then making change, in songs like "Freedom," "All Night," and "Formation." As song number six in an album of twelve songs, "Daddy Lessons" is at that point of structural transition. I'd like to suggest that as we watch Beyoncé move first within her father's framework of justice as retribution to something outside of that frame, beyond those past entanglements, justice is transformed.

The second half of the album meditates upon the collective legacies of slavery, healing, and redemption, and moves outward, beyond the album's tight focus on the heterosexual romantic couple, marriage, and the nuclear family. By the time we get to "All Night," the eleventh song on the album, we have been taken on a journey of critical looking, catharsis, and healing. As Beyoncé puts it at the opening of "All Night," "My torturer became my remedy . . . so we're going to heal, start again." "All Night" takes us back to the personal, this time with couples of different races and sexualities, performing everyday acts of commitment and restoration: working a garden, getting matching tattoos, shopping at a neighborhood grocery store, caring for children. "All Night" also directly restores the tensions suggested by "Daddy Lessons." The sequence includes a home movie from Beyoncé's and Jay-Z's (real-life) wedding, and we see not only that couple restored, but also Beyoncé dancing with Mathew Knowles, her father and one-time manager. One phrase from the song's lyrics on healing could come from a daughter, a daddy, a lover, or a community: "Trade your broken wings for mine. I've seen your scars and kissed your cries." We need "Daddy Lessons," then, to take us through the grieving process, to name the problems and contradictions of patriarchy and perhaps move beyond them.

AT AGE FORTY, I decided a little later than most that I wanted to become a mother. I hadn't even entertained the idea of becoming a daddy. When my partner Annie and I planned to adopt, we went through a nine-month training period with the agency and the state. We learned how to diaper a newborn, how to administer CPR, how to talk about adoption with a nosy neighbor or someone in the supermarket. We discussed some of the particular struggles around identity that adopted children might face in a same-sex and multiracial household like ours. As we got closer to being matched with a child, we worked with a social worker who also asked us to envision what our household might look like from day to day. During one session, she asked us who would be in charge of laundry, who would buy groceries, who would be in charge of discipline or cooking. We rated ourselves for each job that we'd take up. Our answers were all over the map, and we often answered that we'd do each chore together, which seemed to panic our social worker. Neither of us identified as particularly butch or femme, and in our lives together, we were all over the spectrum of gender in the things we did, our clothing, our ways of connecting with each other and the world. Somehow, though, something must have worked, because our darling Cece came home to us one beautiful, rainy May day.

But for the first few years, I sometimes found myself acting the "daddy" in spite of myself. When Cece brought home a great drawing from preschool, I'd hear myself saying, "I'm proud of you, Cece," in a voice that slipped into a register lower than my natural speaking voice. Despite my unreliable back, I'd offer piggyback rides up the stairs for bed like the dad in the Berenstain Bears series and found myself competing with the dads at the playground to push the swings just as hard. Annie likes to build things with Cece and has taught her which screwdriver to use and how to disregard the written directions on her Legos. But despite these queer daddy moments, we've realized that we each need all of our selves that we can bring to the job: our energy, our smarts, our nurturing, our sense of fun, our sense of justice. And when trouble comes to town, in the form of bullies or the casual racism of a teacher, or in navigating the injustice happening in the larger world, our work has been to reach both inward and outward: giving hugs, asking questions, and talking things out, making community with other folks who are struggling, showing up at meetings and protests, and seeking justice by writing about the world we want to see.

As our daughter figures out the world for herself, and how to get the justice that she deserves, we hope that our lessons of care and curiosity and problem-solving will serve her well. I imagine Cece like Beyoncé, riding her own horse through the rough terrain of the world, guided by the outlaw lessons that we've provided her and by her own seeking.

CHAPTER FOUR

VALERIE JUNE, GHOST CATCHER

I'M WATCHING A VIDEO of Valerie June's 2015 appearance on "An Evening at Elvis'," a performance space housed in Elvis's former digs on Audubon Drive in Memphis. Valerie June begins upbeat.[1] In "Tennessee Time," she talks about her vision for making art, makes wisecracks on her own misunderstood and perpetual lateness, and introduces the audience to her banjo, mini-ukulele, and guitar, which she's winsomely nicknamed the Mama, the Baby, and the Stranger, respectively. Even the lonesome "Somebody to Love" is punctuated by a giggle. She performs her version of Jim Reeves's southern gospel single "This World Is Not My Home (I'm Just A-Passing Through)," lending it her own spacey, funky-fey quirkiness, and explains that it was her favorite hymn growing up: "I never felt like I was an Earthling. I don't know, maybe I was from some magical faerie land that had lots of sparkling turquoise things flying around," she says. I find this confession endearing, one of the many ways I hear in this charismatic performer twenty years younger than I an echo of my own Black queer nerdy self. With her feet tapping out the beat on a tambourine set on the floor, I think of tent revivals, folks sweating out sin through the sheer joy of music. But with the next song, June moves to another kind of otherworldliness. She slips a metal guitar slide attached to a floral silk handkerchief onto her pinky finger, flips her long dreadlocks over her shoulder, and, still smiling, says, "The thing about organic moonshine roots music is, you have to play a murder ballad after a gospel song because just a little wrong keeps you right." "Organic Moonshine Roots Music" is June's special take on country, blues, and gospel music—an approach shaped as much by past artists as by her own ingenuity and creativity. June laughs, and the audience and I laugh along with her. Then we all grow quiet, respectful. This one will be a murder ballad from a female perspective, she tells us. It's a chance for Valerie to join a chorus of other haunted voices, in a tradition dominated by men in blues and in country: Elvis Presley and Jimmie Rodgers, Johnny Cash and Jimi Hendrix, Woody Guthrie and Bob Dylan, and, of course, Robert Johnson. Some notable women have tried their hand at murder ballads, too, including Nina Simone and Ma Rainey. June closes her eyes and calls them all forth. The temperature in the room shifts to a dank chill, and my fingers tingle as she breathes out the first line of "Shotgun" a cappella:

Oh, baby. You know that I love you, baby.
I'm in love with you. Yes I am.

It's a simple defense, the only one offered: a ghostly wail whispered as if from the grave, which it turns out to be. The chords inch along a spooky, bare-bones blues. Her face grim, eyes somewhere else, her voice raspy with grief, she shares with us her plan—to get her shotgun and have revenge. June conjures the motherless-child loneliness of blueswomen Geeshie Wiley and Elvie Thomas, the hollowed-out grief of Leadbelly. Next, the song breaks into a fast, furious run, and at the end of each line, her fingers wring vibrato from the neck of the guitar she calls the Stranger, as if it were human. She skids to a stop as if she's seen her own ghost. After three beats, these lines come out as an exhausted sigh:

Well, late last night they laid you in your lonesome grave.
And don't you know tonight they lay me beside you.

She gives the strings one more wallop, then she hangs her head
in silence.

IT IS THE MID-1990S, and my mom and I are walking just outside
of State College, Pennsylvania, in search of the graveyard that was
said to house the graves of the Black slaves who ran away to freedom. It has been a year since I've moved to Penn State, my first job
teaching English out of grad school, and this was my first visit from
my mother, who is here from Chicago. Mom is dressed in jeans and
jaunty red Keds high tops, ready to explore. Her cornrows are tied
back with a red bandana (all the better to be sighted by the hunters,
I think to myself). I have not yet told my mother of my struggles
with my new job, the way that this new school and especially the
new town nestled deep in a verdant valley have left me lonely deep
in my bones. As we walk up the ridge, eyes scanning the ground for
grave markers, I venture, "I just feel sad here sometimes, Mom." But
her own thoughts seem to be somewhere else: her struggles at work,
perhaps, or on my sister, who has just moved back home with her
two young children, her marriage on the rocks. "This is so peaceful,"
she says, scanning the graveyard and the green just beyond it. "I'm
glad to see you settled here. It's such a relief to me," she tells me. A
little later, we find the grave markers that we've been searching for.
We almost missed them because the road has been built right up
to the edge of them, so that there are only a few narrow inches of
ground before the gravel and then asphalt. I think about those slave
bodies, wonder how they feel jammed up against the road. I wonder
if anyone knows who they're driving over as they pass.

I think of all the Black lives that have been crowded out,
pushed back, kicked out, "moved on up" and out, jailed, gentrified,

relocated, priced out, starved out, terrorized, erased. Every state in the United States has its history of "racial cleansing" of Black people, from the sunset codes of Washington and Oregon to redlining in Illinois to the downright stealing of land in Florida. Pennsylvania has its own history. It's been both a stop on the Underground Railroad and a witness to night terrors that have driven whole Black communities out. Any place with that kind of history is bound to have its ghosts.

VALERIE JUNE IS a ghost catcher. She takes on elements of risk and tenderness in her work, honoring moments of mortality and struggle in the music she admires and giving it back to us, with her own spin—whether it's her version of Jimi Hendrix's tender "Little Wing" or her own "Shotgun"—to create something new that honors the past. Just as I attempt in this work, June uses both an artist's and a scholar's tools to help the listener hear and feel and understand connections between experiences and cultures that, we've been told in the past, are separate. Her music is an exercise of freedom and will and risk. Her sartorial style—one part retro, one part hippie—her high-femme beauty, her unapologetic Blackness, the ways these things are put together in settings sometimes hostile to Blackness: all might be a mask of protection. But they also draw us in. She shows us a way to enter dangerous places of history and the heart and how to be brave.

In Valerie June's music, I see a powerful example of African diasporic music's ability to hold culture in the body and voice, making manifest erased or otherwise lost musical memories. In her embrace of her voice's "perfect imperfections," recalling the styles of lesser-known Black female country blues artists of the past, such as Jessie Mae Hemphill and Elizabeth Cotten, among others, June also makes use of it to call up spirits, to conjure the ancestors.

The musicologists Nina Sun Eidsheim and Mandy-Suzanne Wong write that "to play music, especially to improvise, is in part to bring oneself under the influence of other bodies from the past. We perform memories, our own and those of others. . . . To improvise, then, is to call on the resources of our bodies and catapult ourselves beyond the confines and capacities of our singular bodies."[2] Eidsheim and Wong coin the term "corporeal archaeology" to think about both the ways that individuals understand their bodies through music in light of these social forces and the ways that societies in turn understand and value that music. For me, Eidsheim and Wong's analysis brings to light how performance can capture both what is social about music and what can be deeply personal. In addition, I hear in Valerie June's performances a demonstration of music's power to hold unrecorded histories that glimmer beyond us, not quite reachable through other means.

A self-taught musician, June brings together multiple Black, white, rural, and roots musical traditions in her vocal and performative style. June has mastered not only multiple instruments, including guitar, banjo, and ukulele, but also the techniques of known and obscure musicians from the past, particularly 1920s and 1930s country blues artists, thanks to her archival listening work in the Library of Congress and the Smithsonian. June's voice creates a variety of textures and timbres, from the husky rasp that sometimes graces "The No Draws Blues" to the deep and direct frankness in "Workin' Woman Blues" to the higher nasal keening that easily blends into a yodel in "Tennessee Time" and "Astral Plane." June uses her vocal flexibility to convey multiple stories, moods, and textures across lines of gender, race, place, and genre, and laces her performances with stories, hums, and laughter, honoring past traditions while also giving her own spin on them. In these ways, she makes powerful use of another form of "manifest"—like the ship's archivist, tracking a ship's comings and goings, official passengers as well as stowaways. June is rooted in—and rooting for—those who are known as well as those who remain unnamed. This has particular significance for African American culture. As June tells *Austin City Limits'* Antonette Masando in a 2017 interview:

> When I find something that I like, I study it and I go as far into the root of it as I possibly can, because I want to know how did we get to where we are today in music, and I want to know that whole journey . . . I'm curious about the root. And how that leads us to now. That's what I do. I study all the different kinds of music that America has.[3]

June's willingness to consort with ghosts is one of the many ways she participates in an Africanist aesthetic. In their introduction to the volume *Black Performance Theory*, Thomas F. DeFrantz and Anita Gonzalez include as an aspect of an African aesthetic the willingness "to include the voices of those gathered in the fabric of the event."[4] Riffing on shared traditions, June engages the audience in terms of both sharing the feeling of past and known resources and involving them intellectually in the process of revealing difference, a dynamic that LeRoi Jones (Amiri Baraka) calls the "changing same."[5] This call and response includes listeners in the audience as well as any ancestors who might be listening.

In a 2013 interview with NPR, Valerie June describes her hunger to know and understand music from a historical vantage point, one that is interested in the varieties and innovations of folk music in everyday life. She remembers the childhood experience of going to church and listening to the variety of voices—perfect and imperfect—around her. She describes soaking in these different, nonprofessional voices as a means of understanding the role of interpretation and personal idiosyncrasy in music. As for many African American artists, church was June's first resource for hearing heartfelt music *and* the varieties of beauty to be found in nonprofessionalized human voices: "I found that if I sat beside different people I would hear something totally different on the same song. . . . I just started to mimic what they would do with their voices. It was just a silly, playful way to learn how to use my voice as an instrument."[6]

Along with Elizabeth Cotten, June cites Bessie Smith and Nina Simone among her many influences, as well as lesser-known performers of the southern blues and gospel traditions collected by John Lomax and others, and uses her skills as a musician, performer, and interpreter to "overstand" their work. For example, she describes the influence of Jessie Mae Hemphill, a contemporary country, blues, and folk artist who recently passed away: "She didn't have the traditional voice that we expect to come out of a woman from the South, or a Black woman from the South, in particular. And neither did Elizabeth Cotten, Ma Rainey, Bessie Smith. All of these women just had beautiful voices that were perfectly imperfect; they had a lot of emotion and a lot of character. And I shouldn't feel bad that I don't sound like, you know, the number-one pop singer or the number-one soul singer. I should just feel good that I sound like me."[7] When curating a list for a Smithsonian Folkways Records website highlighting lesser-known songs from their collection, June praises white gospel folk-singer Polly Johnson's cough in the middle of her song "The Three Maids": "I love it when recordings have perfectly imperfect things in them," she writes. The sound of Polly's cough is not only a mark of the recording's folk "authenticity," but also a mark of Johnson's presence, a sign of this struggling human life that has come and gone.

ONE DAY, I VISITED a neighborhood bar in Bellefonte, Pennsylvania, which is about ten miles from State College, the town where I lived and taught. I had a girlfriend who lived in Bellefonte, on a street of modest homes uphill from the town center. When I'd drive to visit her, I'd have the feeling that others were peering into the car to see me, shaking their heads over the two of us together, as much because of our races, Black and white, as that we were two women together. Maybe no one assumed that we were even a couple, but sometimes when we were in her apartment, H. would swear that she heard the same car circling as if checking in on us. The only Black person I ever saw in Bellefonte was at the gas station near that first exit into town, a small dark-skinned man in a university windbreaker, putting gas in his car. As I gassed up, the man stared openly at me but didn't say hello. I don't know what I expected. Friendliness, at least. Some sign of the southern-at-the-heart-of-the-Southside-of-Chicago connection that I was raised with, I guess. In the same way, I'd go to diners in search of soul food, or at least some good pie, but never found it. But one day, I went into this bar in Bellefonte. The bar was in the base-ment of a downtown building, and as I went down the stairs, I saw these photographs of Black men, professional stills in black and white. The men were in tuxes, arranged in a pyramid, crooning into a microphone, with close haircuts that could only be called "smooth." "Those are the Mills Brothers," the bartender called out to me. "They were from here," he said, then went back to drying the beer glasses. I asked him if he knew anything more, and he just shrugged. This wasn't the first time I had heard of the Mills Brothers. I remember my grandmother singing "If I Didn't Care" as she worked on Sunday dinners in my Chicago childhood home. I knew that the Mills Brothers produced the soulful crooning that would give birth to doo-wop. But I had trouble connecting them to Bellefonte, a place that seemed so distinctly white to me. Pitts-burgh, maybe, or Philly, for sure. But where was the evidence of the Black lives who lived in Bellefonte? Where were their neigh-borhoods? Where were the plaques and the childhood homes? When I saw these photos, it was the late 1990s; the 1930 and 1940s were not ancient history. Where was everyone?

Later on, I learned that Bellefonte had been a major site for the Underground Railroad, and Black folks who had been enslaved settled there. Bellefonte and the surrounding area were on the "Jefferson Route" of the Underground Railroad, and the area beckoned because of its hills and greenery, great for hiding, and for the population of Quakers and Free Black People who lived there and provided shelter. The Mills Brothers were descendants of those first fugitive slaves. Their grandfather ran a barbershop right there in downtown Bellefonte, part of a community of Black-owned businesses that are no longer there, and preached in the St. Paul's African Episcopal Church, which still stands. On the local news, Donna King, current pastor of St. Paul's, who also leads Underground Railroad tours in the area, states that the all-Black church is the last of its kind in Bellefonte. The church now only has a handful of parishioners, but from one hundred years ago up through the Great Depression, it was a busy meeting place for Black folks in town, including those ex-slaves who settled there.

According to the census, in the late 1990s, African Americans made up 1.5 percent of the population of Bellefonte. Out of 6,187 people in total, that's 92 people (really, 92.8 people). That's not as bad as I thought. In a room, in a bar, or in a church, 92 is not a bad crowd. Ninety-two people could feel like a community. Back in my department at the university, I was one of six Black professors. (Sometimes people would also mistake me for Christine, who taught in the French Department upstairs from mine—even though we looked nothing alike. So, for the sake of numbers, I'll make Christine an honorary seventh.) Sometimes we felt like a community, grabbing drinks at the campus bar. But then we'd scatter to our homes, and the lonely was still there.

VALERIE JUNE IS a ghost catcher. Her voice slips through our ribs, like a ghost, attracted by our hunger, by the space made for her in our shrunken, unfed bellies. Her voice is the ghost, or it conjures up ghosts. It makes my hands ache as she snatches at my heart, mistaking it for a ghost, and weaves through the cathedral of hard bone that protects me.

Joseph Roach has written about the ways that performance can "sing" erased bodies into history: "Performances so often carry within them the memory of otherwise forgotten substitutions— those that were rejected and, even more invisibly, those that have succeeded to be erased."[8]

In *Valerie June: Manifest* (2015), a seven-minute documentary by Alan Spearman, audiences are introduced to a figure with whom they might not be overly familiar: a young African American country and roots artist who describes her music as "vibing off spirits." Songs, she says, "are where I began my spiritual journey in this life. They are the root." The video first aired on MTV as part of its short-lived Reality TV show, *$5 Cover Amplified*, about struggling musicians in Memphis. June is the only African American woman and certainly the only Black country music singer featured on the show. The video presents her doing yoga, laying out tarot cards, exploring a swamp and touching the roots of the trees as they rise from the water, practicing her guitar on an unmade bed and on top of a clothes washer in a basement. The video asks us to see her as a study in the active process of reconciling tradition and self-invention, as both grounded and otherworldly. I am aware of how the video seems to be in love with her beauty; her open face and connection to nature make her seem more spiritually enlightened than the rest of us, and I find myself wondering what of this is real. But even as I think of this as a performance, I admire the deliberateness and care with which she integrates these gestures of everydayness into her process of creativity.

June seems to be negotiating her relationship with her family to find her own place within this rich spiritual world. She sweeps and soaps the bricks on her family's front porch in Jackson, Tennessee, her hometown, and we watch as she cooks and eats with her parents and grandmothers in a dining room surrounded by photographs of ancestors. The video highlights the sometimes-comic drama of intergenerational misunderstanding—a hook, perhaps, for humanizing her and for making her art more universal. We watch June explaining the meaning of her song, "No Draws Blues" to her mother, who assumes it's "just a raunchy song about thongs." In her lyrics, she sings, "I want to be free," rebelling against the constraint of bras, pantyhose, and thongs. Her mother nods warily at her explanation, and we get the sense that she's just not buying it. A little later, June's mother shows to the camera an old photograph of June in high school. In the photo, June's hair is pressed and curled, and she is wearing a preppy crewneck sweater and a conventionally winning smile, a contrast to her current long dreadlocks, green and golden hippy wear, and dreamy look. "This girl here," she says, shaking her head, proud and puzzled both. Still, it's noteworthy that even though the film tries to universalize June's experiences—a reflection perhaps of its aim of translating June's aesthetic for mainstream audiences, she grounds herself in a particular history of African Americans in southern rural life: sewing, growing herbs, making her own soap, rising with the sun, praying, conjuring, writing down the hymns—all practices that link her to her grandmothers and greats.

Valerie June is a ghost catcher. How is she able to sound like both your mama's voice calling you in when the streetlights come on and yourself singing to yourself while you fold laundry? A split voice that sounds like that growl mamas get when they're salty, and like the quiet voice you use when you're all alone and no one can hear you.

AFTER THAT TRIP to the Bellefonte bar, I decided to let myself be haunted by this place. I began to frequent antique stores and used record marts, fingering through the debris of folks' everyday life in this region, looking for a sign of "us." I once took home a church pew from my favorite thrift store in Lockhaven just because it was painted black and white and reminded me of the gaudy décor of Leak and Sons Funeral Homes on Chicago's South Side, in the neighborhood where I grew up.

Unlike my great-grandmother from New Orleans, who had many stories of spiritual encounters with haints and visitations, mine are limited. But thrift stores were, for a time, the place where I would court the spirits of those who came before me. For a while I was drawn to the grotesque smell of decaying wood, of dust and someone else's old skin and sweat. Chair seats woven in leather shiny with the grime of others. I was haunted by loneliness and sought out company, living or dead. Maybe I could learn something about survival from those ghosts. Sometimes, like my real-life courtships, these courtships of spirit were met with anger, resentment: chilly breezes that filled me with sadness and grief; once, the touch of a cold hand and a vision of green that filled me with fear.

On Saturdays, after cleaning my apartment, I'd get into my car to explore antique shops in the towns around me. Sometimes I'd go with a friend, and sometimes I'd go alone. I'd sift through these leftovers from other people's lives, looking for something solid and familiar, making what I hoped would be a stronger sense of home in the present from others' pasts. I had standards, though. When I looked through old sets of dishes, I'd avoid ones with cracks. I didn't mind resting with other people's dirt, but I wasn't sure if I wanted to ingest it. Looking for the perfect couch, I went by smell, buying one that had a busted spring just because it smelled the nicest of the bunch.

One day, I ventured out with Rich, my brother-from-another-mother, to a new place an hour out of town, following a sign for an antique store posted by a highway exit. At times like this, Rich's cracked sense of humor and his empathy made my negotiation of the world beyond our campus more bearable. (I still remember our trip to buy a used car, and the salesman's confused look when we entered the shop, Rich and his partner Amy and I, a white couple and a Black woman, dressed up in matching flannels). The antique store, a dusty storefront set off from the main road at a jaunty angle, seemed to be the only place open for miles. The proprietor, a white man with a mangy dog at his feet, wouldn't make eye contact with me. It took a minute for my eyes to adjust to the dim light, but when I did, I noticed a table of Nazi paraphernalia: copies of *Mein Kampf*, banners of red and white and black. I let out a small "Oh" at the same time that Rich whispered "Fuuuuuuuuuck," and we hightailed it out of there.

JUNE SINGS, "I'LL BE SOMEBODY. Will I be somebody? Will I be somebody to love?" and I worry about her. I know what it feels like to be the only one for miles around. I think, "Are those people good to you, the ones who come to listen while they drink, the ones in your band?" Watching her perform live in 2018, even here in Chicago, June and I were among a small handful of Black women. I worry about how free she is, whipping her locks so they fall in her face as she dances on stage, hiding her eyes. She loops them around her ears like a puppy. I worry that she's forgotten who's out there. Sometimes I worry that she's gone too far in her life among the ghosts.

ANOTHER NIGHT, I'M WITH my friends, driving somewhere outside of town to a bonfire. I don't know where I'm going, embrace, in fact, that feeling of not being able to see what's in front of me, not knowing how to read the signs. I can't really explain my hunger to get outside of that town, the way I catapulted myself into the context of dangers, woods, unpeopled roads. Me, raised by my mama to be so watchful. The bonfire was Jeffrey's idea, a sweet hipster from Milwaukee. But Nan was afraid. Sure, she brought the bourbon, the consummate Kentuckian, in a silver flask, along with Dixie cups for all of us to share by the fire, but she told us that she was afraid for us, going to a bonfire in the woods made by people we didn't quite know, but especially for me, the only Black person in the group. Nan is a historian and has written about white terrorist movements in the South. "I don't trust white people," she said, ignoring for the moment that she herself was white, or maybe informed by that fact. But I laughed off Nan's comment, the same way I laughed off driving home so drunk one night from the one gay bar in our town that the road wavered, when the difference between waking life and sleeping safe at home in my single bed seemed very dim. As I saw the flames leap up between the trees, I heard those voices of warning, too, inherited from my mother and her mother and hers. But with each month here, something was being eaten away, that caution replaced by the urge for sensation and beauty and danger, the leaping glow of the bonfire itself.

Camille Dungy, a Black female writer and academic, knows this feeling and writes about it in her essay "Tales from a Black Girl on Fire, or Why I Hate to Walk Outside and See Things Burning": "Now and then something startling broke loose and knocked hard on my rear window, my moon roof, my windshield. An acorn. Maybe a pinecone. A twig. Dead ropes of kudzu dangled here and there, and all my people's horror stories worried through my head. Why was I out in the country at night? Didn't I know better?"[9]

It's a ghost of a feeling, that lonely feeling that you don't tell others about, that you yourself can't look at, lest it take your heart and squeeze the life right out of you.

Some nights, alone on a drive when I couldn't sleep, I'd watch the yellow lines passing and find myself bending toward them.

VALERIE JUNE, GHOST CATCHER

Once I had to pull over because it scared me. I couldn't feel myself in the car anymore, no sense of the seats or my seatbelt holding me in, no sense of the speed of the car anymore. I had joined the darkness. The rhythm became like it feels when you say the same word over and over again, danger, danger, danger, danger, danger. Until it means nothing but sound, nothing but the curve of a word over and through your mouth, what your teeth feel like as they scrape your tongue, the way the *r* sound seems to go on until it ends in a breath or until your breath gives out.

You've got to be careful with ghosts. They can grow bigger than you, whip you. But June is brave. She sings to grow brave, and so you sing with her, too. She catches the ghosts before they catch her.

When a fear is revealed to me, I dare myself to feel it fully. I challenge myself to mentally walk up to it, let it roar in my face, knock me down, shatter my heart, drown me trembling in sea-soaked tears, and rip through me like a tornado, leaving no tree trunk rooted and no tower untouched. It is only after I do that [that] I awaken to the reality that though the world may have broken my heart, there is still a stillness within that has not been moved.[10]

June's attention to ghosts and spirits is part and parcel of her Afro-futuristic vision—one that is firmly rooted in the past as it invents and envisions the future. As Daphne Brooks discusses in her book *Liner Notes for the Revolution: The Intellectual Life of Black Feminist Sound*, in June's work, we can hear at once an archivally informed conjuring of musical and other ancestors, like Jesse Mae Hemphill and Elizabeth Cotten and the Black country people she grew up with, while she also envisions new expressions of freedom drawing from these roots. This insistence on recognizing the past while not being a prisoner of history is at the heart of June's Black feminist spiritual practice, Brooks insists:

> Hers is an Afrofuturist archiving that faces forward, that leans toward new conditions of black possibility: "I could read certain books about slavery and certain books about our history, but I learn most of it through the songs. And then I try to say, okay, well how can we move beyond that? How can we grow?"[11]

We can hear June's Afrofuturist roots vision and sound in all her albums, but this bringing together of past and future is most explicit in her dreamy, expansive, and translucent 2021 album, *The Moon and Stars: Prescriptions for Dreamers*, and in her book of poetry, *Maps for the Modern World*. These works embody June's brave balance of catching ghosts while not becoming one of them too soon.

I LEFT FOR Chicago before I had the chance to solve the mystery of the Mills Brothers and the other missing Black people of Bellefonte. I needed Black folks and Brown and queer folks, all kinds of folks and languages around me. I needed community. I needed someone to love me back. I found it and made a home, a life more full than I had even imagined for myself, with good work and a child and love. I hoped when I left that at least one person would miss me, even if that person wasn't among the living. That would be enough for me.

> I am a ghost catcher, too.
> I've walked among them, sung with them,
> heard them on the radio between the static
> in the whine of a bottleneck guitar.
> I've wanted to be a ghost sometimes, too, and so they trust me.

They look out at me from photographs, from the flames of a
    bonfire;
From the worn pages of a book and the bottom of a chipped cup.
I've slept among ghosts and they've pulled me
out of my dreams. I've courted ghosts.
They've tapped me on the shoulder, brushed my hand,
Asked me to listen to their stories. Sometimes
I've wanted to be a ghost, too, and so
They know they can trust me.
Like June, I've courted ghosts.
    —**Francesca Royster**

IN VALERIE JUNE'S organic moonshine roots music, we can hear
that coming together of the ghosts of the ancestors and the presence of spirits in everyday embodied life. We hear the clearheaded
rootedness of the ways that June uses traditions passed down, musical and otherwise, in her music. And she opens up new routes
with the hallucinatory, playful, and intoxicating aspects of moonshine—another kind of spirit, a drink that is homemade, nonstan-
dardized (and therefore unpredictably potent!). You can hear these
layers of memory and nowness and experiments for the future in
her duet with the Memphis soul queen Carla Thomas in "Call
Me a Fool," taking the call and response of doo-wop and blow-
ing the top right off of it, letting those reverberations fly out into
the stratosphere. Sometimes growling, sometimes yodeling, sometimes humming deep in the throat, even in her speaking voice,
June wanders on and between scales, exploring the liminal textures
of twang and blues. Always, June seems to be listening while she's
singing or speaking for what can't yet be heard, to create an experience that touches beyond our everyday intelligences, even as she
calls upon what we once already knew.

Is there a light
You have inside you
You can't touch?
　—Valerie June, "Astral Plane"

Listening to June and to some of the older musicians she's learned from, I've realized the power of music—Black country music—to recognize the ghosts that haunt us. Music helps us meet our demons, name them, humor them, and maybe exorcise them. It can be a tool for awakening our own spirit—that light inside that we can't quite touch. And by connecting us to a line of other struggling human beings, Black country music helps us feel a little less lonely.

CHAPTER FIVE

CAN THE BLACK BANJO SPEAK?

Notes on *Songs of Our Native Daughters*

All of us in some capacity have lived life on the in between of . . . not being Black enough, or not being white enough. . . . If someone is moved by music or move[d] by something, they should be able to like it. There shouldn't have to be a birthright to be able to enjoy your love of something, but just in case, here is the historical backstory of this instrument . . . that more or less blasts away the myth of like, "what is Blackness?"
   —**Amythyst Kiah**

CAN THE BLACK BANJO SPEAK? Stand with one pants leg rolled up, leg hitched, to follow those broken stoned paths again, the old songs and uncanny melodies that take us to forgotten, shamed places; tunes and words just beyond the selves we have always been told we should make? To play it for our daughters, to guide their fingers so that they can play it, too? Can the Black banjo speak and be heard? Can we afford the risk that our pleas will not be

understood, not by our loved ones or the police? Can the banjo de-
liver the bad news that the bloody time we find ourselves in is the
bloody time that we were in long ago? Is it queer to take the time
to really learn this language of flail and drone, to find the old tunes
and make new tunes, to make ourselves in this homemade music?
To take the time to learn it all by ear when there is work to be done
and bills to be paid? To wear again this old quilt that kept us warm
once when there was no coal, made up of scraps stitched together
into a crazy quilt with our blood? Is it queer to find comfort in
this music, to wrap ourselves in it or to sit by a stream and strum
while watching the stars? Is it queer to claim birthright where our
place has long been occupied by our enemies? To play a duet with
our enemies, or with a bird that happens to fly in our window?
To claim a love beyond birth, beyond blood? Can the Black banjo
speak and be heard?

WHEN I ASK in this chapter's title "Can the Black Banjo Speak?,"
I am borrowing from Gayatri Chakravorty Spivak's groundbreaking essay on postcolonial identity, language, and power, "Can
the Subaltern Speak?"[1] In Spivak's essay, she questions whether
working-class voices of colonized peoples can be heard through
the static of capitalism and academic language. Inspired by Spivak, I am asking both whether Black banjo players can effectively
use the banjo and country music, a sound, genre, and idiom so
thoroughly controlled by white culture, to tell their own stories,
and if we can be heard by one another. After such a long time
of being estranged from the banjo, of "putting the banjo down,"
can African Americans hear ourselves in this music? To borrow
a phrase from one of my favorite thinkers, Audre Lorde, can the
master's tools dismantle the master's house? Audre says an em-
 phatic no.[2] But for me, the answer lies in the discovery that the
master's tools were never only his own. In this case, he borrowed

them, or rather, stole them, shaping them to his own purpose. The answer, as Audre Lorde would agree, is to always take the risk of speaking truth to power in the best ways that we can. And that means taking back the tools. *Songs of Our Native Daughters*, an album project first initiated by the multi-instrumentalist Rhiannon Giddens in 2018, together with Smithsonian Folkways, and including Amythyst Kiah, Leyla McCalla, and Allison Russell, is an example of taking back the tools. The album amplifies the banjo as a past and contemporary medium of Black women's expression, protest, and healing.

To use the banjo as a central tool for an album that centers on Black women is risky, precisely because of the ways that Black people have been written out of its history. As Rhiannon Giddens tells her audience in her 2017 keynote address to the International Bluegrass Music Association:

> To understand how the banjo, which was once the ultimate symbol of African American musical expression, has done a 180 in popular understanding and become the emblem of the mythical white mountaineer—even now, in the age of Mumford and Sons, and Béla Fleck in Africa, and Taj Mahal's "Colored Aristocracy," the average person on the street sees a banjo and still thinks *Deliverance*, or *The Beverly Hillbillies*. In order to understand the history of the banjo and the history of bluegrass music, we need to move beyond the narratives we've inherited, beyond generalizations that bluegrass is mostly derived from a Scots-Irish tradition, with "influences" from Africa. It is actually a complex creole music that comes from multiple cultures, African and European and Native; the full truth that is so much more interesting, and American.[3]

As Giddens explains in her liner notes for *Songs of Our Native Daughters*, the banjo, the instrument first of West African griots—traveling poets, musicians, and storytellers—and then just regular people was to become a creole medium of expression and song for the multiple ethnicities of enslaved peoples coming from Africa, first to the Caribbean and then on to the United States. As the scholar Dena Epstein documents in her game-changing book, *Sinful Tunes and Spirituals: Black Folk Music to the Civil War*, the banjo traveled with enslaved Black people on ships during the Middle Passage. Sometimes captives were forced to exercise with their own instruments on board in order to keep themselves alive and to battle deep depression at the horror of their conditions.[4] Banjos were incorporated into everyday life for enslaved Black people in the United States and the Caribbean, at times of rest and socializing as well as work. For its first one hundred years in the United States, the banjo was seen by white commentators as primarily an instrument of Black people, until it became a center-piece of American popular culture through blackface minstrelsy, a parody of Black life performed by white working-class men. Min-strel shows were a way for white men, especially white immigrants, to perform and establish their white identity, through what the historian Eric Lott calls the "love and theft" of Black musical tra-ditions.[5] The banjo, together with fiddles, tambourines, and bones, was featured prominently in these shows, and with the success of minstrel shows came the emergence of white performers who had mastered their semblance of Black banjo styles, like Dan Emmett and Billy Whitlock of the Virginia Minstrels. This first generation of minstrel performers, in order to master Black banjo styles and repertoires, served as apprentices to Black musicians, closely ob-serving them and even playing with them. But with the increasing commercial success of blackface minstrelsy, a separation eventually developed and led to the eventual erasure of the banjo's connec-tion to actual Black people in the popular imagination—or at least whites no longer had to prove that they had learned their banjo skills from Black people.[6]

After emancipation, many Black banjo performers found out that if they wanted to make money performing, they, too, had to blacken their faces, and they did so on minstrel and vaudeville stages and for medicine shows, for performances on showboats and in circuses, and for other entertainment spaces in the North and South. Some, like Bert Williams and George Walker, who advertised themselves as "two real coons," took the foolishness to heart and capitalized on it. For some artists, this was the ultimate humiliation. Gus Cannon, an itinerant musician and the son of formerly enslaved Black people, played banjo and fiddle with medicine shows around the region, performing together with doctors and hucksters to provide musical and comic relief while the "doctors" sold their wares. In order to perform, Cannon had to blacken his face and paint his lips white, and he recalled that the only way he could manage it was by becoming blind drunk beforehand.[7] But for some other Black musicians, like Horace Weston for example, perhaps the most celebrated Black banjo player in the late nineteenth century, and troupes like the Genuine Colored Minstrels, performing in minstrel shows in blackface was an opportunity to reinforce the association between Black and banjo in a new way, and to expand and open up minstrel songs, shifting their meanings, especially when they performed for Black audiences.[8] Other Black musicians and composers between Reconstruction and the Jazz Age grappled with the stereotypes of the minstrel tradition and developed ways to draw on folk traditions while finding a place at the center of American culture. For example, the early twentieth-century musician James Reese Europe created his Clef Club Orchestra, an orchestra of all-Black musicians who performed without blackface. The Clef Club Orchestra played spirituals and other religious music, classical music, and "plantation songs" at Carnegie Hall and throughout Europe. The orchestra included a section of banjos, together with other instruments.[9]

While the thread to earlier Black banjo traditions has never been fully broken, and can be heard in gospel and early blues and jazz, many Black people "put the banjo down"—and for some of us, this was an out-and-out rejection of the instrument.[10] As consumers and as musicians, we are still feeling the effects of the early record industry's segregation of popular music into "hillbilly" records (marketed to white people), and "race" records (marketed to Black people), even though there were Black musicians who performed on "hillbilly" recordings and sometimes white performers on "race" records, and some of the repertoire was interchangeable.[11] Even Rhiannon Giddens, born and bred in a community where banjo traditions are still passed down, says that when she first began performing the banjo, "[it was] like I was 'sneaking' into this music that wasn't my own."[12] With the Great Migration, some Black people saw and heard the banjo as linked to a painful past that they didn't want to hear, creating instead new sounds like blues and jazz. Tony Thomas, a Black banjo scholar and member of the group the Ebony Hillbillies, suggests that past banjo revivals have left out many Black people because of their often-uncritical nostalgia for a Jim Crow South.[13]

Songs of Our Native Daughters uses the banjo in new ways but is very aware of this history. The music of *Songs of Our Native Daughters* reminds us that we can't understand the past through archives and texts alone. We need music to help us tap into the imaginations of those lost to us. We need music to process the heaviness and pain of the realities of Black enslaved and apartheid life—and what better music than what was with us from the beginnings in this country, and which has been lost to us for so long? *Songs of Our Native Daughters* offers the stories that have been erased, together with old and new musical sounds and techniques. The Black banjo can provide both a lens and a balm. We can call the ones who came before us with music and joy.

IN THE SUMMER OF 2019, when I heard that Giddens and Our Native Daughters were going to play at the Smithsonian's National Museum of African American History and Culture, in Washington, DC, I quickly bought tickets for my small family: my partner, Annie; our college-aged niece, Demitria, who was living with us that summer; and our daughter, Cece, who was then seven. We planned a road trip that would also be a research trip, weaving from Chicago to Cedar Point, Ohio, to Pittsburgh, Pennsylvania, and then Washington, DC, catching up with family and old haunts along the way. In Rhiannon Giddens's liner notes for *Songs of Our Native Daughters*, she writes that one of her inspirations for taking up the project was a trip to the Smithsonian's National Museum of African American History and Culture with her daughter, Aoife, who was also seven at the time. I had been listening to *Songs of Our Native Daughters* nonstop that summer and playing it for anyone who would listen. And that same summer I began the journey to learn to play the banjo myself, swallowing my pride and Black girl awkwardness every week to eke out a slow, painful version of "Cripple Creek" and other tunes, invoking my own small gesture at Black banjo restoration. The lessons were helping me to hear and feel the banjo differently, to recognize the interwoven layers, the percussive power of the clawhammer, the funk that could be captured if you were skillful enough (which, admittedly, I was not).

My thoughtful teachers at the Old Town School of Folk Music here in Chicago, Chris and Dan, have led me to new discoveries of Black banjo musicians, including Sana Ndiaye and the other Senegalese players of the akonting, one of the banjo's African cousins;[14] the extraordinary Jerron "Blind Boy" Paxton, Jake Blount, Taj Mahal, and Reverend Gary Davis. Later, with lessons from Súle Greg Wilson, multi-instrumentalist, performer, and teacher, I have been absorbing firsthand the important lessons of apprenticeship in the Black banjo tradition as a way of tapping into the instrument's inherent funkiness. Even through the distance of Zoomed meetings from Arizona to Chicago in the months of the COVID pandemic, the funk of this music comes through in Súle's playing and his teasing laughter.

I wanted to join my story to the stories of struggle highlighted in *Songs of Our Native Daughters*. I had begun through memoir the work of bringing together my writerly self with my everyday life as a Black queer mother: adopting and raising a Black girl child with my white partner in Chicago, the city that I once swore, shivering on a bus stop as a teenager, that I would move away from to somewhere warm and never return; navigating the racism and classism and other tensions of our gentrifying neighborhood and then recognizing that I might be a gentrifier, too, even when I felt nervous walking past the police station around the corner; and doubling our efforts to combine our blood and chosen family to make community as a way of coping with all these complexities.

Annie and I had been planning a trip to Washington, DC, since the National Museum of African American History and Culture first opened in 2003. But we had been daunted by the legendary long lines and also by the intensity of the content, especially now that we had Cece. As we prepared for the trip that summer, my father warned us to steer Cece away from the museum's exhibit of Emmett Till's casket. At the age of twelve, my father and his all-Black Boy Scout troop had been forced to attend Till's open-casket funeral in Chicago, and it remains one of his most vivid memories of racial trauma. Cece had already been learning about slavery in her classroom and at the annual Black History month assemblies at her school. More significantly, she had experienced her own body as raced as a Black girl in her mostly white school. In her very first week of kindergarten, she had been bullied on the playground by an older white boy—a fifth grader!—who told her and her best friend Maya, also Black, that "Black girls are nasty!" Cece had gone through a period of shame about her own dark skin, a few shades darker than mine, and Annie and I worked hard to nurture in her a sense of pride and beauty. We wanted Cece's education about our nation's racist history to be as thoughtful, accurate, and gentle as we could manage.

I feel like what I do as an artist is bridge things. I bridge classical and secular. I bridge Black to white. I bridge country to blues. Even though that stuff doesn't really need bridges, that is something that I do.[15]

Rhiannon Giddens was born in Guilford County, North Carolina, and raised by musical parents, her mother, African American and Native American, and her father, white. She and her sister Lalenja grew up listening to folk, rock, soul, jazz, and classical music as well as the bluegrass and country music of her region. Giddens got interested in singing classical music after performing in an all-state children's chorus, and eventually attended Oberlin's Conservatory of Music to sing opera. But after graduating from the conservatory, she burned out on opera and came home to North Carolina, not quite sure what to do. She became increasingly interested in what she calls "homemade music" as a local and a global phenomenon. Back home in Greensboro, North Carolina, she performed in a Celtic band and got involved in the local contra dance scene as a caller. In 2005, she became deeply involved in the Black Banjo Gathering, a banjo festival featuring African American musicians at Appalachian State University, building the website, serving on a planning committee, and even performing in a benefit concert there, which proved to be life-changing for her. It was there that she met the musician who would soon become her mentor, Joe Thompson, a Black musician in his eighties from

Mebane, North Carolina, who played old-time fiddle and banjo. Thompson yearned to keep alive this pre-blues, pre-country style of Black music and to teach it to others, and Giddens found a great affinity for the instrument as well as the culture of apprenticeship of old-time led by Thompson. Giddens tells Mike Seeger, "It was the banjo first for me, when I first got exposed to old-time music. There was something about it. Just the plunkyness of it. The only banjo I'd been exposed to was bluegrass banjo. And I was just fascinated with the difference of clawhammer banjo, old-time banjo."[16]

She and two other friends from the Black Banjo Gathering, Dom Flemons and Justin Robinson, began to go to Joe Thompson's home for regular jam sessions and lessons and, with musical collaboration and support from Súle Greg Wilson and Taj Mahal, eventually formed the band the Carolina Chocolate Drops. As part of the Carolina Chocolate Drops, Giddens sang and played clawhammer-style banjo and fiddle and danced. The Carolina Chocolate Drops (named after a 1920s Black string band, named first as the Four Keys, then renamed with the racist name by white promoters as the Tennessee Chocolate Drops) toured for ten years, using traditional Black musical forms, including country, bluegrass, blues, and folk to explore voices, performance techniques, and other innovations that have been segregated, caricatured, and erased over time. Along with country music, bluegrass, and old-time, the Drops embraced as their archive opera, Celtic and Scottish music, minstrel shows, vaudeville, and hip-hop. The members were musicologists of sorts, drawing from archives at the Library of Congress, integrating oral histories of former slaves as well as memories of performances from their own families and communities, and reworking contemporary songs into their music. The band's membership was fluid, with some musicians joining for specific albums, including Leyla McCalla, who would eventually rejoin Giddens as part of Our Native Daughters.

After releasing five albums and one EP, and earning a Grammy Award for *Genuine Negro Jig* in 2011, the band members went their separate ways. Giddens developed her solo career. Her first post-Drops solo album, *Tomorrow Is My Turn* (2015), produced by T Bone Burnett, features the songs of her biggest female influences across a wide range of genres, including Odetta, Dolly Parton, Patsy Cline, Sister Rosetta Tharpe, and Nina Simone. Giddens has gone on to win multiple awards, including a MacArthur Genius Grant; composed a ballet, *Lucy Redux*, on the life of Shakespeare's "Dark Lady," and an opera, on the life of Oma Ibn Said, an enslaved Muslim African man who was brought to Charleston, South Carolina, in 1807; co-starred in "Keep a Song in Your Soul," a Chicago-based theater event at the Old Town School of Music; created *Aria Code*, a podcast on opera; appeared in small television roles in *Parenthood* and *Nurse Jackie* and a recurring role in *Nashville*; provided songs for movie soundtracks, including *The Hunger Games* and *The Great Debaters*; and collaborated with many other artists, including Bob Dylan, Elvis Costello, Marcus Mumford, the Kronos Quartet, Yo Yo Ma, and the jazz drummer and composer Francesco Turrisi. And she has become a vibrant and accessible public intellectual, sharing her knowledge about the banjo's Black history on social media and other platforms such as Myspace, YouTube, Instagram, and Patreon. She is a contemporary folk hero in the truest sense.

Collaboration, whether with the living or the dead, is something that Giddens does best. For her *Songs of Our Native Daughters* project, Giddens realized that she needed other Black women's voices with her on her journey, so she called on friends that she had admired from afar and past collaborators to bring this project home: Allison Russell, of the Americana/folk band Birds of Chicago, who brings a gut five-string banjo to the album, together with a lilting, honeyed voice and presence; Leyla McCalla, solo artist and past Chocolate Drops member, who brings her tenor banjo and lovely multilingual storytelling voice as well as her cello; and Amythyst Kiah, an out-and-proud queer solo guitarist with a chest-deep singing style that she calls "Southern Gothic, alt-country blues," who contributes vocals, guitar, and a steel-string banjo. Giddens brings her fretless minstrel banjo, a reproduction of a model from the 1850s; her fiddle; her crystalline, multifaceted voice; and her production skills. All contribute vocals and songwriting for the album. All bring deep musical and historical knowledge to the songwriting and performance, including the multiple languages, histories, and legends from their own homes across the Black diaspora: Black Appalachia, by way of Johnson City, Tennessee, and the Piedmont region of North Carolina; the Caribbean nation of Grenada, by way of Montreal; and Haiti, by way of New York City.

On this project, Giddens uses her privilege as a successful artist to help others speak truth to power: "To be able . . . to have a platform for these ladies to say some things that they don't always get to say, you know? Because we're too angry, and we're too strident, and we're too forceful and we're too—every single damned thing that we get told when someone else is doing it, they're like, "'Oh yeah. Right on.'" But you know, all of the sudden, we're [told we're] angry. . . . We have a lot to say and we haven't had a lot of opportunity to say it. Not in the folk world."[17]

The importance of *Songs of Our Native Daughters* for Black women's and girls' collective healing is reflected throughout the album and linked to the album title itself, *Songs of Our Native Daughters*. We very rarely speak of African American women as "native" to the United States, most obviously because of our capture and forced migration, and the ways that Black identity is often grounded in a sense of the continuous movement of the African diaspora. And yet, Black women's identities, like banjos themselves, are formed out of the bloody history that informs this nation at its core. Our unpaid labor was a necessary part of this nation's founding and economy. Family wealth built from the slave trade founded schools, banks, corporations, monuments, and other institutions that are still sources of wealth, luxury, and power today, from the boards of Ivy League schools, to Tiffany and Co., to J. P. Morgan Chase (the bank that I pay a mortgage to every month).[18] Even (or especially) the White House was built by slave labor. To claim ourselves as native, together with our white and Indigenous sisters, is to acknowledge the ways that our lives, work, and creativity are indelible parts of American life, culture, economy, and history.

"I HOPE WE DON'T run into Trump here," Cece wished out loud as we entered the museum. She had been worried about Trump since we arrived in DC. "Don't worry. I really doubt that he'd come here," I reassured her. Though most of the crowd was African American, we saw many kinds of people there: old people, young people, many different races and languages and nationalities. We were all dazzled by the stylish teenagers in diamante-studded jeans and with neon-threaded braids; snazzily dressed elders in tweed, despite the heat; different-sized bodies and rates of motion. And no Trump in sight.

The museum is organized into five floors, ascending historically through the galleries, beginning at the very bottom with the Middle Passage and rising through to the present, with Culture and Art at the very top. Knowing we might not get through everything, we decided to split up for a while, Annie and Demitria exploring independently while Cece and I worked our way as far as we could get through the history galleries. We'd meet up at the soul food cafeteria for lunch.

As we crowded into the hot, stuffy elevators and lurched downward to the Middle Passage exhibit, the festive atmosphere evaporated. Faces looked grim, some a little panicked. A tour guide, an older African American woman, joked that maybe in this crowded elevator, "we might feel a little taste of what those old Africans felt." A few of us chuckled uncomfortably.

Cece was drawn right away to an exhibit of a beautiful African queen, Queen Nzingha of the Ndonga region in the Kongo, now Angola—a brown-skinned, well-accessorized beauty in a bright green robe. The sixteenth-century artist who drew her gave her intelligent, querying eyes, high cheekbones, and full, pursed lips. Queen Nzingha, the exhibit told us, was a sixteenth-century leader and strategist negotiating the growing presence of Portuguese slave traders in her region. This image of Black humanity, even glamour, in the middle of an exhibit on slavery was startling. I was excited that Cece was learning about another kind of queen after a diet of Disney. Take that, Elsa and Anna! But Nzingha's history is complex. The exhibit told us that at times she and her kingdom fought against the traders, and at other times, negotiated with them. It made me want to know more of her story. What painful decisions did she make? Did she feel as though she had a choice? Could she have anticipated what was going to happen for the next four hundred years?

As we moved along with the crowd, we saw an image more familiar to me: a wall-sized diagram of the hold of a slave ship during the Middle Passage: Black bodies stacked horizontally and vertically to take up every inch of space, like so many cords of wood. I wondered if this was the first time Cece had seen this image. We stood close enough to see that the faces of the bodies were nonindividuated on the sketch. Cece ran a finger along each body: one after another, after another. I gave her a squeeze, and we kept moving. In the cases all around us was the evidence that slavery was well planned, calculated for maximum profit: bills of sale, well-constructed shackles and chains, the huge cotton sack larger than a grown man—all so deliberate in its strategies to make the most of its investments: human beings made into objects.

As we made our way through the Middle Passage section, I noticed that Cece was beginning to move more slowly, until her feet were dragging. I saw her eyes linger longingly at another little girl seated on a side bench with a portable Gameboy. "Do you want to take a break?" I whispered to her. "Yes, please," she said. We sat down together on another bench and snuck some animal crackers, looking at my phone. We clicked through the photos from our road trip so far: riding the roller coasters of Cedar Point with her cousins, our multiracial family a rainbow of browns; Cece and Demitria sharing a set of earphones in the back seat of our Honda Fit, surrounded by snacks and stuffed animals; snaps of ourselves posing inside the wacky, colorful, and unapologetically queer brownstone-turned-art-installation, Randyland, in Pittsburgh, and then in front of the mural of the Obamas along DC's African American heritage Trail on U Street. Looking over Cece's shoulder and taking a breath myself, I realized that absorbing the history that the museum provided was hard and melancholy work. I could feel weariness deep in my muscles and bones, and I sensed that Cece felt it, too.

IN THE VIDEO on the making of "Mama's Crying Long," from *Songs of Our Native Daughters*,[19] we are taken into a small North Carolina home studio on a rainy winter morning full of shadow. Rhiannon Giddens sings the song a cappella for her bandmates, something she wrote based on a found slave narrative. In the song, an enslaved woman who has been raped repeatedly by her master finally has enough one day and stabs him to death with her knife. The overseer and the law find her dress, covered in blood, and they take her to a nearby tree and they hang her. This is all told from the point of view of a child—her child, who first finds the dress covered in blood, and who watches her mother being captured by the men. The child sees her mother die, and watches her spirit leave her body. The story is told in the form of a children's rhyme, a hand-clapping game. Giddens tells her listeners that the song came to her in one take, as if it was waiting to be written, waiting to be sung. "But I needed y'all to do this," she tells them.

The three women watch and listen from a worn flowered couch, heads nodding, some crying quietly. Giddens stares out the window as she sings, as if watching her own mother, no longer in the room: "Mama's flying free. Mama's flying free." The last lines linger in the silence. After the song is over, the three women ask Giddens a few questions and then sketch out a bare-bones arrangement on the spot: where to come in with their response to her solo, where to add a few small tweaks to the lyrics. Then the four get to work.

The singers form a ring, the familiar shape of call and response. Leyla McCalla has her hands folded on her stomach as she sings and stares into the middle distance, channeling an unseen source the way Mahalia Jackson used to do. Allison Russell watches the others' faces with care as she sings, a young mother hen. Amythyst Kiah hangs back a little from the others, eyes hooded, going into herself to bring out the resonant voice that will provide the bottom. Jamie Dick, the drummer and, for this song, the only white man in the ring, hovers over his drums, his face hidden, and then, when the music starts, throws his whole body into each beat. Through the magic of technology, Giddens both sings the lead and joins the circle, together with the other women, animated now, no longer alone. A recording of Rhiannon clapping is layered into the mix. Like Octavia Butler's time travelers, we listeners are pulled into the violence and emotional intensity of the slavery past, regardless of whether we are ready to surrender to it:

Mama's cryin' long [Rhiannon starts]
And she can't get up [the circle answers]
Mama's hands are shakin' [Rhiannon continues]
And she can't get up [the circle repeats, raising the tension]

Giddens and the circle take us into this child's mind and vulnerable heart to see this lynching feelingly. With each stanza, we get a variety of feelings: confusion, horror, frustration, abandonment, awe: "Mama's in a tree / and she can't come down. Mama's in a tree / and she won't come down." As a mother, I can barely listen to the song's bare-bones pain, and I am reminded that Giddens is also a mother of a girl the same age as my own. In the presence of that raw feeling, the response circle is vital to confirm the child's truth, to finish the lines of the story when it gets to be too much for her, and to help hold a space of healing when the song is done. Giddens's claps, with the support of Jamie Dick's drum, do more than keep time. They help stir up the air to make the conjuring possible. They give the air shape and help create the necessary space between beats so that they all can breathe.

Watching the work of this circle of singers digging deep into the past, I am reminded of the ring shout, a stripped-down ritual of music, dance, and worship based in West and Central African cultures and brought to the United States by enslaved Black people. The ring shout was a meeting place that could happen anywhere where the heart of African spiritual traditions survived slavery, carrying the polyrhythms, layered harmonies, and call-and-response lyrical structures of older traditions. Sometimes the music of ring shouts included drums, and sometimes it was made up of just the voices of the singers, the rhythm of their feet, and the pounding stick of the stickman, the rhythmic lead. Ring shouts were expressions of resistance that did much of their work under the radar of white masters.[20]

Rhiannon's claps also remind me of the handclapping games of my girlhood, their use of chants, rhythms, and the ring to explore and exorcise difficult and impactful experiences, all in the name of play.[21] It's something to do on a hot summer day, before the sun is high enough in the sky for the sprinkler or the open hydrant to come on, or at recess, or to do with your sister while you're waiting for a long car ride to be over. You stand in a circle or, if there are two of you, you face each other, one palm up, one palm down. Or you wait for the perfect rotation of the rope. Then you call each other in: "Little Sally Walker," "Mary Mack," "Brown Girl in the Ring." Once the circle gets going, sustained by the rhythm of the clapping or the turning of the rope, there's a story to tell through song that looks simple only on the surface: asking your mother for fifteen cents to see the elephant jump the fence when you know she might not be able to spare it; heading to Mexico and running into the police; not having enough water to wash your dishes; dreaming of fishcakes when you're hungry; suffering flus and chest colds; missing playmates. Deep in the story there's shame, an event that you have no control over. And beneath the shame, there's pain. But always, afterward, there's the invitation to break it down: to dance, to strut, to jump the rope hot-pepper style. "Rise, Sally rise," the circle beckons. "Dry your weeping eyes." You might be shy, your heart might be pounding, but you are buoyed up by those clapping girls around you. "Put your hands on your hips and let your backbone slip." Then something magical happens: you do a dance that you saw your mother do once, feet moving without your brain, or you make up something new right on the spot. You might find yourself laughing or you might find yourself crying.

"Mama's Cryin' Long" calls on these traditions of hand-clapping games and ring shouts as a way to highlight the power of the circle as a means of collaboration and to explore and exorcise the traumas of slavery and its aftermath. It is of a piece with the whole of *Songs of Our Native Daughters*, which uses historically informed music as a way of understanding and animating and amplifying Black women's lives. As Giddens says in one interview, "Even though we came from this place of a lot of research and reading and engaging with academic material, I think we've been living in our skin our whole life and that's a part of our experience. We've inherited some of this trauma in different ways and we represent different parts of the African diaspora. And so it made sense for us to come together and try to process this together."[22]

BACK AT THE MUSEUM, after our rest, I found myself searching for the physical evidence of our resilience, the rituals that fed our spirit and imagination despite the brutality. The concert on my mind, I was drawn to the musical instruments: there was a drum from Charleston, South Carolina, carved from the trunk of a single tree. The placard explained that the drum had been a part of the Stono Rebellion that happened in 1739, a large uprising of enslaved African people, who were heard to chant "Liberty" to the beat of their drums. The uprising—in which twenty white people were killed and roughly an equal number of Black people, too—led to tougher slave codes, including the outlawing of drums and other musical instruments in that region. The outlawing of drums became the de facto law of the land, and banjos, fiddles, and tambourines took their place. The Stono drum had a round face carved on its side, the open eyes and mouth conveying to me the power of the drum to both sing and speak. There was a nineteenth-century drawing of a homemade banjo, and with it, a sketch of a ring shout, with a banjo player at their side. We saw a fiddle resting in a glass case, and despite the fingerboard worn from playing, the wood dulled in places where hands may have held it close, the instrument seemed to still thrum with life. I told Cece how those instruments were vital for our survival, to keep our bodies and spirits alive, to communicate, to stay connected to our African past, and also to resist—so much so that laws were enacted to control their use. This is what infuriates me when I see images from minstrelsy of people playing banjo as "Happy Darkies," how the relationship between music and resistance is downplayed and overlooked. Given its power, the fiddle seemed surprisingly small, and I imagined a child playing it. I imagined it being passed along from generation to generation until it reached Cece and me.

The concert felt so necessary. We needed a space to commiserate, to put into words our own feelings of outrage and sadness and loss awakened by the exhibits, to heal and connect. After we left the museum, our bellies full of the peach cobbler and fried chicken that we enjoyed at the museum café, we congregated in front of the building, playing freeze tag on the grass until we saw a line forming for the concert.

The clouds congealed, and it began to rain. As the crowd got wetter and more impatient, a guard was sent out from the museum to announce that people who were not carrying purses could enter the building first, since their security searches would ostensibly go faster. A group, mostly men, stepped up to the front of the line. An outraged young African American woman, wearing a now soggy but still lovely African print pantsuit and carrying a large leather handbag, sputtered with fury at the guard, who was also an African American woman, a few years older. Both seemed as though they had had a long day. The guard carried her heavy body with grace, but you could tell by the way she walked that her feet hurt in her heavy uniform shoes. The angry woman stepped under the guard's umbrella, pointing a finger in her face. As her voice rose, her body becoming more taut, I watched first in horror and then empathy. I willed both of them some waves of calm.

IN THAT MOMENT, I found myself thinking of "I Knew I Could Fly," a quiet, perhaps easily overlooked song on the *Songs of Our Native Daughters* album, penned by Leyla McCalla. It is a song about transcending the struggles of the moment and having confidence in that possibility despite being underestimated by others:

I don't know why
I knew I could fly.

You see what you see
You think you see me.

McCalla says that she was inspired by the playing style and quiet resilience of the guitar and banjo of the African American elder Etta Baker. When she was only four years old, Baker was taught guitar and banjo by her father, Boone Reid, and she played music all her life. Some of her music was recorded on the 1956 collection *Instrumental Music of the Southern Appalachians*, but since she was forbidden to perform by her husband, and she was compensated little for the instrumental music album, Baker never became a household name. Instead, she spent many decades raising children and grandchildren and playing her guitar and banjo every day in her garden. And then, when her husband died when she was seventy-eight, she released her first record with the help of Taj Mahal. Like her peer Elizabeth Cotten, Baker became a performer late, playing into her nineties, influencing performers like Mahal, Bob Dylan, Rhiannon Giddens, and Leyla McCalla. McCalla's "I knew I Could Fly" captures Baker's ingenious plucking technique epitomized in tunes such as "Railroad Bill" and "Carolina Breakdown," where Baker gives her own spin to old-time and blues styles. And the sound as well as the lyrics capture Baker's resilience, her combination of groundedness and otherworldliness. This is felt in the layer of birdsong heard on "Carolina Breakdown," where, according to the liner notes for Baker's recording, a bird actually flew into the window to sing a duet.

McCalla, like Baker and the bird that sings with her, knows the secret of flight, the necessary arithmetic of struggle and dreaming that we might have needed in that concert line. The lyrics feel like a wandering, ruminating conversation with an elder, capturing this act of self-exploration, reflection, and imagination in everyday terms, following the stars, and dreaming and resting by a stream. Each stanza is a slightly shifting meditation. McCalla sings dreamily, her fingers weaving light but strong threads of guitar, pulled together with Giddens's plunky minstrel banjo and Dirk Powell's mandolin. With each repetition, two, three, and four times, the implications of the lyrics deepen as McCalla gives a slight variation to the melody, giving the song a sense of trance. The song is in the tradition of African American songs about flight, from the spiritual "I'll Fly Away," to Parliament Funkadelic's "Mothership Connection," to Kanye West's "Spaceship."[23] As with these songs, the secret to flying is in the music itself.

I willed this knowledge to the upset woman in the concert line, who might not have been angry just about the line. If we all were able to access Etta's spirit, maybe we wouldn't turn against one another in our anger. Do not mistake my gentleness for weakness, the song seems to warn. But also, we can and must teach one another to fly.

WE WERE FINALLY let into the museum again, and we shook off the rain and the altercation and made our way to our seats for the concert. Most of the audience was white, the reverse of the visitors to the museum, but in the front row, I noticed a group of well-dressed Black people in suits and stylish dresses, hair in fresh fades and beautiful locks. They were wearing name tags, and I saw that some of them were connected to the museum and some to a local radio station. We saw other Black people there, too, and I smiled at them, and we gave each other the nod that Black people often give each other in mostly white spaces. Some gave Cece a special twinkling look, as the only Black child in the room. We, as people of culture and color, recognized one another.

I noticed that many of the white people were dressed considerably more casually than the Black people I saw, in T-shirts and shorts or simple sundresses. Maybe this was just a reflection of the exceptionally hot weather that day, or the aesthetics of the folkie community of DC. But I did get the sense that the significance of this event was felt differently across lines of race. (It reminded me of the way that on planes sometimes, I see older Black people dressed to the nines for their flight.) This concert was an Event for us. My family had traveled seven hundred miles to be there, and we were dressed casually but with the best accessories we could muster from our suitcases. And the other Black people, a minority in this crowd, were also similarly dressed. I could smell that sense of an Event in the lingering scent of Egyptian Musk in the air, the buzz of familiar chatter, the hugs of "Hello" and kisses on the cheeks, the glow of freshly oiled skin, the swish of fabric and clicking heels as one of the Black concert organizers walked past.

A white man sitting behind us wearing an Indiana Jones hat and Georgetown T-shirt tapped me on the shoulder and smiled at Cece, who was sitting between Annie and me. We nodded back and continued our conversation. He tapped Cece this time. "I like your hair," he said to her. His smile and eye contact lingered, as if waiting for a response. I saw his hand moving as if about to touch her hair, and Demitria turned to him and gave him her best glare. His hand faltered, but he spoke again, a little louder, talking to his companion this time, a white woman. "Doesn't she have the best hair here?" "Oh, yes," the woman cooed. Cece was often stopped by people, usually white people, who would ask her about her hair in public spaces, and sometimes tried to touch it. Today, it was styled in a dreadlocked ponytail, high and to the front so it draped over her forehead. She had added glitter to it in the bathroom that morning. We wanted Cece to feel proud, but we also taught her that she didn't have to feel obligated to respond when people complimented her. It was her choice to respond. And that no one—NO ONE—should touch her hair, unless she wanted them to. Cece answered with a quiet "Thank you." You see what you see. / You think you see me. Cece and Demitria quickly left to get some popcorn at the concessions table. Annie and I sat taller in our seats, hoping our backs would create an unapproachable wall. When I snuck a look back at the man a few minutes later, he was nodding to the beats of Toots Thielemans's harmonica coming over the loudspeakers, smiling as if he hadn't a care in the world.

FOR THE SONG "Black Myself," which Amythyst Kiah wrote, she drew from her struggles coming of age as a Black and queer girl, and that feeling of not being seen. She writes in *Songs of Our Native Daughters*' liner notes, "I thought of my experience as a Black girl in a white suburban neighborhood in the 1990s, and how, once puberty hit, the doors of my neighbors would suddenly close on me. And thus the refrain and the title of this song are intended to be an anthem for those who have been alienated and othered because of the color of their skin." Kiah sings the lead, and with each stanza, she extends the meanings of Blackness. She goes from instance to instance where her body—in its darker-than-a-paper-bag Blackness, in its butch gender queerness, in its working-class southernness, as a woman who desires other women, as someone who decided to pick up the banjo—is seen as wrong by others:

> You better lock your doors when I walk by
> 'Cause I'm Black myself
> You look me in my eyes but you don't see me
> 'Cause I'm Black myself

Kiah's song acknowledges the lived experience of all of her identities in the flesh, the desires that are denied by white society, even while it refuses the racist messages that it is *she* who is wrong. It's significant that some of the prohibitions that Kiah names in the song, particularly around sexuality, might come from some "respectable" Black folks, too, even while reflecting the codes of white supremacy. Black LGBTQ folks have often been told to be silent about their sexuality, and that their difference is dangerous for a unified Black freedom movement. For a notable example, Bayard Rustin, the Black civil rights leader who spearheaded the 1963 March on Washington, was often silenced about his gayness by civil rights leadership. Given these histories, the song's turn to self-love and community in the final verse is very important to the song and to the album as a whole, "surrounded by many loving arms." Kiah's Blackness is central to her sense of self, in all of its dimensions, and the song is a gesture of self-care. It's significant that Rhiannon Giddens and her coproducers chose this song to be the first on the album because it honors a complex and inclusive Blackness. And I am reminded of one of the publicity photos for *Our Native Daughters*, where Kiah, usually the shy one that hangs in the background, is thrust to the front, with Giddens, Russell, and McCalla standing smiling behind her.

At the 2018 performance of the song for the Americana 18th Annual Honors, presented by *Austin City Limits*, "Black Myself" is the chance for the whole group to jam country music—anthem style, all in the name of a Black womanhood that is queered.[24] Kiah wears a black tuxedo-inspired jacket and black-and-white tie, which is complemented delightfully by Giddens's black lace minidress. They are flanked by Russell and McCalla, who both wear dresses in variations of gold. Kiah stands out as the only butch in a group of femme women, the contrast adding a crackle of electricity to the song.

I hear in this performance a rebuttal to country anthems that assert white countryness, masculinity, and a revved-up patriotism, from Lynyrd Skynyrd's "Sweet Home Alabama" to Toby Keith's

"Courtesy of the Red, White and Blue." I hear in Kiah's performance the tough and tender command of queer Black folk divas like Toshi Reagon and Tracy Chapman. I hear the strong voice and moral authority of Fannie Lou Hamer, testifying to Congress about her jail-cell abuse during the 1964 Freedom Summer.

Kiah plays her acoustic guitar here with a powerful defiance, locking her audience in a direct gaze as she sings. Giddens, Russell, and McCalla provide a spirited chorus, punctuated by claps, hops, and pointing fingers for emphasis. The band behind them, all men, give the song everything they've got, blasting their horns and popping their drums in support. Dirk Powell's accordion provides a kind of answering "Amen" to each of Kiah's lines. By the end of the song, the crowd gives an immediate and enthusiastic standing ovation.

AT LAST, IT WAS TIME for the concert to begin. Cece, Annie, Demitria, and I took two last family selfies, one serious and one goofy, capturing our excitement for the show. As the lights lowered, the members of Our Native Daughters appeared on stage, each carrying a banjo like a weapon. All four women were wearing matching jeans jackets with a colorful design of four black silhouettes, a banjo, and the letters OND. "We're a girl gang now!" Giddens shouts, to our cheers. Giddens described how powerful it was to wear the jackets as they toured the museum earlier that day, making them feel bolder. We reveled in their style, each with their own take on beauty: Giddens, with loose silk purple tunic and bare feet, hair streaked purple and in a ponytail; Russell in a bright flower-patterned halter dress; McCalla, laid-back in a green and red kente cloth summer frock; Kiah in black suit pants with suspenders and porkpie hat. The warm red and orange stage lights brought out the varying browns of everyone's skin and gave the audience our own dose of melanin. Each took turns telling stories, teaming up with one another on the songs that they had cowritten. Their pleasure in playing together was evident in their appreciative gazes, in their inside jokes and flirtations, and in their shared seriousness as they listened to one another play. As the band launched into "Moon Meets the Sun," I got what I had been waiting for all day at the museum. I yearned to know what was happening inside to the enslaved women and men. How did they survive? The song offers their story and their resilient spirit. First, Giddens names the damage:

Ah you steal our children
But we're dancing
Ah you make us hate our very skin
But we're dancing

Russell deflects the shame, leaving the judgment up to God, while Kiah embraces the stealth of the rabbit and the spider: "the smallest will still prevail." And with each chorus, those lines "But we're dancing" answer the lament, backed by the bottom of that minstrel banjo. Resilience. We can feel it in their own dancing as they sing to us, grounded like Giddens's bare feet. They invite us into the circle, to "step into the ring." The women's voices give testimony to resistance to the separation and erasure of home, to the lessons of self-hate. Music and dancing keep us going, connect us to others, they remind us. This is the recipe for survival. With each song offering a new call and response, a new chance to unburden ourselves with song, I could feel the crowd around me releasing its tension.

The concert came to a close with the song "You Are Not Alone," a lullaby by Allison Russell, written, she tells the audience, for the young daughters that the women left behind to go on tour, and perhaps for her own younger self. And it was a lullaby for us. With Russell's voice, tender then swelling with feeling, the rhythms rising and falling in a waltz, the song itself is a circle. I thought of Cece's yearning to learn more about her birth family that summer. My own yearning, too, for ancestors whose histories have been lost. I thought of how excited I am whenever I meet an African person in Chicago and they claim me as their own. The woman in the Ethiopian bead store who giggled as we both struggled to get a string of amber over my very large head, and she said, "You must be Ethiopian. You have a head like ours." How happy that made me. As Russell sang the lines "In the cradle of the circle / All the ones who came before you / Their strength is yours now / You're not alone," Kiah's and Giddens's banjos plucking feather-light, a cobweb subtle but strong, McCalla's melancholy cello woven in between, Cece whispered, "It feels like they're singing to me."[25]

CHAPTER SIX

THIRTEEN WAYS OF LOOKING AT LIL NAS X'S "OLD TOWN ROAD"

When the blackbird flew out of sight,
It marked the edge
Of one of many circles.
> —Wallace Stevens, "Thirteen Ways of Looking
> at a Blackbird," stanza 9

WHY CHOOSE LIL NAS X'S SONG "Old Town Road" to close this book? For some critics, the song has become a test case for the boundaries of country music's definitive sound—and which songs and performers belong on Billboard's Hot Country Songs lists, or on stage at the Grand Ole Opry.[1] (The song got unceremoniously kicked off Billboard's country music charts after one week, going on to break the record for the longest consecutive run as number one on the Billboard Hot 100 chart, for nineteen weeks.) The rejection by some country fans of Lil Nas X as a country music artist, including boycotts of Wrangler Jeans for partnering with Lil Nas X, reveals the racial tensions at the core of the genre.[2]

But beyond this controversy, I am intrigued by the song as an example of Black creativity that is boundless, using fantasies of mobility, strength, and reinvention to create a song and a set of videos that keep on giving. Created with beats purchased for $30 on a YouTube DJing store, boosted by Twitter and Reddit, gone viral on TikTok, the song demonstrates the ways that young artists have been changing how music is being made and shared, bringing their songs together with fans, other musicians, stylists, and dancers outside the confines of the recording industry. Lil Nas X in total made seven remixes of the song, working with a diverse roster of musicians, including Billy Ray Cyrus, Diplo, BTS's RM, Young Thug, Mason Ramsey, and Cupcakke. Collaboration is at the heart of Lil Nas X's music making and, in that way, might offer a blueprint for inclusive social change. But Lil Nas X also just plain seems to be enjoying himself. Like many Black writers before me, including Morgan Parker (in her poem "13 Ways of Looking at a Black Girl") and Henry Louis Gates Jr. (in his book *Thirteen Ways of Looking at a Black Man*), I am reengaging Wallace Stevens's poem "Thirteen Ways of Looking at a Blackbird"[3] to think about the multiplicity, variation, and reinvention that Lil Nas X's "Old Town Road" presents to me. I turn to it, because even though Stevens wrote his "Thirteen Ways" poem in 1917, there is definitely a hip-hop spirit to its interest in remixing and revisioning. Stevens, taking this often underestimated bird, explores the malleability of language and symbol and, with it, offers up a meditation on the ways that Blackness in particular offers meaning in excess. Lil Nas X, with his fringe and glitter and many, many remixes, offers an example of excess as a sign of possibility.

1: SONGS OF SUMMER

I'm writing this essay in August 2020 during what sometimes seems like a summer that beats all summers in the contest to be the worst yet, though the historian in me knows that's not true. I have never experienced a global pandemic like COVID-19 so close to home, but the world has lived through plenty of pandemics already (the Black Plague, deadly flus, and more recently the Ebola virus, just for starters). Bad presidents, ones disdainful of the value of the lives of folks on the margins, are unfortunately not new. And the kind of police violence that killed George Floyd and Breonna Taylor is not new either. The evil snake of white supremacy has been with us from the birth of this nation. Just a glance at the summer news from a year ago reminds me that many of the things that ail us right now were ailing us then. We didn't have the coronavirus to contend with, but we had an unequal health system, made worse by the slow chipping away at the Affordable Care Act. That summer, scientists declared its July to be the hottest on record (only to be beaten by this summer), and we woke up to images of Hurricanes Barry and Dorian and Imelda ravaging those to the south of us. In El Paso, a young white man barely out of his teens shot and killed twenty-two folks of Mexican descent in a Walmart Parking Lot—his own protest over immigration—and of course, such white vigilantism continues, whether by the police or everyday citizens. In 2019, Annie and I went to bed each night worried about the gun violence in Chicago that seemed to explode in the summer months, hoping that what we were hearing was firecrackers. The city's gun violence betrayed the deeper problems of a lack of gun control, unemployment, and divestment in education and other aspects of our communities—all problems that have only deepened with the pandemic.

Last year, like this year, it was hard to feel the promise and release that a typical summer song might offer. Summer songs are often a mix of pleasure and of the impending endings of summer and the romance that comes with them. Melancholy can threaten even the cheeriest songs like the undertow of quinine in a gin and tonic, or like the way the light can change suddenly as the sun moves behind a cloud. But the summer of 2019's top pop songs had that melancholy in surplus: the ache of inevitable heartbreak in Shawn Mendes's and Camilla Cabello's "Señorita"; Miley Cyrus's sad conversation with her lover in "Slide Away" ("You said everything changed. You're right. We're grown now. I'm not who I used to be"); Lewis Capaldi's heart-wrenching hopelessness in "Someone You Loved" ("I'm going under this time and there's no one to save me"). Even Khalid's "Talk," an upbeat, let's-fall-in-love (maybe) kind of a song, is cautious: "Can't we just talk? Talk about where we're going. Before we get lost?").

That's why in summer 2019 I found myself leaning on "Old Town Road" kind of hard. Together with Solange's "Binz" and Lizzo's "Juice" ("Ya ya yee!"), "Old Town Road" seemed evidence, somehow, of Black love, Black optimism, and room for collective Black weirdness, especially in the presence of Lil Nas X himself, his open-faced joy, his apparent pleasure in the music, and his success in sharing it. I felt propelled by the song's sense of motion, its satisfying polyrhythmic bounce, and its sheer goofiness, only renewed with repetition. I heard it everywhere that summer: pumping out of car windows, from the outdoor loudspeakers at the Dairy Queen, here at home, on my computer as I scrolled through Facebook or got lost in musical wormholes on YouTube, a soundtrack of optimism that always made me say "Heeeeeeeyyy!" when I heard it, whipping my imaginary horse's rump, waving my hands in the air, making lassos—moves that were guaranteed to embarrass my daughter Cece if we were in public. While it was released several months earlier, and hit Billboard's Hot 100 Pop Chart back in April, its duration at the top position (nineteen weeks!) throughout the summer has become legendary, and by August 2019, it was still going, bobbing and weaving through that summer's struggles. Even now, in this summer of masks and social distancing, when I seldom hear a car drive by with the radio turned up at all, when I'm afraid to go to the Dairy Queen at all, and when beach days are carefully choreographed, in this summer of pandemic and loss, I find myself captured again by "Old Town Road," by its ability to make a way out of no way and then some. We need the new songs, too, like Beyoncé's "Black Parade" and Anderson.Paak's "Lockdown," to heal us. But I also want to write Lil Nas X to ask if he has room for one more remix.

2: THE LIL NAS X MULTIVERSE

Lil Nas X, whose real name is Montero Hill, said he wrote "Old Town Road" last fall, after staying with his sister while avoiding his parents as a college dropout. When his sister finally sent him on his way, he imagined his future.

"I felt like a loner cowboy," he said. "I wanted to take my horse to the Old Town Road and run away. The horse is like a car. The Old Town Road, it's like a path to success. In the first verse, I pack up, ready to go."[4]

There is a place where certain young Black men go, at least at some point in their lives. Their bedrooms, if they have them, become their retreats. On the walls there might be a Dark Side of the Moon–scape, a post-apocalyptic western, sketched out in pencil on their walls, done so faintly that a mother with aging eyes might miss it; velvety posters that come alive with black light, of a leaping tiger or a reclining Black lady, Afros and cleavage full or a blocky Minecraft-style self-portrait. There are books stacked by the bed: *Dune, The Hobbit*, the westerns of Louis L'Amour, *The Autobiography of Malcolm X*, or a *Harry Potter*, fat books about other young men who are figuring out the hard way which way to go. On the TV set, there might be a Kung Fu movie playing or Cartoon Network or a constant game of *Fortnite* taking place with virtual friends. The smells: Dakar mixed with sweat or Harold's fried chicken with fries and hot sauce, now soggy, mixed with fresh laundry washed and folded by a loved one; pine air freshener or incense to hide whatever was smoked there. "Funky London" was what we called my uncle's room, where we females were barred from entry. And if the young man is lucky, this room would have an excellent sound system, bass too powerful for the thin walls. In my uncle's version, I would hear from those vibrating walls my first Kiss, my first taste of "Maggot Brain," but I can imagine that these days one might hear the rolling percussion of a trap drum.

This retreat has special meaning for young Black men, who seem these days more than ever to be always watched, always suspect by the outside world.

You can knock but you cannot enter without an invitation, because this is a retreat from do-anything-for-you mamas and hotheaded daddies, from opinionated siblings or nosey nieces or ghosted girlfriends. It is a space hard won—maybe it was once a pantry or a mud room, cut off from the rest of the house and from the benefits of a radiator. Maybe it's the borrowed room of a grown-up sister or a grandma's ex–sewing room. This retreat is a way to get away from the things not quite finished: a GED, a job search, a chore list. It is a place where unchecked dreaming can happen, a place to hide a dream, the tiny still-curled-up green leaves of a tenderest self, not yet dried up by the sun.

In the first moments of Lil Nas X's performance of "Old Town Road" at the 2020 Grammys, it would seem that we're entering a retreat just like this one.[5] We see Lil Nas X stretched out on a worn orange velour couch, legs a little too long for it, a cartoon airing in the background. He's strumming a guitar, and there are posters on the wall, clothing strewn on the furniture.

But then as the room begins to turn on some hidden Lazy Suzan, we have to question what we thought we were seeing—the signs of an idle slacker. On closer look, those posters on the wall turn out to be of Lil Nas X himself, his own appearances on the covers of *Billboard*, *Variety*, and *Time*, markers of his miraculous

rise to fame. We are reminded that this unassuming kid strumming his guitar is up for six Grammys that evening—more than
any male that year. The shirt strewn on the couch turns out to
be not just any shirt but Kobe Bryant's jersey, number 24. Kobe
had just been killed in a helicopter accident, along with his young
daughter, that afternoon, and the inclusion of the jersey is a salute
to another Black man with astounding skills, another star. Kobe's
jersey is a gesture of respect for this other Black struggler, and it is
a great example of Lil Nas X's thoughtful use of cameos that we'll
see in "Old Town Road (Official Movie)," too: fellow rappers Rico
Nasty and Vince Staples, comedians Chris Rock and HaHa Davis,
Dutch record producer YoungKio, Diplo playing his heart out on
the washboard, and Billy Ray Cyrus, of course, the Louise to Lil
Nas X's Thelma.[6]

Lil Nas X is wearing a silver suit, and it looks and feels like a
kid's homemade alien suit made out of tinfoil, until he stands up
and our breath might catch as we see how it hugs his long lines
stunningly.

Then the room revolves some more and Lil Nas X opens a door
and we see that we are now in a Lil Nas X multiverse, a series of
dreamscapes and people, all excited to sing with him: the K-Pop
group BTS surrounded by a cityscape of what could be Atlanta
or New York or Los Angeles or Seoul; a sparkling pink glitter
barn, with Diplo and another even younger internet upstart, Mason Ramsey, a thirteen-year-old yodeling sensation; a green slime
room to suggest to fans-in-the-know Young Thug, another collaborator on one of Lil Nas X's remixes; Billy Ray himself; then some
dancers who are doing some cool voguing moves in black patent
leather, then the rapper Nas (no relation), dressed in white, showing in person that there are no hard feelings about their shared
name. The Grammys production demonstrates (with the help of
Jed Skryzpczak's set design) Lil Nas X's creation of a world that
is peopled with others who want to work with him. Spaces that

had once been confining or mundane (bedroom retreat, barn) have been recast, all lit by the lightning bolts of electricity that may be conducted by Lil Nas himself in that foil suit.

If "Old Town Road" is a song of survival and success that might have been cooked up in the fantasy space of a man-child alone in his room, fed by video games, movies, and waterlogged novels, the 2020 Grammys dramatizes a vision of Lil Nas X's own boundlessness and sociability, the power of his multiverse. All the different kinds of masculinities, all the goofy enthusiasm. There *is* a place for us, the performance insists.

3: THE PSYCHIC POWER OF BLACK COWBOYS

In its best, most optimistic form, the cowboy and the wild west can be the perfect flickering movie screen to project a more inclusive, more compassionate, still-wild narrative of what it means to be a pioneer. Ironically, something so tied to a specific traditional look—boots, hat, jeans—might be the medium right now to reinvent, to put LED glow-in-the-dark lights on, to tell the story of new frontiers and underdogs succeeding that people never grow tired of hearing.

    —**Kelsey Lawrence, "Why Young Designers Are Reclaiming Cowboy Culture"**[7]

Lil Nas X and the "wranglers on his booty" isn't the first time Black folks have discovered cowboy hip. At my majority African American high school in Chicago in the 1980s, cowboy style was taken on and integrated with Black bourgie chic, our own angle on the *Urban Cowboy* craze. We wore Levis, though, not Wranglers, and pricey, slick-bottomed Frye boots or Tony Lamas—tall ones that reached your knee were all the rage, to be mixed and matched with Fiorucci New Wave and Izod preppy; cowboy hats were placed carefully on well-picked 'fros or well-pressed asymmetrical bobs cut at the Vidal Sassoon salon on Rush Street, styled with some made-in-Chicago Pink Luster hair oil. Some of my favorite funksters mixed cowboy style into their looks during the mideighties: Rick James and Con Funk Shun; Earth, Wind and Fire; and the Commodores—all rocking fringe and sometimes cowboy hats on *Don Kirshner's Rock Concert* or MTV. Cameo's song "Word Up" featured a sample from the theme for *The Good, the Bad and the Ugly* ("Ooooweee ooooweee ooooo!"), and the video for Cameo's "She's Strange" takes place in an abandoned Old West saloon. This style was a Black cowboy style without really needing the cowboys.

So watching Lil Nas X rocking his yellow and black wasp-sleek cowboy leather pants and shirt at the BET Awards[8] and watching the audience of Black people singing along, doing their own syncopated lasso loops in the air, I felt nostalgia, a throwback to a specifically Black cultural phenomenon and style rather than a knock on the door and a request for admission into a white cowboy/western culture and style.

But Lil Nas X's claims to the Black cowboy in this cultural moment has its own distinct resonances. In this political climate, cross-racial and cross-class alliances are often tense, have often been eroded by sectarian politics, delicate alliances blown. Country (and western) continues to be a staging ground for some of those splits, as we see in some of the debates around Lil Nas X's legitimacy as a country star, including his removal from Billboard's Hot 100 Country chart after one week. And so the appearance of Black cowboys, which has been frequent in Black popular culture lately, is more pointed, more intentionally critical.

Black cowboys and Black cowgirls are about talking back to historic and present erasure—reclaiming a Black past as well as a Black future. Present-day Black cowboys and Black cowgirls are popping up all over the nation: Chicago's Broken Arrow Riding Club, on the South Side of the city; the Compton Cowboys of

Compton, California, and to the north, the Brotherhood Riders Club of Stockton, California; the New York City Federation of Black Cowboys; the Cowgirls of Color of Maryland; and Chicago's viral sensation Adam Hollingsworth, aka Dreadhead Cowboy, riding down the Dan Ryan Expressway on his horse in protest of police brutality.

Don Flemons, the Carolina Chocolate Drops cofounder, brings Black cowboy history alive in his own way in his 2018 album, *Black Cowboys*, with songs from the archives and new ones that he's written bringing Black cowboy history to life, from "Texas Easy Street," a 1929 ragtime blues song about cowboy life, to "One Dollar Bill," a song written by Flemons to capture the vivid images of Black cowboys featured in Hollywood westerns.

Other artists have turned to photography and film to bring the Black cowboy alive in our imaginations. In 2017, the Studio Museum in Harlem featured an exhibit, *The Black Cowboy*, curated by Amanda Hunt and featuring documentary photographs by Brad Trent, Ron Tarver, Chandra McCormick, and Deana Lawson. The exhibit also includes *Wildcat*, a short film by Kahlil Joseph, one of the directors of Beyoncé's *Lemonade*, on the annual Grayson, Oklahoma, Black Rodeo.[9] The photographer Rory Doyle has captured the continuing subculture of Black cowboys in the Mississippi Delta in his 2019 exhibit, *Delta Hill Riders*.[10]

But just as important as these historical interventions are the uses of the Black cowboy to inspire fantasy. Lil Nas X's fantasy cowboy is in keeping with what the young Black Dallas blogger Bri Malandro coined "the yeehaw agenda" the year before "Old Town Road" hit the charts to highlight Black cowboys and cowgirls as images of creativity and empowerment in popular culture.[11] The yeehaw agenda reflects an aesthetic that informs Solange's *When I Get Home*, Beyoncé's *Daddy Lessons*, Cardi B. in chaps and hat, Megan Thee Stallion riding bareback on a liquor bottle bronco, the folks of the Afropunk community, young designers like Pyer Moss and Telfar, and other expressions of Black cowfolk star quality amplified by Black Twitter, TikTok, Instagram, and Facebook.[12] Lil Nas X's activation of the cowboy seems to be partly a way of claiming the psychic power of the cowboy, the masculinity and achievement, for Black people and using it as a stage for dreaming new futures.

4: HIGH FASHION: "HAT IS MATTE BLACK / GOT THE BOOTS THAT'S BLACK TO MATCH"

Lil Nas X wears his clothes with such casual charm that it's easy to imagine him just strolling into some big walk-in closet and improvising them on the spot. But like many celebrities, his style is a team effort, a combination of his own performative use of space and body (gesture, facial expressions, movement) and the skills of his stylist, Hodo Musa, a thirty-four-year-old Somali Swedish young woman, a transplant to Los Angeles, an outsider like him. Lil Nas X and Musa together manage to make each photo opportunity a dip into the archive of Black masculinities, sampled and remixed.

When we see Lil Nas, resplendent in sunshine-yellow or orange latex, in licorice-whip-red leather pants, in gorgeously dripping embroidered western wear (one part cowboy, one part geisha), is it his desire or ours that we are seeing?

Framed in orange fur all around, a close-up of his face. Slow smile that he makes look easy. Against blown fur, the texture of skin, lips. In his left ear, a Black power fist of gold.[13]

A three-strapped harness in Barbie pink. Cowboy hat, pants, jacket, and mesh shirt, all in pink leather. Lil Nas holds two Grammys up to his ears. Can he hear the ocean?[14]

Lime-green suit, with green and black zebra stripes on the shiny shirt underneath. A city Easter look. These are the cheeks that Oprah wanted to grab: "Mama's baby."[15]

White suit, black hat, long and lean. No shirt. With longhorn's horns and chains. Loose fists almost pumping. Man at work, working manhood.[16]

Sky-blue leather pants and boy-band vest, a sunset of flames at the border. Arm flung wide to hold us.[17]

5: TECHNOLOGY

Some people are like, "A kid accidentally fell into this." But this is no accident. I was pushing this. Hard. The internet is like my parents. I was raised picking up on stuff. I had to learn how to use it, you know, in my own way.

—Lil Nas X in "'Old Town Road': Diary of a Song,"
   told to the journalist Joe Coscarelli[18]

Internet technology is everywhere in "Old Town Road," from the instrumentation itself: its sampled drums and banjo and auto-tuned voice and layered beats; to distribution: from YoungKio's beat store on YouTube, where Lil Nas X first found the sample, to Sound Cloud, where he first posted the song, to the ways that he cultivated listeners and fans on Instagram, TikTok, and Reddit. Once the song caught fire, it was taken up by everyday fans who posted videos for others to watch of themselves dancing and dressed up in cowboy gear, nudged by social media influencers like @elitelife_KD and @nice Michael_. And behind all these movements is Lil Nas X himself, who reached out to his Twitter hive to find Billy Ray Cyrus and invite him to collaborate, and who continues to promote the song with fans and shape the way the song travels and reaches others. With "Old Town Road," user-made social media set the terms, with older, slower media—like newspapers, magazines, television, record companies, award shows—always playing catch-up.

6: NOVELTY SONGS, COUNTRY SONGS, AND COUNTRY NOVELTY SONGS

Who is laughing at "Old Time Road"? The kids are. They delight in the pleasurable combination of cowboy and beat, the reference to boobies and having to go pee when you're riding on your tractor; the sound of a heightened twang, the familiarity of the cowboy, and the familiarity of the rapper; the delight of a sing-along rhyme. They revel in the swapping of clever verses, some kid-friendly, some not: Billy Ray's line "Baby's got a habit," Young Thug's craving for a chill pill and his bragging that women let him into their "back doors." Even if those lines might go over the kids' heads, there's always that line "Can't nobody tell me nothing," which you've got to sing with your arms waving in the air, together with your friends.

And as the remixes continue and grow, add in Lil Nas's ability to stay on the charts week after week after week, outlasting the pop kings and queens at that number-one Billboard Hit 100s spot (beating out Daddy Yankee and Justin Bieber, beating out Mariah Carey and Boyz II Men). Recognizing the song everywhere you go: walking down the street, on your own earphones, piped into your favorite restaurant—there's a kind of giddy delight to be found in that, too.

When I laugh during the official video of "Old Town Road," which I do, always, it is about the transcendent beauty of Lil Nas himself, his embodiment of the song, his sweet boy face, and his graceful control over his body as he does a quick two-step; his "look what I did grin" as he shows off his rings and beautiful Lil Nas X rodeo suit. When Billy Ray takes the stage for his solo, Lil Nas seems to be having so much fun that he forgets himself, mimicking the flight of a bird.

When I laugh at "Old Town Road," which I always do, it is also the laughter of recognition. That feeling that maybe he, like you, has been born at the wrong time, in the wrong place. He knows what it feels like to be watched, too. Or to be interrupting a game already in progress. The feeling of being an outsider among strangers and at home. What it feels like on the other end of a stare. Before we get to the credits, to the bloopers from Chris Rock and HaHa, when Lil Nas is posing with folks in the bingo hall and everybody's showing off their suits, Lil Nas X is embraced by a kindly white lady. The white lady looks up at Lil Nas with wonder and delight, and maybe like he's a tasty treat that she's about to devour. Lil Nas X doesn't return her look, but instead looks out at us. His smile—how do I read it? A sweet yearbook-ready smile, gentle, and a little . . . pained. The smile says to me, "You see this, right?" The smile says, "I get this all the time. Don't you?"

Maybe it's the song's humor, its success in taking over attention and the airwaves, its presence in public spaces for so long: in stores, in schoolyards, from the windows of passing cars, riding till it can't no more, and those moments of sly recognition that got the gatekeepers so riled up. When Wrangler, knowing a good thing when they heard it, teamed up with Lil Nas X to create a line of jeans and T-shirts together: white T-shirts with "Wrangler" on the front and a big red X on the back—shades of Malcolm?—the jeans with the line "Wrangler on my booty" dripping off the pocket in white paint, or even better, just a pair of booty shorts with "Wrangler" across the butt (the infamous song lyrics in action), some folks got pissed. One country fan, ostensibly white, wrote on Instagram, "Really? Supporting an artist that so clearly is mocking country music and the lifestyle it represents? Bad move Wrangler."[19] Lil Nas X, through it all, seemed to take everything in stride. He responded, "Ya'll boycotting Wrangler? Is it really all that deep?" When asked by the *New York Times* journalist Joe Coscarelli if being booted off the charts seemed racial to him, he responded, "I think it's more like, 'If we let that slide, what's next?'" Without calling out racism, Lil Nas X points to the paranoia, the fear of the new, the fear of a loss of white self at the heart of the boycott.

If it's novelty that's the problem, if it's mockery, then of course country music must look at its own history. As I discussed in my introduction, country has deep ties to minstrelsy, to coon songs and other "humor" about Blackness—not only in country's long past but in its more recent, twentieth-century past—including the blackface acts by Uncle Dave Macon and Lasses and Honey that were a part of the live *National Barn Dance* and the *Grand Ole Opry* shows as recently as the 1960s.[20]

Country music can also mock country whiteness, too, with shows sending out their own stereotypes through images of the hillbilly and the redneck at work on *Hee Haw* every week, for those who watched it. But what happens when those Black bodies talk back to you, taking pleasure in taking up space until you aren't sure which space is yours and which is theirs anymore? What happens when they revel in the excesses in ways that you used to laugh at, and sell them back to you? The answer, perhaps, is a scramble to protect the genre's "country elements," the language that Billboard used to justify its exclusion of "Old Town Road" from its Hot Country charts—even though Black artists have very much been a part of those elements from the beginning. As Charles Hughes has pointed out, "Black artists have been influential in country a long, long way back. But country has rewarded white artists that have taken advantage of those influences without giving black artists the same opportunities."[21] But in many ways, whether Billboard accepts Lil Nas X's "country trap" as sufficiently country music has become more or less irrelevant to the life of the song, which is perhaps at the heart of Lil Nas X's ability to let the whole debate roll off his back. "I'm going to do what I want to do. I'm going to make the music I want to make, and if people like it, then they like it. If they don't, then they don't," he tells genuius.com.[22] Ultimately, Lil Nas X, along with his collaborators and his ingenious producers Young Kio and Jozzy, has bigger fish to fry. As the DJ and novelty song maven Dr. Demento wisely puts it: "Novelty isn't just about being funny—it's also about being new. . . . And 'Old Town Road' is a very inventive piece of music."[23]

7: COUNTRY TRAP

And what about the banjos that open "Old Town Road" (even if they're synthesized banjos sampled from Nine Inch Nails, not a group known for country music)? To rely on instrumentation and even rhythm to define country is a slippery enterprise, to be sure. Country music has swapped and traded with multiple genres, including ranchero, blues, soul, gospel, hip-hop, and Hawaiian—all of which betray its truly creole roots.[24] And while the banjo may be a signature country sound (as well as a slide guitar and maybe a fiddle), such signature sounds have traveled widely across genres and multiple roots.

Billboard justified its decision to remove "Old Town Road," in an article by Joe Levy, by calling up Lil Nas's own definition of his sound as "country trap."[25] But given other songs that have mixed country and hip-hop and are still included as country music, including hick-hop, why is "country trap" the element that broke the camel's back?[26]

Trap is a subgenre of hip-hop that has its roots in the Atlanta music scene, and its signature sound is its layered use of hi-hat drums, tuned kick drums, and a long decay. Trap is sexy and cool and mimics the sound of a clock ticking against a heartbeat. Trap is the sound of precarity, the underground.[27] The brilliant cultural critic and self-described trap feminist Sesali Bowen defines "trap" as "Atlanta slang for the specific dwelling or neighborhood where drugs, guns, or other illicit products or services are sold. The term is multifaceted and flexible. When used as a verb, 'trapping' means hustling."[28] While many early songs by T.I. and others were grounded in images of urban realism and underground economy, the sound of trap drums has traveled widely in hip-hop, from Drake to Kendrick Lamar to pop music at large, including Ariana Grande and Miley Cyrus. So when Lil Nas X insists on referring to "Old Town Road" as "country trap" as an Atlantan, he's rooting a song in a specific home region and a distinctly Black subcultural sound, and even though the sound has traveled widely, it is still a sound of risk.

Perhaps Lil Nas X's insistence that his song is country trap, together with his methods of production and distribution outside of traditional record companies and radio, at least initially ally him with the underground, with a world beyond, and maybe even bigger than, the charts. And for some, that just might be claiming "too much dip" for his chip. But this boldness has become the catalyst for a whole new genre of country trap, including Black artists like Breland ("My Truck"), Young Thug, and RMR.

8: TWO MEN AND A BABY

In the "Old Town Road" video, Billy Ray Cyrus and Lil Nas X escape the men on horses who are chasing them across a wide golden prairie. They have stopped at a lean-to built of dark gray, worn wood. The house looks empty, the eyes staring blankly. "This should be fine. We'll settle in here for the night." The two share a moment of quiet. "Whoo, that was rough," Billy says. He walks over to a bale of hay and grunts as he sits, his leather pants tight around his hips. Billy takes out a round brown leather water bottle and hands it to his friend, then lets his hands dangle between his legs. His hands are relaxed. Lil Nas X refuses a seat and goes down into a squat near the dusty ground. He takes the bottle, wetting his lips, his long legs cradling a fat white bag of money. Lil Nas X, Billy, and the bag of money make an inverted triangle: a family. Lil Nas X takes a long drink of water. Then Lil Nas X stands, looking down at the ground, away from his friend. He shakes his head. He swallows his water. "I don't know, man." He takes another sip. "Last time I was here, they weren't too welcoming to outsiders." There is time for one inhale, one exhale. Billy says, "You and me this time. Everything's going to be all right." Lil Nas holds the water bottle in his hands, not yet ready to return it. Heart muscles constrict, then release. But then the gun shots pop. Lil Nas X turns his head away from his friend and runs toward a cave, a big black hole, and leaps, signifying an Afrofuturistic travel to a new era.

9: MARLBORO MAN

When I watch Billy Ray in the "Old Town Road" video, it's as if he's wearing a heavy disguise that weighs down his body, pulls his face down. Even his hair seems heavy. He is carrying that flesh disguise with him everywhere, but I get the sense that he wants out. He keeps his eyes covered with sunglasses and a tilted-down hat. "I'm like a Marlboro Man so I kick on back" he riffs, but on camera he can't quite seem to relax. But when he stands next to Lil Nas X, his body leans a little toward him, and when Lil Nas X sings, he tilts his head toward him as though he's a father listening to a child. When they get on stage at the bingo palace, I hear Billy digging into his verse, digging into feeling, so that when he changes from the beat on the two to the beat on the one, at the line "Got no stress, I've been through all that," he swings it. I hear his desire to escape, to be free, too. Billy strokes his white guitar, and his load seems a little lighter.

At the June 2020 BET Awards, Billy Ray Cyrus and Lil Nas X ride up on their brown horses to the entrance of LA's Staples Center. "Reckon this is it?" Billy asks. "Yeah, man," says Lil Nas X. Lil Nas and Billy burst into the door of a salon on set, Billy following Lil Nas's lead. The doors hit him just a little. Billy gets them started with the first verse of the song while Lil Nas makes his way to center stage. When it's time for his solo, Billy pulls down his hat and mostly sings standing in place, but when he sings, "I want to get back to that Old Town Road," he does bust out a quick Elvis hip thrust, like he did on the video for "Achy Breaky Heart." The audience roars with approval. The audience is spilling over the stage in the effort to dance with them. O the lassos! The shimmies and the pops! It's all going so fast. Billy's playing a black guitar this time. His face is bare of sunglasses. He seems surprised but pleased, as though he had been transported there by some Star Trek beaming device. Every once in a while he looks up, and his blue eyes catch the light.

The day after the performance, a rumor circulated on Twitter that Billy Ray Cyrus had attended an HBCU—Howard, in particular. He was that good.

A month later, Billy Ray is singing "Old Town Road" at the Grand Ole Opry. Lil Nas X is not there. Maybe he wasn't invited. Billy seems lonely. Another guy sings Lil Nas's part, a tall white guy in jeans and flannel, taking his voice an octave lower than Lil Nas X and giving the song the Oakridge Boys "Elvira" treatment. Billy Ray seems lost again. Even when young Mason Ramsey joins him and contributes his yodeling "Old Town Road" verse ("Aye-o, aye-, yippee-o-ki-yay / If you ain't got no giddy up then giddy out my way") and the crowd laughs and claps, there seems to be something missing. Still, when it's time for Billy's big solo, he digs in again, getting those not-so-Grand-Ole-Opry growls in there. He doesn't have Lil Nas X there, but maybe he's conjuring him, a memory carried with the song.

10: THE HORSE

The other collaborator that I left out is important, of course. He is the conduit to dreams, the source of mobility. He might not have a say about where Lil Nas goes, but his participation is crucial. He is solid, reliable, animal, and he keeps his own council. He is a being in and of himself. In the fantasy, the horse is the marker of the West, the keeper of rhythm, the sound of his hooves on road or pavement marking time.

Whether real or make-believe, horses take us to the cross-roads—those Four Horsemen of the Apocalypse could not do it alone.

Lil Nas X's horse is black.

Is the horse the ability to transcend race, to go beyond it? I don't want to say what Lil Nas X is feeling, or especially what Montero Hill might feel in the face of racism, but I think if there were a mechanism to be even faster, even wilier, than your most racist detractor, to be free, who wouldn't choose it?

Is that black horse, mane flowing with wind and motion, will, resistance, creativity, the internet, the imagination? A shimmering flowline to freedom?

When a group of school kids in England get to interview Lil Nas X, asking anything they want, they ask him what his favorite animal is, and he says, "Horses." When they ask him if he prefers dogs or cats, he says, "Horses."[29]

"I'm gonna take my horse to the Old Town Road. I'm gonna ride it till I can't no more."

Horses can aid and abet escape, resistance, resilience. I think about Toni Morrison's legendary Black and blind horsemen in her novel *Tar Baby*. The horsemen are a race of men who live in the hills of the Isle of Chevalier, the place where Morrison's characters, American and Haitian, rich and poor, meet and clash. Maybe they're related to the real-life maroon soldiers, enslaved

Black people who escaped into Haiti's hills and then fought for Haiti's independence from France. On Morrison's fictional island, the horsemen are a race of blind people, descendants of the first captured African slaves who went blind when they first saw the island. When the slaving ships on which they're being transported to France sink near the island, slaves, horses, and sailors are all cast into the water. Some slaves and horses survive and hide in the hills. You can still hear them, making love to the swamp women and riding in the hills:

> Lickety-split. Lickety-split. Looking neither to the
> left nor to the right. Lickety-split. Lickety-split.
> Lickety-lickety-lickety-split.[30]

When I did a Google search with the words "Black men on horses," the first story that comes up is about Bill Picket, an early twentieth-century cowboy, rodeo rider, and creator of "bulldog-ging," a rodeo event in which a rider rides next to a steer, leaps off his horse, grabs the steer by both horns, and wrestles him to the ground. Pickett was the first African American voted into Oklahoma's Cowboy Hall of Fame, in 1971—an example of strength and creativity and, for once, recognition.[31]

But what also comes up is a story of a Black man in Galveston, Texas, being escorted by two white police officers on horses, teth-ered to them by a blue nylon rope tied to his handcuffs. One of the police officers is heard to say on the police bodycam video footage, which has since gone viral, "This looks so bad."[32] This spectacle happened during the August 3, 2019, arrest of Donald Neely, for trespassing. Family lawyers said that he was known by city police as someone who suffered from mental illness and regularly slept on the streets.

I also find a story on the Compton Cowboys, and Walter Thompson-Hernandez's book about them. *The Compton Cowboys* chronicles the lives of ten Black men who are friends, who decide to take up the legacy of the original Compton Cowboys, who were a mainstay in the city for thirty years. They ride their horses in part to teach the kids of South Central Los Angeles, their own neighborhood, about horses and freedom, to share the history of Black cowboys, and to just have fun. Thompson-Hernandez, a journalist who grew up just ten minutes from Compton, speaks to the power of his first memory of seeing these Black men on horseback that inspired his book:

> He was about five or six in the backseat of his mom's car, and there was this cowboy riding bareback with a quiet confidence, his back long and strong, taking command of this urban landscape. Thompson-Hernández would roll down his window to hear the click-clacking of the horses' hooves on the concrete.
>
> And it was only as he got older that Thompson-Hernández realized these men on horses signified something even deeper: the endless possibilities of what he could do in this world as a Black man.
>
> "I'm the son of a Black man and [a] Mexican mother, and so for me, I grew up seeing Mexican cowboys, a lot like brown men on horses, was a normal thing," he says. "But also seeing Black men on horses, to me, was very important. That was a part of the story that wasn't told to me in school, and I felt like it was a part of history that I would have wanted my teachers to have told me about—and it never was."[33]

In the "Old Town Road" video with Billy Ray, after Lil Nas X time-travels from 1890 to a present-day "Old Town Road," a Black community that looks like South Central Los Angeles, a young man asks him, "I think I know you. You're from Compton, right?"—an insider joke about these real-life legends.

11: COMING OUT

In September of 2019, Lil Nas X goes on *Ellen* to come out, but he's really already done it himself on Twitter. The landscape of coming out as a celebrity has changed a lot since Ellen's controversial "Puppy Episode" in 1997, when her character came out and kissed another woman on her show and she faced bomb threats and boycotts. Since 1997, of course, gay marriage has been legalized nationally. And while LGBTQ homelessness for young people, especially young people of color, is still high, and though the protection of civil rights, especially trans rights, is still at risk, there's an "of course love is love" quality at least to Hollywood conversations about sexuality. Chatting with Ellen in a white flight suit, Lil Nas X is relaxed and matter-of-fact. He tells Ellen he decided to come out because he thought it was "the right thing to do" and that he told his father and sister that same week, just to give them a "heads-up." He says that he "wasn't in the position to before," a very low-key way of referring to the often fraught experiences of other stars who have come out in both country music and hip-hop. When Ellen asks him if he's in a relationship right now, he shrugs and says, "You know, it's complicated." Love, Lil Nas X seems to suggest, might be more complicated than sexual identity right now.

Of course I have to mention Lil Nas X's much-debated and, by many queers, much-loved 2021 video for "Montero (Call Me by Your Name)," in which Lil' Nas X explores through lyrics and pole dance his relationship drama with the most extreme crazy boyfriend imaginable, Satan. Talk about complicated.

The video for "Montero" has been the subject of debate for many, who have worried over its explicit performances of collective gay pleasure and desire, images of Satan as love object, and overall raunchy glee. But in his essay "I Grew Up Afraid. Lil Nas X's 'Montero' Is the Lesson I Needed," Ashon Crawley shows us how

Lil Nas X takes his performance of outlaw sexuality beyond prov-ocation, to name the ways that fear and condemnation (by parents, church, community, and the state) get internalized into self-hate and weaponized against oneself and others. Lil Nas X plays each part: the "sinner," the judges, Satan himself, showing us how we can become our worst critics. The song offers as antidote the joys of the material world: the flesh—your own and others'—fashion, outra-geous wigs, color, laughter, and beat. Crawley argues that Lil Nas X's "Montero" is about both outrageousness and outrage, sharing a Tweet that Lil Nas X made soon after "Montero's" release:

> i spent my entire teenage years hating myself because of the s*** y'all preached would happen to me because i was gay. so i hope u are mad, stay mad, feel the same anger you teach us to have towards ourselves.
>
> In other words: *You say we're going straight to hell. What if we've already been there?* Because what is more terrifying than living and loving a queer Black life in an anti-queer, anti-Black world? What do you have, in terms of power to control, when the thing you try to wield against us ain't a thing we're afraid of? You got outrage, anger, Twitter fingers, gullible Facebook posts. But you don't have the truth, and you don't have peace, and you don't have joy.
>
> In the end, he slays the devil, refuses to live with the myth. In so doing, he overcomes the power others receive by attempting to coerce him to fear. And he reminds me that fear does not have to determine your possibilities—that fear might, in fact, show you how to love yourself.
>
> A teenaged Ashon could have used that message.[34]

With a swagger that still might have a little bit of cowboy, Lil Nas X raises the stakes of his earlier genre busting with "Old

Town Road," using the platform of his fame to demand a more explicit naming and rejection of the hate that binds us, including homophobia and racism.[35] This naming and claiming of self in Lil Nas X's hands is entertaining and memorable, and it's also a matter of life and death. (Indeed, the Trevor Project, a national nonprofit project that focuses on suicide prevention for the LGBTQ community, recently honored Lil Nas X with its first suicide prevention award for his discussion with his fans of suicide and mental health on social media.[36]) As Crawley writes, Lil Nas X has reminded us through "Montero" that "pleasure and joy are serious work."

This raucous and seriously joyful queer spirit continues and amplifies with each skillfully released new single and video from the *Montero* album. In the video for "That's What I Want," Lil Nas X recasts himself in an updated Black and Brown homage to *Brokeback Mountain* (cowboys again!). And in the publicity video for the release of the *Montero* album that has flooded social media, a pregnant Lil Nas X gives birth to the album, the cover a Black and queer reimagining of Genesis, Lil Nas floating above Eden outstretched, naked, and gleaming. In these ways and more, the embrace of what the cultural critic Jason King calls "post-respectability,"[37] including joy, pleasure, excess, and possibility that we saw and heard first in "Old Town Road" and its remixes, has become the roadmap for his future career.

12: CALLING THE AUTHORITIES

How are we listening to young Black men? Can we really hear them?

Is listening a form of love?

"I can't breathe."

13: ON THE SCHOOL BUS

My daughter, Cece, age seven, is on the school bus with the rest of her YMCA camp, listening to "Old Town Road." I picture them, some sitting, some standing, some bouncing, breaking down the different layers of beat, some doing the drums, someone taking on that Nine Inch Nails banjo sample, someone attempting Nas's twangy baritone. What kid wouldn't want to sing that song with your friends on a school bus in the middle of July, "Can't nobody tell me nothing," arms waving in unison, on your way back from the water park or the children's museum or wherever the Y has taken you, fingers and mouths dusted with orange fluorescent Takis or Cheetos dust? Some people have pointed to the fact that kids love this song as a sign of its weakness, but we all know that kids can be tough critics, especially kids on a school bus. This group has its own high standards, and they can be tightly patrolled with noogies, spitballs, name-calling, or just being ignored. Cece's Y cohort is a group of mostly Black and Brown kids from all over the world, reflecting the highly diverse population of Chicago's Rogers Park neighborhood. (According to our community business alliance, over eighty languages are spoken here.) That all of them would be willing to put down their snacks and their LOL dolls, their lanyards or their phones (if they're lucky enough to have them), after a day in Chicago humidity and 90-degree overbearing sunshine and sing "Old Town Road" is a testament to the power of the song to energize. And it might also reflect the ways that this particular group of kids might be the hope of a generational shift, where categories like genre don't really matter.

But as Cece tells me, it might just be that it has a good beat.

BLACK COUNTRY MUSIC AFROFUTURISMS

Mickey Guyton, Rissi Palmer, and DeLila Black

Country music is gone! Black people already took
country music back. Keep up! Keep up!
  —**Electro-mountain-country noire-punk-country-
  roots-rodeo musician DeLila Black**

THE BLACK COUNTRY MUSIC up-and-comer Mickey Guyton
stands in a white, brown, and gold kaftan in a friend's sunny LA
studio, the African mud cloth–inspired patterns framing her
rounded, growing belly. At the time of the recording, Guyton is
expecting her son, Grayson. In the background, she's set up an
altar of sorts, a trail of breadcrumbs, an offering for any of us who
want to join her and see ourselves in her music, whatever our racial
loyalties: *Patsy Cline's Greatest Hits* on one and Whitney Houston's soundtrack to *The Bodyguard* on the other, Whitney's face
in lush close-up. In the far background is Dolly Parton's *Coat of*

Many Colors.[1] Guyton shares the best of these three icons: Whitney's gospel chops and sweet melisma; Parton's skillful, vulnerable storytelling; and Cline's verve and appeal to a nostalgic country femininity. Light-blue hand-knitted baby booties are lovingly propped up next to a worn paperback copy of John Howard Griffin's 1961 book about standing in another's shoes, *Black Like Me*, which Guyton says inspired her writing of the song. The light suggests a new morning dawning.

In this November 2020 NPR Music Tiny Desk (home) concert performance of her song "Black Like Me" and other hits, Guyton creates a new space in country music. As Ann Powers, a feminist music critic and producer of Guyton's Tiny Desk concert comments about this performance in particular, "A star for our times claims her space."[2]

The concert comes at a moment of great cultural change. We are not in the NPR Music's traditional Tiny Office, because we are in the middle of the COVID-19 pandemic and lockdown. We are also at a point of great racial tension and protest: those last nine seconds of George Floyd's life still haunt our dreams, catching our breaths. Guyton's performance seems to evoke both of those experiences of struggle in the current moment. Indeed, CNN's John Blake calls Guyton's "Black Like Me," whose timely lyrics captured a wide audience's interest after being posted on Instagram, as "the most powerful song about race in 2020."[3] This performance marks a moment of change for Guyton personally, too, a push toward greater national visibility after a ten-year process of working within the country music industry. And it's a moment when attention to Black artists in country music has grown in and outside of the industry.

In this performance, we see Guyton's ability to build bridges—something that has been important for Black country music stars before her, like Charley Pride and Darius Rucker and Rhiannon Giddens—but on her own terms. The tone of her storytelling in

"Black Like Me" is gentle but unapologetic in its racial and classed critique, daring to claim the space of blue-collar identity—the space of white authenticity in many country songs—as also being a Black experience of life being "twice as hard."

My daddy worked day and night
For an old house and a used car
Just to live that good life

Rather than keeping this storytelling in the past, a childhood struggle or that of an earlier generation, Guyton brings it to the here and now, where nothing has changed. Yet the song is also a plea for understanding, and there's vulnerability as well as urgency in her voice that feels distinctly Black feminist, as she ends with a claim to freedom, with pride, repeating "Black Like Me."

Her voice and her belly both lending her authority, she pulls at her listener's conscience. Guyton's plaintive face when she sings, her thin brows yielding up and opening the rest of her face, framed by honey brown straightened hair, reminds me some of Tina Turner on the back cover of *Tina Turns the Country On!*—the promise to tell us stories of difficult emotional truths.

This feeling heightens as she's joined in the performance by Lynette Williams, a keyboardist who also plays with Childish Gambino and Leyla Hathaway and who knows how to raise roofs, bringing rousing funk and church to pop music. But for "Black Like Me," Williams's playing is spare, insistent, and moving, taking us through a simple architecture of chords. As Guyton introduces the song, Williams listens appreciatively. She cracks a proud smile as Guyton mentions her first as a Black woman performing an original song on the Academy of Country Music Awards stage. As the song begins, Williams's face refocuses on the keyboards, going deep into the song, and together they create a quilt of sound and warmth.

In interviews, Guyton breaks the code of silence that past Black country music artists in the industry have faced, even while still on the cusp of stardom. Guyton has shared her experiences of the stresses of trying to break into the country music industry, describing insomnia and a period of heavy drinking. And as she's moved up in notoriety, performing "Black Like Me" at the 2021 Grammy Awards, being the first Black woman to be nominated in the solo country music category, and cohosting the 2021 CMA awards, Guyton is also aware that her role as a model for other artists of color is vexed, and perhaps her power is limited:

> "I've been putting my neck on the line, saying you can sing country music and be accepted," she says. "There was a part of me that was also like: but can you?" I've encouraged so many amazing, talented, beautiful people. But I want to protect the people I'm leading into this, too.[4]

What Guyton reveals in her shrewd analysis of the risks of performing country music as a Black woman, and in her insistence on singing songs that are making a political intervention, is an overstanding of the country music landscape that I see in other performers that I explore in this book. "Overstanding," a term that some trace to hip-hop, some further back to Rastafarian and bebop roots, has to do with a knowledge and awareness of the presence of anti-Blackness, based on lived experience. Guyton's work is Afrofuturist in that it is critically interested in what it means to be Black in the country music industry in the present and is guided by an investment in its future.

Since I began my journey to write this book, a shift has occurred in the country music industry and the media toward recognizing the erasure of Black talent, creativity, and resistance awakened by the Black Lives Matter movement and response to the blatant disregard for Black life that we see addressed so poignantly in Guyton's song "Black Like Me." But whether these changes will make a lasting impact on the industry is still an open question, given the dangers of co-optation and appropriation of the freedom work of Black artists in country music by the music industry. As the country music scholar Leigh H. Edwards suggests:

> You can now see a trend of some segments of the industry undertaking a neoliberal appropriation of diversity, equity, and inclusion language for the purposes of public relations but without making meaningful structural changes. Witness DEI framing in promotion or awards show appearances involving BIPOC artists, such as co-hosting performances by Kane Brown, Darius Rucker, and Mickey Guyton, or for LGBTQ+ artists such as Brandi Carlisle or for white cisgender heterosexual female artists.[5]

Rather than simply asking for a place at the table, the artists in this book are using country music as a way of exploring a more complex Black identity. Part of that social change is also listening to and seeing one another differently and including country music among the ways that Black people address the struggles and triumphs of Black life together as a community.

You can hear this feeling of recognition in the following conversation about Black country music in the February 2, 2021, episode of the podcast *Hear to Slay*, hosted by Roxane Gay and Tressie Cottom, with special guest star Rissi Palmer, country music singer and creator and host of her own podcast, *Color Me Country*.[6] The podcast *Hear to Slay* is a weekly conversation that explores the social, cultural, and political landscape of Black life, centering Black women's insights and experiences. In this warm-up to the interview with Palmer, the three begin with some chatter, one part cultural analysis, one part commiseration, and one part trash talk, clearly enjoying one another's company:

TRESSIE COTTOM: I am really over the narrative of this being white people's music because I listen to a lot of Black people making country music.

ROXANE GAY: Umm hmmm. I think a lot of times people want to see country music as the purview of whiteness, and I understand why, because they want to be comfortable and say, "We're just good ol' aw-shucks kind of people. And this is what we do." But guess what? Black people are, too. And frankly, country music would not exist without us. It's not a window into whiteness; it's actually a genre that's historically ostracized Black talent, if not completely erased it.

COTTOM: Umm hmmm.

GAY: I'm sorry, but there's no way that you could grow up in Nebraska, at least where I grew up, and not have a familiarity with country music. Yes, I'm going to dance to Brook and Dunn's "Neon Moon" now. I'll see you later!

COTTOM: And I vaguely remember you hooking up at a country music line dance bar, do I not?

GAY: I did. There used to be—actually, unfortunately it recently closed—but there used to be a gay bar there called The Q, and they would have a line dancing night every night and I met one of my exes there.

COTTOM: And one of the infamous exes!

RISSI PALMER: Line dancing! Exactly!

GAY: . . . and we were two Black lesbians, dancing around! And listen, we can line dance because we have the "Electric Slide." And all the line dances are just—we created the line dance! You think we can't handle that?

PALMER: I was getting ready to say, it's all just the "Electric Slide!"

COTTOM: There is only just one line dance. Everything else is just an iteration of the "Electric Slide."

PALMER: Right!

COTTOM: I don't know where people come up with this. It's either the "Electric Slide" for people who can hear the bass line, or for people who cannot.[7]

I am interested in this moment on *Hear to Slay* because it speaks to the humor, spontaneity, intimacy, and testimony of lived knowledge about country music by these three Black women in one another's company: the cultural critic and creative writer Roxanne Gay, the sociologist and cultural critic Tressie Cottom, and Rissi Palmer, country music singer, archivist, and tastemaker. *Hear to Slay* centers Black women as experts on country music and beyond, so this conversation marks a change in the cultural landscape, wherein Black involvement in country music and country life is presented as the common ground for a properly educated and "woke" populace.

The conversation also testifies to a relationship of care among Black women that is important to Black country culture's continued existence. Over the course of the conversation, Palmer not only talks about her current podcast but also divulges the struggles in her past country music career before she left her label and rebooted her career as an independent. As Palmer details the earlier part of her life in country music in Nashville, snagging a record deal with a major label while in her twenties, recording her first major hit—2007's "Country Girl" (the first song recorded by a Black female artist to hit Billboard's Country charts in twenty years)—and appearing onstage at the Grand Ole Opry, she complicates what might be seen from the outside as a Cinderella story of success. Palmer describes the daily surveillance and fashioning of her body, clothing, and sound by country music executives ("They were scared of my hair," she tells Cottom and Gay); she describes tense conversations with fellow songwriters in the writing of "Country Girl," some of whom pressured her to change her lyrics that named her own Blackness; and ultimately, she shares the pain of her loss of ownership of her masters and the professional use of her name to her record label. Palmer eventually went to court to regain control of her own name and, in the process, underwent a grueling and also shame-inducing public debate over her artistry and integrity in court—a conversation that felt so personal that she called her mother to warn her of what might come out in the press. Ultimately Palmer regained her right to use her name but lost the control of her masters. She quit country music for a while, but she eventually decided to begin her career again as an independent artist, creating her own label, recording her children's album, *Best Day Ever* (2017), then a country soul solo album, *Revival* (2019), and in late 2020, launching the *Color Me Country* podcast. Palmer has also created the Color Me Country Fund, together with the journalist and radio host Kelly McCartney, which provides a source of sustainability for Black, Indigenous, and other artists of color within the country music community.[8]

Over the course of the *Hear to Slay* interview, Palmer's voice is intimate and often vulnerable with feeling as Gay and Cottom coax the story of her journey out of her. Cottom asks Palmer why she keeps working in country music, despite the pain she's experienced in the industry:

PALMER: Nashville the industry is something completely different from country music, for me. Country music is all the CDs in that closet over there. And it's the way I feel when I listen to them, and it's the way I feel when I sing these songs. This morning, I was walking around singing "Rodeo" by Garth Brooks.

COTTOM: Yeah.

PALMER: It was what happened to be in my head. And that's what I love. The industry, I hate.

COTTOM: Umm hmm.

PALMER: I just think it needs to be burned down and started all over again.

COTTOM: Huh.

PALMER: But I keep fighting, and I keep caring about it because while I figured out a way to have a career and a life and be happy outside of it, people that look like me and anybody else, if that's what they want, they should have it.

COTTOM AND GAY TOGETHER: Umm hmmm.

PALMER: That's why I still care.

COTTOM: That's such a quintessential Black woman answer, to me. I mean, how many times on this show and in our lives, especially in my work life, over and over again, when we talk to Black women about how we survive hostile institutions, whether it's academia, the tech industry, publishing, we've covered all of them on this show, finance, we've covered all of them, and it's the same story. Every industry, every institution, it's the same story, that "it is hostile to us, but I care about the people coming after me."[9]

In Gay and Cottom's web of care, Palmer doesn't have to justify either her love for country music or how her analysis of her experience highlights racism and sexism intertwined. There's room for all of these complexities in this conversation. These experiences are the fuel behind Palmer's fire that we see at work in her podcast, *Color Me Country*, her passion underlying the effort to set the historical record straight.

Palmer's struggle to control her music puts her smack in the history of other Black country artists in the twentieth and twenty-first centuries, from country music's DeFord Bailey and Linda Martell (the namesake for her show) to artists outside of country like Little Richard, Marvin Gaye, Stevie Wonder, and Prince, in the struggle for control of one's own masters, a say in one's profits, and artistic credit for one's songwriting. While Palmer has touched on some of these experiences before on her own show, there's something important happening in the *Hear to Slay* conversation. Gay and Cottom make space for Palmer to go deeper into the feeling of her story, with the encouraging "umm hmmms" and the "go ons," and in the analysis that they provide as a framework, making frequent connections to other Black struggles in this political moment. This is important Black feminist restoration work, with an eye to care, what Christina Sharpe calls "care work"—the necessary next step to restoring self and community for Black people after a history of nonfreedom.[10]

In the meantime, Palmer's *Color Me Country* podcast has changed the conversation about Black country music, making room for new musical futures. Palmer has interviewed current and past Black, Brown, and Indigenous country music stars like Darius Rucker, Miko Marks, and Star De Azlan; interviewed Dr. Cleve Francis and Frankie Staton, the founders of the Black Country Music Association, a short-lived but visionary organization created in the 1990s by and for Black country music artists navigating the Nashville-based country music industry; hosted roundtable discussions on the country music industry and country music studies in academia; delved into the early history of Black country music with the Carolina Chocolate Drops cofounder Dom Flemons and the blues gospel performer Queen Esther; and raised up new country music female artists of color with her "Class of 2021" episode, featuring Ashlie Amber, Kären McCormick, Camille Parker, Kathryn Shipley, and Julie Williams.

Perhaps predicting the future of Black country music is always an exercise in finding yourself behind the times. Maybe this is because of the very fast movement of trends in popular culture. As we saw with the insurgent power of Lil Nas X, Black-culture making sometimes follows its own timeline, outside of the schedules of recording studios and radio play. As we think about Black interventions in country music, the speed of change and unpredictable innovation of Black art forms can be tactics to subvert appropriation and the control and constraints of white supremacy, especially as they take advantage of new platforms and forms of distribution.

So in a March 16, 2021, interview over Zoom, when I asked the UK-based country-punk musician and performance artist DeLila Black, a Londoner by way of New York and Port-au-Prince, whether Black country music is Afrofuturistic music, she reminded me that Black people are always inventing new ways to survive the unfreedoms of white supremacy, and this includes country music. (This is actually a central idea of Afrofuturism: imagining a Black future while also looking back at the history of Black struggle.) As Black puts it:

In my head I think Black people, we're in the future already. We've got to live in all the spaces because we're forced to, you know? We've got to think ahead. We're already teaching our kids what to do if you're stopped by some goon. You're constantly playing games to keep yourself safe. There's a different way that you speak on the phone or speak when you're going for a job. When Black people get together, the conversation is about one thing and then when white people are present, there's another, so we're made to always be thinking and moving. We've got to be on it all the time. And even if you have nothing—you create it. Like my father made his own furniture. It wasn't great-looking furniture, it looked crazy, one piece of wood there, some plywood there, but it worked. Black people, they just get on with it. Black people, we have to make a place for ourselves. So there's always innovation. We have to be innovative because we don't have a choice, and because of those innovations, we're already in the future. And that's why we're in the future. Black people are already in the future. We don't have to answer for or answer to. We've done it. Of course we're futurists. We have to be.[11]

In DeLila Black's music we see her power of innovation and reinvention, and her energy seems endless. Because she's working within means that are under her own control, making work in performance art spaces and on Patreon,[12] and supported by a day job that's unrelated to the music industry, she is not limited by questions of genre or the rules of an industry. She calls her own sound "Electro-Mountain Music," "Country Noire," "Punk Country," and "Roots-Rodeo-Rock."[13] As these names suggest, Black uses an expansive and sometimes humorous style to undercut generic expectations and formulas. She uses this off-center position to lobby political critique, using the forms of country to signify on conventions of nostalgia, cultural stagnancy, and uncritical Americanism that are coded into her use of country music style. For example, in the video for her 2020 song "Cain't Git None," a cowpunk mashup that features the New Lost City Ramblers folk icon Tom Paley on fiddle,[14] we see a bored DeLila Black lying on a couch, switching channels between images of whiteness: from a white rodeo cowboy to a white toddler, grotesquely made up for a beauty pageant, to an image of the Confederate flag. Her lyrics suggest the rudderlessness of capitalism, an exhausted American Dream now only interested in pleasure, but even that pursuit is boring. In the song's lyrics, evoking the Rolling Stones' "(I Can't Get No) Satisfaction," Black flips the position from Black girl object of desire that the Stones often hail in their music to Black woman as the bored and disgusted subject:

When I'm shopping in the mall and the music makes me ill,
like my life is over
And I try to pop fingers along
But it's all so dumb.

In this song's video, she positions herself outside, watching the spectacle of the exhausted whiteness evoked by the images and implicated in it.

If in "Cain't Git None" she is bored, and country sounds and Americana images evoke that boredom, that boredom grows more menacing in her 2020 song "Routine," a song Black recorded in October 2020 as a fund-raiser for the Grassroots Law Project, one in which she names the spirit-numbing routineness of police brutality and murder.[15] The lyrics are simple, singsong, childlike:

> She was stopped in the road and asked for her ID.
> We were told it was routine.
>
> They knocked on her door and shouted some things.
> She said, "What for?" It was routine.

The spectacle of violent confrontation is left out of these stories. But it is in the music where we feel the bite of the critique: the sounds are a mash-up of plunking banjos and fiddles, news reports of violence, and, very faint, almost subliminal, the police themselves, shouting to their assailants to "Get on the ground!" Together with her band, the Routine Players (Ben Paley on fiddle, Sean Dillon on banjo, Steve Gerred on acoustic guitar and bass, and Justin Buckley on electric guitar, with Black on vocals and programming), Black captures the feeling of being overwhelmed of an everyday bystander trying to absorb news story after news story of anti-Black violence, excused with the explanation of a "routine" that is supposed to keep all of its citizens safe, but fails. In the video, this feeling of being overwhelmed is emphasized with many—too many—thumbnail photos of Black victims of racist gun violence in the United States, including Trayvon Martin, Korryn Gaines, Ahmad Arbery, Michael Brown, Botham Jean, and Sandra Bland, and ending with the image of George Floyd.

Black switches sonic tactics in her 2021 song "Accountability," moving from numbness and being overwhelmed to swells of sentimental feeling combined with hard-hitting critique. With a country waltz with lap steel guitar played by the legendary B. J. Cole, Black uses a sweet "crying-in-your-beer" vocal style, complete with Hank Williams–esque yodels, to call out white people who avoid taking responsibility for their own violence, and the media that reports it—from mass shooters like Dylann Roof, to police officers who kill Black people like Derek Chauvin, to the everyday Karens who keep popping up on our social media feeds, with their many complaints and accusations to the police of imagined Black threats.[16] In "Accountability," Black goes through a long list of explanations for their violence that white perpetrators offer in the media:

> You blame your mom, your dad, the childhood you never had your friends, your education.
> You blame your job, your home, your kids, your wife, . . .
> Everyone but you. It's never you.

There's always a deferral of responsibility in the end, Black suggests. As she explains to *Adobe and Teardrops* interviewer Rachel Cholst:

> I remember waking up one morning and reading a headline that said "Ted Cruz Blames His Kids for Cancun Trip During Texas Crisis." Really, dude? That sort of kicked it off for me. I'd been waking up to headlines about shooters who were presented as misunderstood youths, violent insurrectionists who were presented as misguided patriots. There was one story after another, "Georgia Officer Says Atlanta Shooter Was 'Having a Bad Day.'" I was following the Botham Jean story a while back. He was killed by police officer Amber Guyer. Her attorneys said that she made a "reasonable mistake." I remember the images of the victim's brother hugging Officer Amber Guyer as she cried.

I remember images of the judge also hugging her, praying with her. There was a viral clip of the bailiff stroking Guyer's hair. The way in which the narrative shifts, I find it very disturbing.[17]

As of this writing, there's no video to accompany the song, but Black has posted the song on her website together with a photo of herself in a romantic pink, polka-dotted, puffy-sleeved blouse and black cowgirl hat, offering the viewer a bouquet of wildflowers, a gesture that belies the fierce message to come.

As we see in the work of Mickey Guyton, Rissi Palmer, and DeLila Black, Black artists are using country and country-adjacent music as a vehicle for freedom and resistance to shape the future. Mickey Guyton uses the personal storytelling and emphasis on feeling of traditional country music for a direct and electric appeal to our shared concerns as a culture. Rissi Palmer insists on not only exploring the history of Black persistence in country music but also exposing how unequal power is institutionalized in the music industry. DeLila Black reaches beyond the boundaries of the music industry to create art that defies the constraints of genre and allows for a playful, if more direct, naming of white supremacy. Black country has been creative and productive within these systems of constraint and appropriation, but these artists are asking for more for themselves and their communities. I'd argue that we need all three impulses: exposing injustice, building bridges, reaching beyond them. All three strategies are necessary for us to see and hear Black people in the future.

EMERGENCE

There are only two things I have to do, my mom taught me, and I can do them in the company of my choosing. The company of

myself, my living, my dead, my folks, my dreams. 1. Stay Black.
2. Breathe.

    —**Alexis Pauline Gumbs,** *Undrowned: Black Feminist*
    Lessons from Marine Mammals

If I started out this book looking for my people at the Windy City
Smokeout, for those of us who love country music and count ourselves as Black, I've found them.

Even if claiming country music in public still sometimes feels
a little like coming out to me, unsure if the Blackness that others
see in me is big enough to include it, I've found my people. I've
found musicians, teachers, students, historians, journalists, and
critics; I've found fans and instrument makers, curators and archivists, and activists and festival organizers. I've found them online,
at shows, in the small print of liner notes, in a book's footnotes.
I've found them among my friends and family. More than a collection of song titles, Black country music is a set of relationships,
a community of people making and listening to Black country
music, whatever else is happening at the Ryman Auditorium or
the CMAs or the Grammys.

You can see this spirit at play at the Black Opry Outlaw House
gathering recently co-organized by the *Black Opry* founder Holly
G. and the journalist Marcus Dowling this past September 2021,
coinciding with the Americanafest in Nashville.[18] A five-day "by
us, for us" gathering for Black country music artists and allies,
the Black Opry Outlaw House brought together longtime Black
country music insiders and up-and-coming artists for day parties
and nighttime singing circles, taking their turns at the mic or just
sitting on the stairs or overstuffed couches and listening to one another sing and speak, nodding, wooting, and adding their Amens.
The gathering was the first of its kind, the chance to come together
to commune, share experiences about the country music business,
and honor one another, relaxed and unguarded. Watching the

highlights shared by Holly G. on Twitter after the event, I was struck by the beauty, the comfort found on those mostly Black and Brown faces; the variety of styles: denim and sequins and vintage velvet; dramatic upsweeps, side shaves, lace fronts, and dreadlocks. The Black Opry Outlaw House seemed like such a familiar Black space to me—a little bit like a rally, a lot like church, and clearly like a very good party, and it was hard not to feel a serious case of FOMO. But maybe my role as an audience member is also a part of this movement for change, by recognizing this moment as Black country music in the making. As Frankie Staton, a forty-year Nashville country music veteran and organizer of the now defunct Black Country Music Association in the 1980s and 1990s, tells the mostly younger audience at the event, "I never would have thought that something like this could ever happen. It's a beautiful thing. . . . But my advice to you is to concentrate on your emerging audience. On the blending of the genres that you do. Find your audience. That is the most important work you can do, not only for yourself, but for the entire country music genre."[19]

The Black Opry Outlaw House is part of an important future, and that future is now. Some of my favorite Black queer feminist thinkers who are also Afrofuturists, Adrienne Maree Brown and Alexis Pauline Gumbs, write about the importance of emergent strategies: creating the world that you want through seeds of small change on the curve of the future and pushing for that change with all the faith you have in the people you love.[20] The artists and fans that I've described in this book are playing and listening around corners, evolving an emergent strategy to shape the future.

We are here, changing what country music looks and sounds like, how it's talked and written about, who gets to name it and who gets to grow it; who gets to be an expert and who gets paid and who gets to represent it; who hears themselves in its stories or is hailed by its tunes; who discovers it by surprise or by inheritance; who makes a community to enjoy it.

Who gets to love it.
We're already here.

Cece picks up the banjo.

ACKNOWLEDGMENTS

FIRST AND FOREMOST, I'd like to thank my series editors, Charles Hughes and Jessica Hopper, and my acquisitions editor, Casey Kittrell, at the University of Texas Press. Thanks for your vision and support for the project and your warm guidance throughout the process. I have been thrilled to be a part of this series! Thanks also to Christina Vargas and Lynne Ferguson at University of Texas Press, for their editing and production help, and to Nancy Warrington for her sharp copyediting eye.

I'd like to thank my colleagues at DePaul University's Department of English, especially my chair, Michele Morano, for her support, friendship, and feedback as I wrote this book. Our walks were often the place where I'd try out some of my newest ideas on her. I've come to rely on Michele's questions and curiosity as I write. I'd also like to thank the DePaul College of Liberal Arts and Sciences and Dean Guillermo Vásquez de Velasco for their support via LAS Summer Research Grants to investigate and develop this work; and DePaul's University Research Council for an academic leave to complete this manuscript.

I have so much gratitude to Súle Greg Wilson, for patiently teasing out the funk of the banjo, for reading my writing, sharing book titles and historical notes, geeking out with me on Black Sci Fi, and for helping me laugh every week during a difficult pandemic year. I also want to thank John Huber and my friends and teachers at the Chicago Old Town School of Folk for the terrific programs and welcoming community they've provided.

I have so many friends and colleagues whose expertise, enthusiasm, community, and care have helped me finish this project: Lourdes Torres, Amina Chaudhri, Jennifer Curley and Choua

Vue, Laila Farah, Misty DeBerry, Nadine Hubbs, Amor Kohli, Julie Moody Freeman, Bill Johnson Gonzalez, Eric Selinger, Barrie Jean Borich, Laurie Fuller, Erica Meiners, Rich Doyle, Elizabeth Wheeler, Paige A. Nichols, Irene Tucker, Jacqueline Shea Murphy, Cynthia Franklin, Daphne Brooks, Nadine Hubbs, Ayanna Thompson, Maya Angela Smith, Maureen Mahon, Robin Mitchell, Janice Monti, Don Hedrick, Deborah Murray and Jerry Dees, Barry Schuchter, Shiren Lee, Kathleen Rooney, Lance Schwultz, LeAnn Fields, Marc Piane, Sanjukta Muhkerjee, Vidura Jang Bahadur, Andrea Solomon, Carolyn Aguila, Aimee Carrillo Rowe, Dan Stolar, Brian Ragsdale, Cheryl West, and Tony Thomas. Many thanks to Julie Moody Freeman, E. Patrick Johnson, Holly G., Willa Taylor and Mary Morton, Erica Pitts, Eric Venable, Robin Mitchell, and Paige May for sharing with me their experiences as fans of country music (and country music–adjacent music). And to my amazing writing group: Miles Harvey, Gail Siegel, Andy White, Lauren Cowen, Laura J. Jones, Peter Handler, Gwen Macsai, Maria Finitzo, and the late Doro Boehme, thanks for providing a supportive writer's community, giving lovingly detailed feedback on drafts, feeding me terrific food and drink (especially Peter's banana bread!), and continuing to listen even as my mind goes into hyperspace. Much appreciation, too, to Halee Curtis, Nina Wilson, Cristena Chanel Brown, and Hanna Wisner for the excellent childcare that they provided during this writing period so that I could have the time and mental space to write.

Thanks to the editors who saw earlier versions of some of these pages and helped me sharpen them, including Aimee Carrillo Rowe and Esther Rothblum at the *Journal of Lesbian Studies*, Susan Fast and Craig Jennex, in *Popular Music and the Politics of Hope: Queer and Feminist Interventions* (New York: Routledge, 2019); and Nadine Hubbs, Eric Weisbard, Robin James, and Esther Morgan-Ellis, at the *Journal of Popular Music Studies*. An enthusiastic thanks to Nadine Hubbs for her invitation to coedit with her our special issue of *JPMS, Uncharted Country: New Voices and Perspectives in Country Music*. Working on this issue plunged me into country music studies in a powerful way, helping me build a community of music critics, musicologists, and journalists. And thanks to our contributors, from whom I learned so much: Chelsea Burns, Kimberly Mack, Karen Pittelman, Shirli Brautbar, Jessica Hutchings, Peter La Chapelle, Clay Kerrigan, Joe Kadi, Wayne Marshall, Sophia Enríquez, Deborah Vargas, Jesse Montgomery, Amanda Marie Martínez, Mari Nagatomi, Ryan Shuvera, and Jocelyn Neal.

Thank you to the musicians, living and dead, who inspired this project, especially Rhiannon Giddens, Leyla McCalla, Amythyst Kiah, Allison Russell, Valerie June, DeLila Black, Rissi Palmer, Darius Rucker, Tina Turner, DeFord Bailey, Blanco Brown, Charley Pride, Beyoncé, Mickey Guyton, Kamara Thomas, Linda Martell, Ray Charles, Bobby Womack, and the irresistible Lil Nas X.

And to my family: my father, Philip M. Royster, whose conversation about home and playing percussion at the Exit/Inn in Nashville in the 1970s sparked this project. Thanks for reading, listening, challenging, and nurturing me. To Phyliss Royster, whose wisdom, care, and humor provides sustenance for me and for all of us. To my sister, Rebecca Royster, for being my partner in crime all these years, for introducing me to Prince and always coming with the Popeyes, and for your fun texts and warm hugs. To Demitria Pates, thank you for your laughter and inspiring ideas about everything from podcasts to music to how to handle the world with verve. To Alexandra Pates, Kaleyah, K.J., and Kennan Keith, Tara Hammond, Barbara Asare-Bediako, all the Roysters, the Harveys, and the Russos, you are my loved ones always. Thank you to our pups, Ruthie and Viva, for keeping life unpredictable and cuddly.

And most of all, thanks to my two sweethearts, Ann Russo and Cecelia Royster-Russo. Cece, you are my treasure! Thanks for all of your great dances, for being willing to sing yet another verse of

"Old Town Road," wherever we are, for your curiosity, for your empathy, and for modeling what Afrofuturist thinking looks like. And to my love, Annie, who has read every page, and whose vision of a loving and accountable community inspires this whole book. Every single day, I can't wait to wake up to have coffee and chai and talk to you, even when it's five in the morning. You're a friend of my mind. And thanks to both of you for putting up with my banjo plunking while we've been quarantined. I love you!

NOTES

INTRODUCTION. WHERE MY PEOPLE AT?

1. That line "In Birmingham they love the governor (boo-hoo-hoo) / Now we all did what we could do" *could* be read as a critique of Wallace and a possible support of Kennedy's move to bring in the troops to support integration, but then later in the song Van Zant ad libs, "Sweet Home Alabama . . . / Where the skies are so blue / and the governor's true." As the Wallace verse continues, the song seems to voice a cynicism and disengagement with the federal government: "Now Watergate does not bother me. Does your conscience bother you?"

2. There's a Confederate flag on stage at this July 2, 1977, performance at the Oakland Coliseum, though it seems to have clouds or maybe flowers superimposed on it. The concert was performed just a few months before the plane crash that killed three of the band's members: Steve Gaines; his sister, backing vocalist Cassie Gaines (of the Honkettes); and lead vocalist Ronnie Van Zant. Ironically, Ronnie Van Zant is wearing a Neil Young T-shirt. Lynyrd Skynyrd, "Sweet Home Alabama," recorded live July 2, 1977, at Oakland Coliseum Stadium, Oakland, CA, YouTube, accessed December 16, 2021, https://www.youtube.com/watch?v=6GxWmSVv-cY.

3. The bombing and burning of the 16th Street Baptist Church where Addie Mae Collins, Carol Denise McNair, Carole Rosamond Robertson, and Cynthia Dionne Wesley died also injured twenty-two others.

4. "Interview—Merry Clayton on Recording the Song 'Sweet Home Alabama,'" November 29, 2013, SuperPopVip, accessed December 16, 2021, https://www.youtube.com/watch?v=-Zj7KrKsW6Q.

5. As Maureen Mahon puts it, Clayton's powerful, gospel-trained voice provided an "audible blackness" that white rock performers sought out to lend authenticity and edge to the music. Maureen Mahon, *Black Diamond Queens: African American Women and Rock and Roll* (Durham, NC: Duke University Press, 2020), 117. For Daphne Brooks, it is the

presence of Black women vocalists like Clayton, King, Darlene Love, and others that's at the heart of white male rock sonic rebellion, though that importance usually goes uncredited. Daphne A. Brooks, *Liner Notes for the Revolution: The Intellectual Life of Black Feminist Sound* (Cambridge, MA: Harvard University Press, 2021), especially page xx. In my listening to Clayton in "Sweet Home Alabama," I have also been inspired by Hanif Abdurraqib's writing on Clayton's transformative performance on the Rolling Stone's song "Gimme Shelter," in his book *A Little Devil in America: Notes in Praise of Performance* (New York: Penguin Random House, 2021), 201–202.

6. The rocker and Black country musician and journalist Kandia Crazy Horse suggests that "there's something enduring to the myth and the spirit and just the funk of 'Sweet Home Alabama' that transcends national and international boundaries in that everybody, no matter where they're from, can identify with this longing for home and the beauty of home." Quoted from the documentary *Sweet Home Alabama: The Southern Rock Saga* (2012), directed by James Maycock. The song has since been covered by a spectrum of performers. Rihanna belted out a verse during a live benefit concert for Birmingham after a 2011 tornado, and the progressive Chicago-based Afro-Indian supergroup Funkadesi sometimes integrates the song into their live performances, as "Sweet Dhol Alabama," with the singer Radhika Chimata adding her own beautiful Hindi flourishes to the chorus. Matt Wake, "20 'Sweet Home Alabama' Covers That Might Surprise You," published March 1, 2017; updated May 18, 2019, al.com, https://www.al.com/entertainment/2017/03/sweet_home_alabama_covers.html; Funkadesi, "Sweet Dhol Alabama," live at SummerDance in Chicago (2007), YouTube, accessed December 16, 2021, https://www.youtube.com/watch?v=ZPPpO2IuL7Y; Ashley Batchelor, "'Feel the Joy': Funkadesi Fills WAC with World Music," *Northwest Arkansas Democrat Gazette*, October 3, 2014, accessed December 16, 2021, https://www.nwaonline.com/news/2014/oct/03/feel-the-joy-20141003/.

7. And my listening to Fender has been deeply shaped by Deborah R. Vargas's essay "Freddy Fender's Blackbrown Country Ecologies," *Journal of Popular Music Studies* 32, no. 2 (2000): 77–94, both in terms of

thinking about the dual influences of Black and Brown musical cultures in Fender's sounds and in the stakes of claiming both to understand the role of racial trauma in Fender's music. Fender's "Before the Next Teardrop Falls" had also been performed by the Black country music singer Linda Martell in 1970, on her album *Color Me Country* (Plantation Records).

8. Holly G., *Black Opry* creator, personal interview with author on Zoom, September 13, 2021, Chicago, Illinois.

9. Diane Pecknold, ed., *Hidden in the Mix: The African American Presence in Country Music* (Durham, NC: Duke University Press, 2013).

10. Claudia Rankine, *Citizen: An American Lyric* (Minneapolis, MN: Graywolf Press, 2014), 32. At this moment of her lyric essay, Rankine is discussing the racial surveillance of the tennis player Serena Williams, but her point is that this experience is one felt by any Black person "thrown against our American background" (*Citizen*, 32).

11. Stephanie Shonekan, *Soul, Country, and the USA: Race and Identity in American Music Culture* (Basinstoke, UK: Palgrave MacMillan, 2015), 2.

12. Alice Randall, quoted in Pamela E. Foster's groundbreaking but neglected *My Country: The African Diaspora's Country Music Heritage* (Nashville, TN: My Country, 1998), 202, which is arguably the first documented history of Black people in country music.

13. See Richard A. Peterson's discussion of these shifts in nomenclature on the part of record companies, radio stations, and eventually performers and fans, in *Creating Country Music: Fabricating Authenticity* (Chicago: University of Chicago Press, 1997), especially 194–201.

14. In R. J. Smith's biography of James Brown, *The One: The Life and Music of James Brown* (NY: Gotham Books, 2012), he describes the "One" as the anchor of Brown's trademark insurgent sound that will continue to shape funk artists that follow him. Brown tells R. J. Smith: "The 'One' is derived from the Earth itself, the soil, the pine tree—ONE two THREE four—not the downbeat, one TWO three FOUR, that most blues are written [in]. Hey, I know what I'm talking about! I was born to the downbeat, and I can tell you without question there is no pride in it. The upbeat is rich, the downbeat is poor. Stepping up proud only happens on

the aggressive 'One,' not the passive Two, and never on lowdownbeat. In the end, it's not about music, it's about life" (5).

15. Eve Kosofsky Sedgwick, *Tendencies* (Durham, NC: Duke University Press, 1993), 8.

16. José Esteban Muñoz, *Cruising Utopia: The Then and There of Queer Futurity* (New York: New York University Press, 2009).

17. Karen Pittelman, "You're My Country Music," *Journal of Popular Music Studies* 32, no. 2 (June 2020): 11–17.

18. Brooks, *Liner Notes for the Revolution*.

19. Holly G, quoted in James Barker, "Profiles in Activism: Black Opry's Holly G.," in *Country Queer*, accessed August 24, 2021, https://countryqueer.com/stories/interview/activism-series-an-interview-with-black-oprys-holly-g/.

20. If, for Geoff Mann, in his essay, "Why Does Country Music Sound White? Race and the Voice of Nostalgia," *Ethnic and Racial Studies* 31, no. 1 (2008): 73–100, country music is a means for white working-class audiences to hold on to older notions of a former white supremacist South, Nadine Hubbs challenges this view of country music's signifiers and its white audience in her book *Rednecks, Queers, and Country Music* (Berkeley: University of California Press, 2014), to ask us to consider a more complex white working-class subjectivity. See also Nadine Hubbs's conversation with Karen Pittelman, Charles Hughes, and Francesca Royster, "How Does Country Music Use Nostalgia to Help Keep White Supremacy in Place?," at the Country Soul Songbook Summit, air date December 10, 2021, Country Music Against White Supremacy, accessed December 16, 2021, https://www.cmaws.org/how-does-country-music-use-nostalgia-to-help-keep-white-supremacy-in-place/. William Peterson, in *Creating Country Music: Fabricating Authenticity* (Chicago: University of Chicago Press, 1997), considers country music's construction of a misremembered past as one that is both fabricated, sometimes by the music industry itself, but is also something that has been socially useful to keep racial, class, and gender stereotypes—hallmarks of white supremacy, I'd add—in place.

21. The Carolina Chocolate Drops also took up stories of the Great Migration as told through the songs of the Chitlin' Circuit and vaude-

ville in their 2011 production, *Keep a Song in Your Soul*, commissioned by the Old Town School of Folk Music in Chicago. "Carolina Chocolate Drops Debut 'Keep a Song in Your Soul': The Black Roots of Vaudeville," *Nonesuch*, November 3, 2011, https://www.nonesuch.com/journal /carolina-chocolate-drops-debut-keep-a-song-in-your-soul-black-roots -vaudeville-chicago-old-town-school-2011-11-03.

22. Mann, "Why Does Country Music Sound White?," 74.

23. John Lingan, "Rhiannon Giddens Is Reclaiming the Black Heritage of American Folk Music," *Time*, February 21, 2019, https://time .com/5534379/songs-of-our-native-daughters-music-review/.

24. But as the contributors to Mark Allan Jackson's edited collection *The Honky Tonk on the Left: Progressive Thought in Country Music* point out, there has also been an ongoing leftist and progressive impulse in country music (Amherst: University of Massachusetts Press, 2018). And in a recent interview, Diane Pecknold warns that making homogeneous generalizations about country music audiences and performers as universally conservative is inaccurate. Reggie Ugwu, "Nashville's Last Taboo? Country Music Stars Are Tiptoeing around Trump," BuzzFeed News, posted on March 2, 2017, https://www.buzzfeednews.com/article /reggieugwu/country-stars-and-donald-trump.

25. Gabe Meline, "Country Music and Race: Something Seems Missing in Ken Burns' Latest," KQED, September 16, 2019, https://www .kqed.org/arts/13866441/in-ken-burns-country-music-an-optimistic -handling-of-race.

26. Louis M. Kyriakoudes, "The Grand Ole Opry and the Urban South," *Southern Cultures* 10, no. 1 (Spring 2004): 67–84, quote on 18, accessed December 16, 2021, https://www.cmaws.org/how-does-country -music-use-nostalgia-to-help-keep-white-supremacy-in-place/.

27. Daphne A. Brooks, *Bodies in Dissent: Spectacular Performances of Race and Freedom, 1850–1910* (Durham, NC: Duke University Press, 2006), 3–9.

28. Dom Flemons, "Can You Blame Gus Canon?," *Oxford American*, no. 83 (Winter 2013), https://main.oxfordamerican.org/magazine/item /160-can-you-blame-gus-cannon.

29. In fact, the website Spinditty finds 127 examples of songs about dancing across races and genres, proving that this topic is a musical

staple; see FlourishAnyway, "127 Songs about Dancing," Spinditty, June
15, 2021, https://spinditty.com/playlists/Pop-Rock-and-Country-Songs
-About-Dancing.

30. Matthew Leimkuehler, "'Blanco Brown: I smelled my own
blood. That's when it all hit me. I gotta stay strong,'" *Tennessean*, March
4, 2021, https://www.tennessean.com/story/entertainment/2021/03/04
/blanco-brown-interview-motorcycle-collision-new-music-ginny
-georgia/6842808002/.

31. @Zandashe, Twitter post, May 18, 2021.

32. David C. Morton, with Charles K. Wolfe, *DeFord Bailey: A Black
Star in Early Country Music* (Knoxville: University of Tennessee Press,
1991).

33. Jocelyn Neal discusses Charles's album as a full circle of cross-
racial borrowing, particularly in terms of soul harmonies. Jocelyn R.
Neal, "'Tennessee Whiskey' and the Politics of Harmony," *Journal of
Popular Music Studies* 32, no. 2 (June 2020): 214–237, https://online.uc
press.edu/jpms/article/32/2/214/110779/Tennessee-Whiskey-and-the
-Politics-of-Harmony.

34. Ray Charles and David Ritz, *Brother Ray: Ray Charles' Own Story*
(New York: Da Capo Press, 1992), quoted in Katie Quine, "How Ray
Charles Shaped Country Music," *The Grand Ole Opry* [blog], updated
August 13, 2019, accessed December 16, 2021, https://www.opry.com
/story/how-ray-charles-shaped-country-music/.

35. Charles Hughes, *Country Soul: Making Music and Making Race
in the American South* (Chapel Hill: University of North Carolina Press,
2017), 133.

36. Quoted in Tim Ghianni, "Ray Charles: Country Music Wouldn't
Be the Same without Him," *Tennessean*, September 17, 2019, originally published in the print edition March 5, 2006, accessed December 15, 2021, https://www.tennessean.com/story/entertainment/music
/country-mile/2019/09/17/ray-charles-country-music-wouldnt-same
-without-him/2291352001/

37. David Browne, "Linda Martell: Country's Lost Pioneer," *Rolling
Stone*, September 2, 2020, https://www.rollingstone.com/music/music
-features/linda-Martellll-black-country-grand-ole-opry-pioneer-1050432/.

38. Hughes, *Country Soul*, especially pages 128–151.

39. Hughes, *Country Soul*, 138.

40. Chelsea Burns, "The Racial Limitations of Country-Soul Cross-over in Bobby Womack's *BW Goes C&W*, 1976," *Journal of Popular Music Studies* 32, no. 2 (2020): 112–127.

41. Ann Powers, "Alabama Shakes' Brittany Howard Has a New Band: Bermuda Triangle," *NPR: All Songs Considered*, July 5, 2017, accessed December 16, 2021, https://www.npr.org/sections/allsongs/2017/07/05 /535630110/alabama-shakes-brittany-howard-has-a-new-band-bermuda -triangle.

42. Discussed at length in Karl Hagstrom Miller, *Segregating Sound: Inventing Folk and Pop Music in the Age of Jim Crow* (Durham, NC: Duke University Press, 2010), 187–214, and in Peterson's *Creating Country Music*, 12–32.

43. Elias Leight, "Lil Nas X's 'Old Town Road' Was a Country Hit. Then Country Changed Its Mind," *Rolling Stone*, March 26, 2019, https://www.rollingstone.com/music/music-features/lil-nas-x-old-town -road-810844/.

44. Kimberly Mack, "She's a Country Girl All Right: Rhiannon Giddens's Powerful Reclamation of Country Culture," *Journal of Popular Music Studies* 32, no. 2 (2020): 148, https://online.ucpress.edu/jpms /article/32/2/144/110773/She-s-A-Country-Girl-All-RightRhiannon -Giddens-s.

45. Craig Havighurst, "The Country Soul Songbook Summit Advances the Inclusion Conversation over Four Days," *WMOT Roots Radio News*, published October 14, 2020, https://www.wmot.org/post/country -soul-songbook-summit-advances-inclusion-conversation over-four -days#stream/.

CHAPTER 1. UNEASY LISTENING

1. Nikky Finney, "Brown Country," in *Black Bone: 25 Years of the Affrila-chian Poets*, edited by Bianca Lynne Spriggs and Jeremy Paden (Lexington: University Press of Kentucky, 2018), 47–54.

2. Tina Turner and Kurt Loder, *I, Tina: My Life Story* (New York: William Morrow, 1986), 9.

3. Maybe this mixture of affection and critique is why it's been taken up so enthusiastically in Australia as a campy line dance, "The Nutbush," and played and performed at school performances, community events, wedding receptions, and Christmas parties. Dancing the Nutbush has even become a Guinness Book of World records event for the most people dancing it at the same time, mostly undergone by folks in Sydney and in Australia's smaller towns.

4. Ike and Tina Turner, "Nutbush City Limits" (1973), *Der Musikladen*, YouTube, accessed December 16, 2021, https://www.youtube.com/watch?v=Io7249JX8w4.

5. Darlene Clark Hine, "Rape and the Inner Lives of Black Women in the Middle West," *Signs: Journal of Women in Culture and Society* 14, no. 4 (1989): 912.

6. Tina Turner, "Honky Tonk Woman" (Live 1982), YouTube, https://www.youtube.com/watch?v=aSROZUsDmpo.

7. Valerie June, online interview with Antonette Masando, *Austin City Limits' Austin Underground*, November 13, 2017, https://www.youtube.com/watch?v=yaax-qduFCU.

8. In *I, Tina*, coauthor Kurt Loder writes that "Tina actually liked the country album . . . even though it didn't sell well" (Turner and Loder, *I, Tina*, 180). The album was a high point of an otherwise barren year, in which the hit that Ike and Tina had was "Sexy Ida," which managed to chart at sixty-five before dying, "the beginning of the duo's decline" (Turner and Loder, *I, Tina*, 180).

9. Turner and Loder, *I, Tina*, 172.

10. Tina Turner at the Chicago United Center, "Nutbush City Limits," October 4, 2008, YouTube, https://www.youtube.com/watch?v=2wMNbPk9obU.

CHAPTER 2. LOVE YOU, MY BROTHER

1. You can watch the Burger King TV ad for the Tender Crisp Chicken Bacon Cheddar Ranch Sandwich here: https://www.youtube.com/watch?v=ctnUCg2Sdqk.

2. Brooks, *Bodies in Dissent*, 3.

3. Brooks, *Bodies in Dissent*, 3.

4. In a 2016 interview, Rucker tells *Rolling Stone*'s Andy Greene that Radney Foster's "Old Silver," together with Al Green's "For the Good Times," are among the five songs that shaped his world as an artist. Rucker says that after he heard Foster's album *Del Rio, TX, 1959*, which includes "Old Silver," "it was when I first started saying 'I want to make a country record someday.' It was all about that album." https://www.rollingstone.com/music/music-lists/darius-rucker-five-songs-that-changed-the-way-i-heard-music-630045/old-silver-radney-foster-630118/. Indeed, when Rucker cut his 2010 country music album, *Charleston, SC, 1966*, he did so as an homage to Radney Foster's *Del Rio, TX, 1959*. Both album titles, giving the time and place of birth of each artist, provide a kind of country music "origin story." In this way, Rucker savvily puts himself in a country music genealogy while also performing his country insiderhood through his knowledge of Foster's much-admired music and songwriting. In that way, Rucker places himself in the Nashville country music singer-songwriter tradition that includes Radney, Nanci Griffith, and Mary Chapin Carpenter. Rucker once appeared on VH1 wearing a Radney Foster T-shirt and, with Hootie, recorded a live performance of Foster's "A Fine Line" on the B side of the single "Let Her Cry." Over the years, their collaborations have been numerous. Rucker provided guest vocals on Foster's 2009 solo album, *Revival*, singing background on the song "Angel in Flight"; has performed at Radney's fiftieth birthday party with other artists saluting his music; and in June of 2021 invited Radney to perform as an opener at a pop-up concert at Charleston's The Windjammer, in support of nurses and first responders.

5. Joe Posnanski, "So I Sing," *NBC Sports World*, October 13, 2015, accessed December 16, 2021, https://sportsworld.nbcsports.com/darius-rucker-sports-fan/.

6. Will Hermes, "Darius Rucker: The Rock Transplants: The Artist Formerly Known as Hootie's Amazing Second Act," *Rolling Stone*, no. 1211, June 19, 2014, https://www.rollingstone.com/music/music-news/darius-rucker-the-rock-transplants-37784/.

7. With a nod to Eric Lott's powerful study of blackface minstrelsy, *Love and Theft: Blackface Minstrelsy and the American Working Class*, 20th ed. (New York: Oxford University Press, 2013).

8. See, for example, this description in the *Huffington Post* of the "bro-iest" neighborhoods: "Maybe they were in a frat, maybe they weren't. Maybe they work in investment banking, maybe they don't. All we're really certain of is that they don't see graduating from college and having a job as a reason not to be doing shots on a Monday night." Matt Meltzer, "America's 12 Bro-iest Neighborhoods, Ranked," *The HuffPost*, May 5, 2015, updated December 6, 2017, accessed December 16, 2021, https://www.huffpost.com/entry/americas-12-bro-iest-neig_b_7213748.

9. You can watch Darius and Brad here: "Brad Paisley Invites Darius Rucker to Join Grand Ole Opry," October 4, 2012, https://www.youtube.com/watch?v=7WPDkiAHko4.

10. You can watch Darius and Lionel here: https://www.youtube.com/watch?v=vaSuqw9itpY; video no longer available.

11. E. Patrick Johnson, *Appropriating Blackness: Performance and the Politics of Authenticity* (Durham, NC: Duke University Press, 2003), 3.

12. Peterson, *Creating Country Music*, 137–155.

13. Peterson, *Creating Country Music*, 150–151.

14. Peterson, *Creating Country Music*, 151.

15. Candice M. Jenkins, *Private Lives, Proper Relations: Regulating Black Intimacy* (Minneapolis: University of Minnesota Press, 2007), 14.

16. Charley Pride, *Pride: The Charley Pride Story* (New York: William Morrow, 1994), 18.

17. Bill Malone and Jocelyn Neal, *Country Music U.S.A.*, 3rd ed. (Austin: University of Texas Press, 2013), 314.

18. Pride, *The Charley Pride Story*, 216–218.

19. Pride, *The Charley Pride Story*, 154–155.

20. Pride, *The Charley Pride Story*, 186–187.

21. Pride, *The Charlie Pride Story*, 176.

22. Since Charley Pride's death at the age of eighty-six in December 2020 of COVID-19 complications, his work as a country music pathbreaker is just beginning to be recognized. He received the CMA's Willie Nelson Lifetime Achievement Award just weeks before his death in

November of 2020, and has been the subject of posthumous tributes by
PBS, NPR, *People*, and the *New York Times*. In the summer of 2021, a
ninety-minute video, *CMT Giants: Charley Pride*, was made, which includes performances by Black artists Rucker, Gladys Knight, and Mickey
Guyton, together with Garth Brooks, Reba McEntire, Alan Jackson,
George Strait, and others. This special makes Pride's sonic impact unde-
niable. But I am still waiting for the more painful aspects of Pride's story
and legacy to be addressed. As Andrea Williams writes in her obituary
for Pride in *Vulture*, "Pride's name is the one trotted out when justifi-
able rebukes are lobbed against the industry and its history, his achieve-
ments upheld as proof that Country Music isn't as bad and backward as
it seems." Williams points out that Pride's sacrifices haven't yet yielded
full transformation of the industry, but change is still possible:

> In the words of Dr. Cleve Francis, a cardiologist turned country
> music crooner who found his own dreams of stardom dampened by
> country music's racism, this is the chance for the industry to get it
> right: "In honor of this great African American artist, the country
> music industry should open the doors that have been closed to
> African American artists for years," he wrote on Facebook. "Mu-
> sic should be about talent and not color—Charley Pride was that
> living proof."

Andrea Williams, "Charley Pride Deserved Better Than What Country
Music Could Ever Give Him," *Vulture*, December 15, 2020, https://www
.vulture.com/article/charley-pride-obit.html.

23. In a November 2020 interview on NPR's *All Things Considered*, the African American country music singer and radio host Rissi
Palmer discusses all the strategy and handwringing that went into making music videos for her first country music hits: whether she should
wear her hair naturally or relaxed, who was cast in the video with her,
whether she should have a love interest, and what race would he be. Usually, the final decision was for her to be cast alone. She confirms that
for Black country music stars, the making of music videos is fraught
and often out of the performer's hands. "Interview with 'Color Me
Country' Radio Host Rissi Palmer," heard on *All Things Considered*,

NPR, November 28, 2020, https://www.npr.org/2020/11/28/939737483 /interview-with-color-me-country-radio-host-rissi-palmer.

24. Though Rucker didn't discuss them often at this time in his career, such racial navigations were definitely a part of his everyday life. For example, Rucker tells *Rolling Stone* that he received a tweet advising him to "leave country music to white people." Rucker tweeted back "WOW! Is this 2013 or 1913?" Beville Dunkerley, "Darius Rucker Making 'True Believers' with Country Music," *Rolling Stone*, May 21, 2013, https://www.rollingstone.com/music/music-news/darius-rucker -making-true-believers-with-country-music-186406/.

25. "Darius Rucker," season 2, episode 8, *Key & Peele*, Comedy Central, November 14, 2012, YouTube, accessed December 16, 2021, https://www. youtube.com/watch?v=FE9PUexeUvo.

26. "Obama's Anger Translator—Victory," season 2, episode 7, *Key & Peele*, Comedy Central, November 7, 2012, https://www.cc.com/video /dogxh2/key-peele-obama-s-anger-translator-victory. The critic Wesley Morris gives some great insights on the power of the "Obama Anger Translator" skit's relevance to the current racial climate that also shed light on the ways that Rucker might be navigating the pressure to Keep Composure While Black: "Luther's meltdowns weren't funny because they were a generic black man's rage. They were funny because Keegan-Michael Key imagined that Luther was Obama inside out. In exposing the president's volcanically aggrieved inner self—a man regularly buffeted by condescension, disillusionment, presumption, willful obstruction, distrust, disdain, and disbelief—Key turned stereotypical Black militancy into a kind of ignoble grace." Wesley Morris, "Race to the Top: The Meaning of 'Key and Peele,'" *Grantland*, September 9, 2015, https://grant land.com/features/race-to-the-top-the-meaning-of-key-and-peele/.

27. Darius Rucker, quoted in Dan Weiss, "Hootie and the Blowfish Talk *Cracked Rear View*'s 25th Anniversary, Being Secretly Political and 'Old Town Road,'" Grammys, July 31, 2019, https://www.grammy .com/grammys/news/hootie-blowfish-talk-cracked-rear-views-25th -anniversary-being-secretly-political-and.

28. Darius Rucker, interview with Lee Hawkins, "Darius Rucker Discusses Race and Country Music," *Wall Street Journal/Video*, September

15, 2014, https://www.wsj.com/video/darius-rucker-discusses-race-and
-country-music/319B4C2D-69FC-434B-BE74-F39E8499D3C4.html.

29. Darius Rucker, "Darius Talks DMAs, Country Music History, and
Race in America," interview with Rissi Palmer, *Color Me Country*, Apple
Radio, episode 6, November 6, 2020, https://music.apple.com/us/station
/darius-rucker/ra.1538223258.

30. Rucker, Dan Weiss interview, "Hootie and the Blowfish."

31. Hanif Abdurraqib, *They Can't Kill Us Until They Kill Us* (Colum-
bus, OH: Two Dollar Radio, 2017), 185–186.

32. Darius Rucker, "If I Told You" (official video), YouTube, October
21, 2016, https://www.youtube.com/watch?v=7LBCFyUw8gM.

33. Amanda Petrusich, "Darius Rucker and the Perplexing Whiteness
of Country Music," *New Yorker*, October 25, 2017, https://www.newyorker
.com/culture/cultural-comment/darius-rucker-and-the-perplexing
-whiteness-of-country-music.

34. Rucker, "Darius Talks DMAs," Rissi Palmer interview.

CHAPTER 3. HOW TO BE AN OUTLAW

1. Audre Lorde, "A Litany for Survival," Poetry Foundation, https://
www.poetryfoundation.org/poems/147275/a-litany-for-survival.

2. "Daddy Lessons" and *Lemonade* as a whole fit a trajectory of Beyoncé's career and image that has become increasingly politicized, from her
support of Black survivors of Hurricane Katrina, to her controversial 2013
declaration of herself in *Ms.* magazine as a card-carrying feminist, to her
support of the Black Lives Matter movement. Janell Hobson, "Beyonce's
Fierce Feminism," *Ms.*, originally published in the Spring 2013 issue;
reprinted March 7, 2015, https://msmagazine.com/2015/03/07/Beyonces
-fierce-feminism/. See also Daphne Brooks, "'All That You Can't Leave
Behind': Black Female Soul Singing and the Politics of Surrogation in
the Age of Catastrophe," *Meridians: Feminism, Race, Transnationalism* 8,
no. 2 (2008): 180–204. Earlier in February 2016, Beyoncé performed at
the halftime show of Super Bowl XLVII, referencing Black Lives Matter,
the Black Panthers, and other Black Power icons; she also referenced the

Black Lives Matter movement frequently during her appearance on the MTV Video Music Awards in 2016, including bringing the mothers of Michael Brown, Eric Garner, and Treyvon Martin—all African American men recently killed by police violence—with her.

3. For more on the Dixie Chicks 2003 controversy and backlash, see Gabriel Rossman, "Elites, Masses, and Media Blacklists: The Dixie Chicks Controversy," *Social Forces* 83, no. 1 (September 2004): 61–79; Emil B. Towner, "A <Patriotic> Apologia: The Transcendence of the Dixie Chicks," *Rhetoric Review* 29, no. 3 (2010): 293–319; and Jada Watson and Lori Burns, "Resisting Exile and Asserting Musical Voice: The Dixie Chicks Are 'Not Ready to Make Nice,'" *Popular Music* 29, no. 3 (October 2010): 325–350.

4. Brad Paisley's well-intentioned, albeit cringeworthy, 2013 CMA duet with the African American rapper L. L. Cool J, "Accidental Racist," caused quite an uproar, particularly on the left, for its "Why can't we all get along?" erasure of difficult histories of racism (i.e., "If you don't judge my gold chains / I'll forget the iron chains").

5. Quoted in Spencer Kornhaber, "What Beyonce's 'Daddy Lessons' Had to Teach," *The Atlantic*, November 3, 2016, https://www.theatlantic.com/entertainment/archive/2016/11/cmas-beyonce-daddy-lessons-dixie-chicks-country-music-awards-race/506375/.

6. Quoted in Randall Roberts, "Conservative Country Music Fans Lash Out at CMA Performance by Beyoncé and the Dixie Chicks," *Los Angeles Times*, November 3, 2016, https://www.latimes.com/entertainment/music/la-et-ms-conservative-cma-beyonce-dixie-chicks-2016 1103-htmlstory.html.

7. While country music has often been claimed as the soundtrack for conservative politics, recent critics have taken on this image and argued that country music has always had progressive streams and that it can continue to be a place for progressive activism. See Peter La Chapelle, *I'd Fight the World: A Political History of Old-Time, Hillbilly, and Country Music* (Chicago: University of Chicago Press, 2019); Jackson, *The Honky Tonk on the Left*; Hubbs, *Rednecks, Queers, and Country Music*; Jason Mellard, *Progressive Country: How the 1970s Transformed the Texan in Popular Culture* (Austin: University of Texas Press, 2013). The work

of Country Music Against White Supremacy, a group of BIPOC and white musicians, fans, and industry professionals, seeks to end white supremacy in country music and to use country music to end white supremacy. CMAWS, https://www.cmaws.org/.

8. Aynslee Darmon, "Natalie Maines Vows to Never Perform at CMA Awards Again," *ET Canada*, July 21, 2020, https://etcanada.com/news/670919/natalie-maines-vows-to-never-perform-at-cma-awards-again/.

9. Mellard, *Progressive Country*, 118–119.

10. Greg Tate, ed., *Everything But the Burden: What White People Are Taking from Black Culture* (New York: Broadway Books, 2003).

11. See Omise'eke Natasha Tinsley's excellent analysis of the ways that misogynoir shaped the critiques of Beyoncé's clothing, movements, and overall image in the aftermath of the CMA performance in her book *Beyoncé in Formation: Remixing Black Feminism* (Austin: University of Texas Press, 2018), 46–47.

12. Alex Abad-Santos, "Beyoncé, the CMAs, and the Fight over Country Music's Politics, Explained," *Vox*, November 4, 2016, https://www.vox.com/culture/2016/11/4/13521928/Beyoncé-cma-awards-controversy-deleted-performance.

13. See Tressie McMillan Cottom's "Reading Hick-Hop: The Shotgun Marriage of Hip-Hop and Country Music," in *The Honky Tonk on the Left*, ed. Mark Allan Jackson, 236–256.

14. Joseph Hudak, "Beyonce's Country Song 'Daddy Lessons' Rejected by Grammys," https://www.rollingstone.com/music/music-country/Beyonces-country-song-daddy-lessons-rejected-by-grammys-119339/.

15. There are plenty of country songs about fathers protecting their daughters with their shotguns, including "Shotgun Boogie" by Tennessee Ernie Ford, "Shotgun Wedding" by Jamie Lynn Spears (Britney's little sister), and the frightening "Cleaning This Gun (Come on in, Boy)" by Rodney Atkins. Evocative of these past country daddies, the tough if tender dad in "Daddy Lessons" also has his rifle and his bible and his whiskey in his tea. But reading "Daddy Lessons" as an unequivocal embrace of a gun-happy father seems simplistic to me, especially in the larger context of the *Lemonade* album's video critique of violence against women and its wrestling with Black women's anger and healing.

16. "Daddy Lessons"'s opening evocation, using second line horns and drums, acts as a spiritual call and adds a layer of both celebration and mourning to the song. As the historian Tyina Steptoe argues in her essay "Beyoncé's Western South Serenade" in *The Lemonade Reader*, edited by Kinitra D. Brooks and Kameelah L. Martin (New York: Routledge, 2019), 183–191, this New Orleans jazz sound intertwines with Texas country to speak to the layered and vexed racial histories of the region, as well.

17. For a terrific discussion of Black and Brown divas, see John Musser, "Radiant Divas: In Pursuit of the Queer Sublime," PhD diss., University of Illinois, 2019, *IDEALS*, http://hdl.handle.net/2142/105144.

18. "Beyoncé's 'Lemonade' Album and Information Resources: #lemonadesyllabus," https://library.highline.edu/lemonade/syllabus.

19. Hilary Moss, "Satoshi Kanazawa Causes Firestorm after Claiming Black Women Are Less Attractive," *HuffPost*, May 17, 2011; updated July 17, 2011, https://www.huffpost.com/entry/satoshi-kanazawa-Black-women-less-attractive_n_863327.

20. Melissa Harris-Perry, "A Call and Response with Melissa Harris-Perry: The Pain and the Power of 'Lemonade,'" *Elle*, April 26, 2016, https://www.elle.com/culture/music/a35903/lemonade-call-and-response/.

21. James Baldwin, "Notes of a Native Son," in *Collected Essays*, ed. Toni Morrison (New York: New Library of America, 1998), 594.

22. Baldwin, "Notes of a Native Son," 594.

23. Love and Protect: Supporting Criminalized Survivors of Violence, https://loveprotect.org/.

24. For more on the Dixie Chicks' use of a feminist critique of domestic violence within the gendered confines of country music, see Delia Poey, "Striking Back without Missing a Beat: Radical Responses to Domestic Violence in Country Music's The Dixie Chicks and Salsa's Celia Cruz," *Studies in Popular Culture* 32, no. 2 (Spring 2010): 1–15.

25. The Combahee River Collective Statement, 1977, https://www.Blackpast.org/african-american-history/combahee-river-collective-statement-1977/.

26. Omise'eke Tinsley, in *Beyoncé in Formation*, 36, suggests that

Beyoncé sharpens the trope of the injured wife by reminding the addressee of Malcolm X's deeper point: a Black man who doesn't value Black women ultimately hurts himself, because he doesn't value himself. "When you hurt me, you hurt yourself / Try not to hurt yourself / . . . When you love me, you love yourself / Love God herself," Bey sings with Jack White. Their lyrics echo the questions that began Malcolm X's speech: "Who taught you to hate yourself from the top of your own kind?—You should ask yourself who taught you to hate being what God made you." The Black man will never be fully human, he inveighs, until he loves every part of himself unconditionally—including "his" women.

27. bell hooks, *We Real Cool: Black Men and Masculinity* (New York: Routledge, 2003), 3–4.

28. Cathy J. Cohen, "Punks, Bulldaggers, and Welfare Queens: The Radical Potential of Queer Politics," *GLQ: A Journal of Gay and Lesbian Studies* 3 (1997): 437–465.

29. Alexis Pauline Gumbs, "Mothering Ourselves," in *Revolutionary Mothering: Love on the Front Lines*, ed. Alexis Pauline Gumbs, China Martens, and Mai'a Williams (Toronto, Canada: Between the Lines, 2016), 21–22.

CHAPTER 4. VALERIE JUNE, GHOST CATCHER

1. "'An Evening at Elvis' Presents Valerie June," episode 3, *The Audubon Sessions*, November 16, 2015, https://www.youtube.com/watch?v=OOvX2vkJ8JM.

2. Nina Sun Eidsheim and Mandy-Suzanne Wong, "*Corregidora*: Corporeal Archaeology, Embodied Memory, Improvisation," in *Negotiated Moments: Improvisation, Sound, and Subjectivity*, ed. Gillian Siddall and Ellen Waterman (Durham, NC: Duke University Press, 2016), 217.

3. Valerie June, online interview with Antonette Masando, *Austin City Limits' Austin Underground*, November 13, 2017, https://www.youtube.com/watch?v=yaax-qduFCU.

4. Thomas F. DeFrantz and Anita Gonzalez, "Introduction: From 'Negro Experiment' to 'Black Performance,'" in *Black Performance Theory*, ed. Thomas F. DeFrantz and Anita Gonzalez (Durham, NC: Duke University Press, 2014), 5.

5. LeRoi Jones (Amiri Baraka), "The Changing Same (R&B and the New Black Music)," in *Black Music* (New York: Da Capo Press, 1998; originally published by William Morrow, 1967), 18.

6. "Valerie June on Learning to Love 'Perfectly Imperfect Voices,'" *The Record*, NPR, August 9, 2013, heard on *All Things Considered*, https://www.npr.org/sections/therecord/2013/08/09/209857975/valerie -june-on-learning-to-love-perfectly-imperfect-voices.

7. "Valerie June on Learning to Love 'Perfectly Imperfect Voices.'"

8. Joseph Roach, *Cities of the Dead: Circum-Atlantic Performance* (New York: Columbia University Press, 1996), 5.

9. Camille T. Dungy, "Tales from a Black Girl on Fire, or Why I Hate to Walk Outside and See Things Burning," in *Guidebook to Relative Strangers: Journeys into Race, Motherhood, and History* (New York: W. W. Norton, 2017), 171.

10. Valerie June Hockett, *Maps for the Modern World* (Kansas City, MO: Andrews McMeel, 2021), iv.

11. Brooks, *Liner Notes for the Revolution*, 409.

CHAPTER 5. CAN THE BLACK BANJO SPEAK?

1. Gayatri Chakravorti Spivak, "Can the Subaltern Speak?," in *Can the Subaltern Speak? Reflections on the History of an Idea*, edited by Rosalind C. Morris (New York: Columbia University Press, 2010), 21–78.

2. Audre Lorde, "The Master's Tools Will Never Dismantle the Master's House," in *Sister Outsider: Collected Essays and Speeches* (Berkeley, CA: Crossing Press, 1984, 2007), 110–114.

3. "Rhiannon Giddens' Keynote Address at IBMA Conference: Community and Connection," September 26, 2017, *Nonesuch*, posted October 3, 2017, https://www.nonesuch.com/journal/rhiannon-giddens -keynote-address-ibma-conference-community-connection-2017-10-03.

NOTES TO PAGES 120-129

4. Dena J. Epstein, *Sinful Tunes and Spirituals: Black Folk Music to the Civil War* (Urbana: University of Illinois Press, 1977, 2003).

5. Eric Lott, *Love and Theft: Blackface Minstrelsy and the American Working Class* (New York: Oxford University Press, 2013).

6. Cecelia Conway, *African Banjo Echoes in Appalachia: A Study in Folk Traditions* (Knoxville: University of Tennesee Press, 1995).

7. Laurent Dubois, *The Banjo: America's African American Instrument* (Cambridge, MA: Belnap Press of Harvard University Press, 2016), 244.

8. Dubois, *The Banjo*, 250.

9. Dubois, *The Banjo*, 255–260.

10. See Dubois, *The Banjo*; Conway, *African Banjo Echoes*; Dena J. Epstein, *Sinful Tunes and Spirituals*; Tony Thomas, "Why African Americans Put the Banjo Down," in *Hidden in the Mix: The African American Presence in Country Music*, ed. Diane Pecknold (Durham, NC: Duke University Press, 2013), 143–170; and Rhiannon Giddens's wonderful liner notes on the album *Songs of Our Native Daughters*.

11. See Karl Hagstrom Miller, *Segregating Sound: Inventing Folk and Pop Music in the Age of Jim Crow* (Durham, NC: Duke University Press, 2010).

12. "Rhiannon Giddens' Keynote Address at IBMA."

13. Thomas, "Why African Americans Put the Banjo Down," 144.

14. Watch Sana Ndiaye at work here: "Sana Ndiaye Performs 'Children' on the Akonting," YouTube, August 25, 2009, https://youtu.be/Pc9Y_uu1KH8.

15. Tommy Tomlinson, "Rhiannon Giddens and the Making of NC's Most Beautiful Voice," *Our State*, September 2, 2015, https://www.ourstate.com/rhiannon-giddens/.

16. In *Just Around the Bend: Survival and Revival in Southern Banjo Sounds: Mike Seeger's Last Documentary* (Washington, DC: Smithsonian Folkways Recordings, 2019).

17. *Our Native Daughters on Their Roots and the African American Banjo Tradition*, Smithsonian Folkways video, 2019.

18. Vernellia R. Randall, "Shocking List of 10 Companies That Profited from the Slave Trade," *Race, Racism and the Law*, August 31, 2013, https://www.racism.org/index.php/articles/law-and-justice/citizen

ship-rights/117-slavery-to-reparations/reparations/1697-reparations 1001.

19. You can watch the video here, released by Smithsonian Folkways: Our Native Daughters, "Mama's Cryin' Long" (Behind-the-Scenes Documentary), posted December 13, 2018, https://www.youtube.com/watch?v=M7PvWw97Cqo.

20. For more on the ring shout, see the post by the UNC dance professor Tamara Williams, "Reviving Culture Through Ring Shout," *Dancer-Citizen*, no. 6, http://dancercitizen.org/issue-6/tamara-williams/.

21. See Kyra D. Gaunt's *The Games Black Girls Play: Learning the Ropes from Double-Dutch to Hip-Hop* (New York: NYU Press, 2006).

22. Nate Hertweck, "American Roots Music Supergroup Our Native Daughters Look Back to Move Forward/Newport Folk 2019," Grammys interview, July 30, 2019, https://www.grammy.com/grammys/new/american-roots-music-supergroup-our-native-daughters-look-back-move-forward-newport.

23. For more on this flying tradition in black music, see Soyica Diggs Colbert, "Black Movements: Flying Africans in Spaceships," in *Black Performance Theory*, ed. Thomas F. DeFrantz and Anita Gonzalez (Durham, NC: Duke University Press, 2014), 129–148.

24. You can watch it here: "Our Native Daughters 'Black Myself'/ACL Presents: Americana 18th Annual Honors," November 21, 2019, https://www.youtube.com/watch?v=vjd9zlSiHZM.

25. Since the release of *Songs of Our Native Daughters* in 2019, the album has enjoyed great success. In 2021, Smithsonian Folkways released a documentary of the concert that my family viewed, *Reclaiming Our History: Our Native Daughters*, which streamed on the Smithsonian Channel and which highlights the spiritual and creative process behind the album. Amythyst Kiah was nominated for a Grammy for Best American Roots Song as a songwriter of "Black Myself." Giddens, Kiah, Russell, and McCalla have all released new solo albums that continue *Songs of Our Native Daughters'* exploration of Black women's sonic traditions of survival through a range of sounds and stories, drawing from past, present, and future: Leyla McCalla's album *The Capitalist Blues* (2019) brings together humor and protest through past and present New Orleans jazz

traditions; Rhiannon Giddens's timely meditation on mortality, grief, and community, *They're Calling Me Home* (2021), made with her partner Francesco Turrisi, engages directly with the shared experience of loss and dislocation of the COVID-19 pandemic; Allison Russell's meditative and joyful *Outside Child* (2021) and Amythyst Kiah's powerful *Wary and Strange* (2021), both reflective of the legacies of personal trauma and healing, promise powerful continued work by both artists. And this work has inspired a new generation of Black musicians who are reclaiming the banjo, including the Chicago-based poet and musician Kara Jackson, the rapper Demeanor (Justin Harrington), and Hannah Mayree, founder of the Oakland, California–based Black Banjo Reclamation Project. These developments make clear the point that *Songs of Our Native Daughters* is part of a larger movement of Black feminist reclaiming, healing, and historic change. As Rhiannon Giddens tells the Black journalist Marcus K. Dowling, "The reclamation of the banjo is not a one-event thing. It's a multiyear and multigeneration process. We still have a lot of work to do." Marcus K. Dowling, "Tonight: Watch 'Reclaiming Our History: Our Native Daughters,' a Documentary about 'Reclaiming Our History,'" CMT News, February 22, 2021, http://www.cmt.com/news/1830600 /reclaiming-our-history-our-native-daughters-documentary-smithso nian-channel-tonight/.

CHAPTER 6. THIRTEEN WAYS OF LOOKING AT "OLD TOWN ROAD"

1. For great overviews of the controversy around "Old Town Road"'s inclusion on the country charts, see Ben Sisario, "Lil Nas X Added Billy Ray Cyrus to 'Old Town Road.' Is It Country Enough for Billboard Now?," *New York Times*, April 5, 2019, https://www.nytimes.com /2019/04/05/business/media/lil-nas-x-billy-ray-cyrus-billboard.html; and Owen Myers, "Fight for Your Right to Yeehaw: Lil Nas X and Country's Race Problem," *The Guardian*, April 27, 2019, accessed December 17, 2021, https://www.theguardian.com/music/2019/apr/27/fight -for-your-right-to-yeehaw-lil-nas-x-and-countrys-race-problem.

2. See Alex Zaragoza's discussion of the Wrangler boycott in "White Country Music Fans Need to Stop Hating on Lil Nas X's Wrangler Collaboration," *Vice*, May 31, 2019, https://www.vice.com/en/article/xwn4ja /white-country-fans-need-to-stop-hating-on-lil-nas-xs-wrangler -collaboration.

3. Wallace Stevens, "Thirteen Ways of Looking at a Blackbird," in *The Collected Poems of Wallace Stevens* (New York: Alfred A. Knopf, 1954) and available from the Poetry Foundation at https://www.poetryfoundation .org/poems/45236/thirteen-ways-of-looking-at-a-blackbird.

4. Ben Sisario, "Lil Nas X's 'Old Town Road' Breaks Billboard's Singles Record," *New York Times*, July 29, 2019, https://www.nytimes.com /2019/07/29/arts/music/lil-nas-x-old-town-road-billboard-record.html.

5. You can watch the performance of "Old Town Road" on the 2020 Grammys here: https://www.youtube.com/watch?v=Q9VjvziNPN8.

6. You can watch Lil Naz X—"Old Town Road (Official Movie)" at https://www.youtube.com/watch?v=w2Ov5jzm3j8. It premiered May 17, 2019.

7. Kelsey Lawrence, "Why Young Designers Are Reclaiming Cowboy Culture," *i-D*, November 27, 2018, https://i-d.vice.com/en_us/article /j5z5xd/why-young-designers-are-reclaiming-cowboy-culture?utm _source=stylizedembed_i-d.vice.com&utm_campaign=3k3vb8&site=i-d.

8. You can watch the "Old Town Road" BET Awards performance here: "Lil Nas X and Billy Ray Cyrus Bring the 'Old Town Road' to the BET Awards Live!" BET Awards 2019, June 23, 2019, https://www.you tube.com/watch?v=amhC8WYgNA4.

9. Emily Raboteau, "Black Cowboys, Busting One of America's Defining Myths," *New Yorker*, January 22, 2017, https://www.newyorker .com/culture/photo-booth/black-cowboys-busting-one-of-americas -defining-myths.

10. Sarah Gilbert, "The Black Cowboys of Mississippi—in Pictures," *The Guardian*, February 15, 2019, https://www.theguardian.com/artand design/gallery/2019/feb/15/the-black-cowboys-of-mississippi-in -pictures.

11. Taylor Crumpton, "A Brief History of the Yeehaw Agenda," *Afropunk*, March 12, 2019, https://afropunk.com/2019/03/black-cowboys -yeehaw-agenda/.

12. Rachel Tashjian, "Welcome to the Yeehaw Agenda: The Black Cowboy Trend behind the Internet's Favorite Song," *GQ*, April 9, 2019, https://www.gq.com/story/old-town-road-yeehaw-agenda.

13. Wesley Morris, "Lil Nas X Is the King of Crossover," *New York Times*, March 11, 2020; photograph by Arielle Bobb-Willis for the *New York Times*, https://images.app.goo.gl/nv9YBFzLaHVAJB4XA.

14. Photograph by Amanda Edwards, Getty Images, accessed December 17, 2021, https://media.gettyimages.com/photos/lil-nas-x-winner -of-best-music-video-and-best-pop-duogroup-for-old-picture-id1202 198308?s=612x612.

15. Photographer unknown, Getty Images, accessed December 17, 2021, https://static.independent.co.uk/s3fs-public/thumbnails/image/2020 /06/18/15/gettyimages-1189836609.jpg?width-640.

16. Photographer unknown, https://images-na.ssl-images-amazon .com/images/I/713y9fSdqfL._AC_SL1500_.jpg.

17. Author unknown, "Lil Nas X: I Prayed That Being Gay Was Just a Phase," *BBC News*, October 1, 2019, Getty Images, https://www.google .com/imgres?imgurl=https://c.files.bbci.co.uk/151DD/production/_ 109039468_gettyimages-1176067846.jpg&imgrefurl=https://www.bbc .com/news/newsbeat-49892179&tbnid=QQ7zvIuUCgYyIM&vet =1&docid=MsI4hWGya7EBRM&w=976&h=549&source=sh/x/im.

18. Lil Nas X, quoted in Joe Coscarelli, "'Old Town Road': Diary of a Song," *New York Times Music* on Twitter, May 10, 2019, https://twitter .com/nytimesmusic/status/1126830559886491650.

19. Quoted in "Country Music Fans Boycott Wrangler Brand Following Lil Nas X's Partnership," *Vibe*, May 21, 2019, https://www.vibe.com/2019 /05/lil-nas-x-partnership-wrangler-boycotted-angry-country-music-fans.

20. See Kyriakoudes, "The Grand Ole Opry and the Urban South," 67–84.

21. Charles Hughes, quoted in Sisario, "Lil Nas X Added Billy Ray Cyrus to 'Old Town Road'"; also see his book *Country Soul*.

22. Lil Nas X, "'Old Town Road' Lyrics—Genius Annotation," *Genius*, accessed December 17, 2021, https://genius.com/Lil-nas-x-old -town-road-lyrics.

23. "'Old Town Road' Is a Record-Breaking, Gay-Pride-Celebrating, America-Unifying Pop-Culture Miracle," *Los Angeles Times*, Tribune

News Service, July 27, 2019, https://www.chicagotribune.com/entertain ment/music/ct-ent-old-town-road-lil-nas-x-20190727-5wnsnfcuf5dbv pi4kmt7vzg6rq-story.html.

24. For more on country music's creole roots and identities, see Peck-nold, *Hidden in the Mix*; Wayne Marshall, "Ragtime Country: Rhyth-mically Recovering Country's Black Heritage," *Journal of Popular Music Studies* 32, no. 2 (June 2020): 50–62; Hughes, *Country Soul*; Sophia M. Enríquez, "'Penned Against the Wall': Migration Narratives, Cultural Resonances, and Latinx Experiences in Appalachian Music," *Journal of Popular Music Studies*, 32, no. 2 (2020): 63–76, https://doi.org/10.1525/jpms .2020.32.2.63; Ludwig Hurtado, "Country Music Is also Mexican Music," *The Nation*, January 3, 2019, https://www.thenation.com/article/archive /country-mexico-ice-nationalism/; Kristina M. Jacobsen, *The Sound of Navajo Country: Music, Language and Diné Belonging* (Durham, NC: Uni-versity of North Carolina Press, 2017); and John W. Troutman, "Steelin' the Slide Guitar: Hawai'i and the Birth of the Blues Guitar," *Southern Cultures* 19, no. 1 (Spring 2013), https://doi.org/10.1525/jpms.2020.32.2.63.

25. Joe Levy, "Inside the 'Old Town Road' Charts Decision," *Billboard Chart Beat*, September 19, 2019, https://www.billboard.com/articles /business/chart-beat/8530110/inside-the-old-town-road-charts-decision.

26. See Tressie McMillan Cottom, "Reading Hick-Hop: The Shotgun Marriage of Hip-Hop and Country Music," in *The Honky Tonk on the Left: Progressive Thought in Country Music*, ed. Mark Allan Jackson (Am-herst: University of Massachusetts Press, 2018), 236–256.

27. For an expansive and complex analysis of trap music and culture, see Sesali Bowen's *Bad Fat Black Girl: Notes from a Trap Feminist* (New York: Amistad Books, 2021).

28. Bowen, *Bad Fat Black Girl*, 5.

29. "Lil Nas X Gets Interviewed by Cute Kids," *Noisey Shorties*, Vice Video, https://video.vice.com/en_uk/video/noisey-lil-nas-x-gets-inter viewed-by-cute-kids/5d2dad79be40771eea21b7a1.

30. Toni Morrison, *Tar Baby* (New York: Random House, 1981, 2004), 306.

31. "Black Legends of the West," *News and Record*, January 26, 2015, https://greensboro.com/black-legends-of-the-west/article_1acf2b85-7a42-575e-9d98-4d4604a52eca.html.

32. Steve Gorman, "'This Looks So Bad,' Says White Texas Cop on Horseback, Leading Black Man on a Rope," *Reuters*, October 3, 2019, https://www.reuters.com/article/us-texas-police-horseback/this-looks -so-bad-says-white-texas-cop-on-horseback-leading-black-man-on-a -rope-idUSKBN1WJ07U.

33. Cristina Kim and Tonya Mosley, "Compton's Black Cowboys Ride to Reclaim Their Legacy," *Here and Now*, WBUR, April 20, 2020, https://www.wbur.org/hereandnow/2020/04/30/compton-cowboys -black-ranch-culture.

34. Ashon Crawley, "I Grew Up Afraid. Lil Nas X's 'Montero' Is the Lesson I Needed," *NPR Editor's Picks*, April 14, 2021, https://www.npr .org/2021/04/14/986466561/i-grew-up-afraid-lil-nas-xs-montero-is-the -lesson-i-needed.

35. In an autumn 2021 interview, Lil Nas X tells Kris Ex that he wouldn't have been able to come out so publicly without the success of "Old Town Road"; see Kris Ex, "Lil Nas X Opens Up about His Battle for Respect in Hip Hop," *XXL*, September 28, 2021, https://www .independent.co.uk/arts-entertainment/music/news/lil-nas-x-out-gay -montero-b1929165.html

36. Rebecca Ruiz, "Lil Nas X Honored for Talking about Suicide, Mental Health," *Mashable*, September 1, 2021, https://mashable.com /article/lil-nas-x-suicide-mental-health-trevor-project.

37. Jason King, "Lil Nas X Is the Boundary-Smashing Pop Revolutionary of 2021," *NPR Music*, December 28, 2021, https://www.npr.org /2021/12/28/1068323960/lil-nas-x-pop-revolutionary.

CONCLUSION. BLACK COUNTRY MUSIC AFROFUTURISMS

1. Thanks to Nadine Hubbs for helping me ID this blurry image!

2. See Ann Power's comments and watch the concert here, from NPR Music: "Mickey Guyton: Tiny Desk (Home) Concert," November 9, 2020, https://www.youtube.com/watch?v=bnbJCEBGvHU.

3. John Blake, "This Black Country Singer Wrote the Most Powerful Song about Race in 2020," *CNN Entertainment*, January 1, 2021, https://

www.cnn.com/2020/12/31/entertainment/mickey-guyton-country
-singer/index.html.

4. Marissa R. Moss, "'The Boat Has Been Rocked': Mickey Guyton, the Grammys' First Black Solo Female Country Nominee," *The Guardian*, March 12, 2021, https://www.theguardian.com/music/2021/mar/12/mickey-guyton-the-grammys-first-black-solo-female-country-nominee.

5. Leigh H. Edwards, "Dolly Parton's Netflix Reimagining: How Her Twenty-First-Century 'Jolene' Revises Country Music's Authenticity Narratives," in *Whose Country? Genre, Identity, and Belonging in Twenty-First-Century Country Music Culture*, ed. Jada Watson and Paula Bishop (Cambridge: Cambridge University Press, forthcoming in 2022). Thanks to Leigh for sharing an early copy of this essay with me.

6. Roxanne Gay and Tressie McMillan Cottom, "It's Our Country, Too," *Hear to Slay* interview with Rissi Palmer, February 2, 2021, https://consumer.luminarypodcasts.com/listen/roxane-gay-and-dr-tressie-mcmillan-cottom/hear-to-slay/its-our-country-too/e4d9a1ff-71aa-470b-a0f5-33cbd4184178.

7. Gay and Cottom, "It's Our Country, Too," *Hear to Slay* interview with Rissi Palmer.

8. Markus K. Dowling, "Rissi Palmer Establishes Color Me Country Fund to Aid Artists of Color," *The Boot*, December 15, 2020, https://theboot.com/rissi-palmer-color-me-country-artist-fund/.

9. Gay and Cottom, "It's Our Country, Too," *Hear to Slay* interview with Rissi Palmer.

10. Christina Sharpe, *In the Wake: On Blackness and Being* (Durham, NC: Duke University Press, 2016).

11. Author's Zoom interview with DeLila Black, March 16, 2021.

12. DeLila Black, Passe Partout, https://www.patreon.com/delilablack.

13. Rachel Cholst, "Five Rounds with DeLila Black," *Adobe and Teardrops*, May 13, 2021, https://adobeandteardrops.com/2021/05/5-rounds-with-delila-black.html.

14. DeLila Black, "Cain't Git None," YouTube, June 3, 2019, https://www.youtube.com/watch?v=gIcbChkuYBY.

15. You can hear and watch DeLila Black's song "Routine" on YouTube, posted October 16, 2020, https://www.youtube.com/watch?v=KqEU-NR4nYk.

16. You can listen to DeLila Black's "Accountability" on YouTube, posted May 13, 2021, https://www.youtube.com/watch?v=5KaVDIG Quws.

17. Cholst, "Five Rounds with DeLila Black."

18. Jewly Hight, "New Roots: Black Musicians and Advocates Are Forging Coalitions Outside the System," heard on *Morning Edition*, NPR, October 29, 2021, https://www.npr.org/2021/10/29/1050322605/new -roots-black-musicians-and-advocates-are-forging-coalitions-outside -the-system.

19. "Frankie Staton Addresses the Black Opry," Black Opry Outlaw House, YouTube, posted October 19, 2021, https://www.youtube.com /watch?v=ZZrMJUdANow.

20. See Adrienne Maree Brown, *Emergent Strategy: Shaping Change, Changing Worlds* (Chico, CA: AK Press, 2017), and Gumbs, *Undrowned: Black Feminist Lessons from Marine Mammals* (Chicago, CA: AK Press, 2020).

INDEX